The Archive Project

Recent scholarship on archive research has raised questions concerning the character and impact of 'the archive' on how the traces of the past are researched, the use and analysis of different kinds of archived data, methodological approaches to the practicalities involved, and what kind of theory is drawn on and contributed to by such research. *The Archive Project: Archival Research in the Social Sciences* builds on these questions, exploring key methodological ideas and debates and engaging in detail with a wide range of archival projects and practices, in order to put to use important theoretical ideas that shed light on the methods involved.

Offering an overview of the current 'state of the field' and written by four authors with extensive experience in conducting research in and creating archives around the world, it demonstrates the different ways in which archive methodology, practice and theory can be employed, and shows how the ideas and approaches detailed in the book can be put into practice by other researchers, working on different kinds of archives and collections. The volume engages with crucial questions, including: What is 'an archive' and how does it come into existence? Why do archival research and how is it done? How can sense be made of the scale and scope of collections and archives? What are the best ways to analyse the traces of the past that remain? What are helpful criteria for evaluating the knowledge claims produced by archival research? What is the importance of community archives? How has the digital turn changed the way in which archival research is carried out? What role is played by the questions that researchers bring into an archive? How do we deal with unexpected encounters in the archive?

A rigorous and accessible examination of the methods and choices that shape research 'on the ground' and the ways in which theory, practice and methodology inform one another, this book will appeal to scholars across the social sciences and humanities with interests in archival and documentary research.

Niamh Moore is a Chancellor's Fellow in Sociology at the University of Edinburgh, with a background in interdisciplinary feminist studies. Her research includes work on ecofeminist activism (*The Changing Nature of Ecofeminism: Telling Stories from Clayoquot Sound*, UBC Press, 2015), the archiving and reuse of data, and community-based participatory research, including with community-food growing projects.

Andrea Salter has a background in sociology and human geography and has held postdoctoral positions at UCL and the Universities of Cambridge and Edinburgh. She is presently Research Facilitator across Arts, Humanities and Social Sciences at Cambridge and continues to research 'documents of life'. Publications include articles and also *The World's Great Question: Olive Schreinerâ's South African Letters* (Cape Town: VRS, 2014, with Liz Stanley).

Liz Stanley is Professor of Sociology and ESRC Professorial Research Fellow at the University of Edinburgh, UK. Her work focuses around conjunctions of theory, methodology and the past. Books include *Breaking Out Again* (with Sue Wise), *The Auto/Biographical I, Mourning Becomes, Documents of Life Revisited*, and *The World's Great Question* (with Andrea Salter). See www.sociology.ed.ac.uk/people/staff/stanley_liz

Maria Tamboukou is Professor of Feminist Studies at the University of East London, UK. Her research activity is in the areas of critical feminisms, auto/biographical narratives and studies in neo-materialism. Writing feminist genealogies is the central focus of her work. Recent publications include the monograph *Sewing, Writing and Fighting: Radical Practices in Work, Politics and Culture*.

The Archive Project

Archival research in the social sciences

Niamh Moore, Andrea Salter,
Liz Stanley and Maria Tamboukou

Routledge
Taylor & Francis Group

LONDON AND NEW YORK

First published 2017
by Routledge

2 Park Square, Milton Park, Abingdon, Oxfordshire OX14 4RN
52 Vanderbilt Avenue, New York, NY 10017

Routledge is an imprint of the Taylor & Francis Group, an informa business

First issued in paperback 2020

British Library Cataloguing in Publication Data
A catalogue record for this book is available from the British Library

Library of Congress Cataloguing in Publication Data
Names: Moore, Niamh, author.
Title: The archive project : archival research in the social sciences / by
Niamh Moore, Andrea Salter, Liz Stanley and Maria Tamboukou.
Description: Abingdon, UK; New York, NY : Routledge, [2016] |
Includes bibliographical references and index.
Identifiers: LCCN 2015042243 (print) | LCCN 2015045949 (ebook) |
ISBN 9781472453945 (hardback : alk. paper) | ISBN 9781315612577 (ebook) |
ISBN 9781317044611 (epub)
Subjects: LCSH: Social sciences–Research–Methodology. |
Social sciences–Archival resources.
Classification: LCC H61.M5865 2016 (print) | LCC H61 (ebook) |
DDC 300.72/2–dc23 LC record available at http://lccn.loc.gov/2015042243

ISBN: 978-1-4724-5394-5 (hbk)
ISBN: 978-0-367-59622-4 (pbk)

Typeset in Sabon
by Out of House Publishing

Contents

About the authors

Niamh Moore is a Chancellor's Fellow in Sociology at the University of Edinburgh, with a background in interdisciplinary feminist studies. Her research includes work on ecofeminist activism (*The Changing Nature of Eco/feminism: Telling Stories from Clayoquot Sound*, 2015), the archiving and re-use of data, and community-based participatory research, including with community-food growing projects.

Andrea Salter has a background in sociology and human geography and has held post-doctoral positions at UCL and the Universities of Cambridge and Edinburgh. She is presently Research Facilitator across Arts, Humanities and Social Sciences at Cambridge and continues to research 'documents of life'. Publications include articles and also *The World's Great Question: Olive Schreiner's South African Letters* (2014, with Liz Stanley).

Liz Stanley is Professor of Sociology and ESRC Professorial Research Fellow at the University of Edinburgh, UK. Her work focuses around conjunctions of theory, methodology and the past. Books include *Breaking Out Again* (with Sue Wise), *The Auto/Biographical I*, *Mourning Becomes*, *Documents of Life Revisited* and *The World's Great Question* (with Andrea Salter). See www.sociology.ed.ac.uk/people/staff/stanley_liz

Maria Tamboukou is Professor of Feminist Studies at the University of East London, UK. Her research activity develops in the areas of critical feminisms, auto/biographical narratives and studies in neo-materialism. Writing feminist genealogies is the central focus of her work. Recent publications include the monograph *Sewing, Fighting and Writing: Radical Practices in Work, Politics and Culture*.

Prologue

The Archive Project is a book concerned with methodology, the methodology of archival research in the social sciences. It has been written in the context of the 'archival turn', the vast surge of interest in archives, memory and traces of the past that has occurred among both popular and academic audiences over the last few decades. 'Methodology' includes method in the sense of techniques of investigation (although is by no means confined to this), theory of both a middle-range and a more abstract social theory kind, and an overarching framework organised around some principles or grounding. The principles underpinning *The Archive Project* are at once political, ethical and intellectual, and we present them under the broad heading of a feminist archival sensibility.

This archival sensibility underpinning *The Archive Project* is elaborated in a range of ways across its composing chapters. It has originated in our ethical, political and conceptual approach to 'the trace', to the remaining signs – on paper, in buildings and street names, in 'zines and oral recordings... – of people, events and times gone by. Our use of the term, as in archival research more generally, accords the trace a foundational status and accordingly it has a grounded and material presence throughout our discussions of methodology matters.

This prologue sets the scene. Chapter 1 explores key ideas, debates and literature associated with the archival turn. It has a particular eye on methodology matters, which are often bracketed or ignored and with the focus instead on conceptual and theoretical issues. Chapter 2 is concerned with opening the 'black box' of archival research methodology and explores practical strategies and tools for investigating traces, documents, collections and archives and the role of rewriting and writing in these activities. Chapter 3 offers a way of thinking about and working with the rhythms of archival practice, and it details a broad narrative methodology grounded in the interweaving of archival processes and products. Chapter 4 explores time and the temporal order in archival research, for time not only marks the traces to be found in archival collections but also structures the practices of archival research methodology, with different temporally grounded ways of reading archival materials this chapter's focus of discussion. Chapter 5 is concerned with further expanding ideas about what an archive is and who archivists can be, by exploring the sometimes blurry line between archival research processes and products in relation to the formation of a community archive. Chapter 6 draws together themes and ideas across the book, starting with the trace, the concept that underlies the whole of the book's discussions, and comments on the archive as an institution, a project and a process. The epilogue rounds things off in considering some important matters touched on in the composing chapters but not previously discussed in a direct way.

The Archive Project has been written so as to combine elements of a workbook, a collection and a monograph. It contains jointly produced chapters which open and close the book and provide a detailed guide to the bigger picture that the other chapters touch on. Chapter 1 was discussed collectively, written by Liz Stanley, then added to and subtracted from collectively; Chapter 6 follows the same approach, being collectively discussed, written by Maria Tamboukou and Liz Stanley and revised and added to collectively. This prologue and the epilogue combine the modes of authorship of Chapter 1. The book also features four individually authored chapters. Chapters 2 (Liz Stanley), 3 (Maria Tamboukou), 4 (Andrea Salter) and 5 (Niamh Moore) introduce and guide readers through some different but mutually supportive ways of putting archival research methodology into practice, and discuss many practical examples in doing so. There is no single methodology or method for archival research, so it is important to us that readers should gain the sense that a range of permissible ideas and strategies can be tried out.

As readers will find, the approach to methodology taken in *The Archive Project* occurs around an attention to the form of the process. By this we mean that all of its chapters open up for discussion the details of the methodological processes involved, and show that these processes have distinctive forms, with four of them elaborated in Chapters 2, 3, 4 and 5. These chapters share many features and guiding principles, while there are also some differences, which are explored in particular in the opening chapter and the epilogue, but will be best appreciated by reading all chapters against each other.

For many people, archival research is almost by definition historical research. Certainly much is. However, many archives and collections are present- and also future-oriented – indeed, a plausible argument could be made that all are, because all archival research takes place in the present and anticipates future lines of inquiry. In addition, historians are by no means the only people interested in archives or who do research in archives, with this book addressed in particular to social scientists in sociology, political science, social anthropology, social policy, social and cultural geography, and science and technology studies. We also hope it will appeal to humanities colleagues and students at all levels, as well as to readers with more general interests in archival research, for books which explore the methodological aspects of archival research in detail remain fairly few and far between, for reasons discussed in our opening chapter.

We hope readers will find *The Archive Project* interesting and a 'good read'. Some additional materials regarding 'the trace' and archival documents, pointed to across its chapters, will be found on the book's website at https://sites.google.com/site/thebookarchiveproject/. And a final point for the prologue: *The Archive Project* has been conceived as an interconnected set of chapters that reflect ideas back and forth and add up to more than the sum of the parts, as 'a book' providing a coherent account of the processes and products of archival research. Consequently, while its chapters can be dipped into and out of by using the list of contents and the index, readers would lose the cumulative argument made which would be gained by reading from start to finish, embracing the different voices and seeing the overall project that retains these differences within a greater whole. They really do add up!

1 In other archives and beyond

Niamh Moore, Andrea Salter, Liz Stanley and Maria Tamboukou

The archival turn

This book is about archival research and ways of crafting methodological frameworks for carrying it out. 'Methodology' signals a framework that harnesses both method or specific research tools, and also theory in the sense of a framework of ideas, and its meaning is fairly settled. The word 'archive', however, can conjure up different things for different people and is a term still very much in the making. Indeed, the interest and excitement around it remains palpable and infectious.

An archive is a repository of some kind; and while for some people this is seen in formal 'archives of the nation-state' terms, in fact it can variously also be a building, cardboard-box, photograph album, internet website, or discourse of interconnected ideas such as community heritage and shared memory; and it holds or contains documents, which can take the form of written texts, photographs, sound recordings, postcards, medical records, printed materials, material objects... and not just official records, nor necessarily things on paper either. For some people, the word conjures up excitement, noise and the Da Vinci Code. For others, it is the New York Public Library or a National Archives Repository with researchers silently focused on their documents of choice. It can bring to mind a group of people sharing a cause, hobby or job who collect materials of some kind and make them available to like-minded others. It can emphasise, as does the UN's convention on intangible cultural heritage, the interdependence between the intangible, the oppression of 'outsider' groups, and the materiality of formalised means of valorising some forms of heritage and memory rather than others. In a more playful register, it might also be that labyrinthine library as infinite as life itself that figures large in the fictions of Jorge Luis Borges (1998). Some of the people associated with archives are professional archivists and historians, the groups most often linked with archival investigations; but cheek by jowl will be found family researchers, genealogists, radical or community activists wanting to make or remake the historical record, journalists, hobbyists, computer geeks, collectors of all kinds, and social scientists and arts scholars, medical researchers, scientists...

Archives, then, are the preserve of none because they are engaged with by many kinds of people, who use or create them in diverse ways. However, there *is* a canonical version that tends to dominate, the state archive version associated with a disciplining view of what archives and archival research 'ought' to be like (and challenged by, among others, Foucault, 1972; Richards, 1993; Derrida, 1997; Steedman, 2001; Farge, 2013 [1989]). It is therefore no surprise that the existence of competing and disparate envisionings of archives should give rise to contrary assumptions about their constitution (a 'proper' state archive, versus new initiatives and countervailing projects), organisation (arcane systems of classification, solitary study and silence, versus the noise of collective endeavour), contents (facts versus fictions, representations versus referentialities), and also concerning what the 'it' is that archival investigations are concerned with (knowledge, understanding, change, commemoration, recognition...). Different examples of what 'the archive' is and what happens in it are discussed in *The Archive Project*, influenced by ideas associated with the archival turn that has taken place over the last few decades. This has involved a general re-thinking and re-visioning of what archives are, who can be an archivist, the purposes archives serve, the character and boundaries of their contents, how these should be investigated, all of which are discussed in this book.

The social science presence within the archival turn has been relatively muted until recently, when there has been an increase of interest in archives and collections as sites for research, and also archiving research data such as meta-archives, ethnographic fieldnotes, recorded or transcribed interviews, numerical datasets and the products of webscraping, twitter feeds and other forms of 'big data' and data mining. It is worth asking why now, in terms of the increased social science attention to archiving and the archive and its experience of the archival turn. Is it just that at long last the social sciences are catching up, or the ongoing renewal of historical sociology, or the rise of interest in big data, or the pull of secondary analysis, or the archiving of qualitative as well as quantitative datasets? We see it as an amalgam of all these, but with particular attention given to the more textual and long-standing instantiations of what 'the archive' is. A lively body of work has emerged here, exploring and debating key issues (cf. Hill, 1993; Burton, 2006; Craven, 2008; Kirsch and Rohan, 2008a; Stoler, 2009; Jobs and Lüdtke, 2010; Tamboukou, 2010c; Valles Martínez *et al.*, 2011; Levy, 2011; Stanley, Salter and Dampier, 2013a; Dirks, 2015; see also Hughes and Goodwin, 2013; Stanley, 2013). Valles Martínez *et al.* (2011) have usefully tabled key questions about archiving, the re-use and re-analysis of existing archived data, digital transpositions, approaches to archival research and other crucial matters. There are, as they point out, achievements and strengths but also areas that need to be further explored and theorised within the horizon of an archival sensibility. *The Archive Project* provides such an exploration, by engaging with key theoretical and methodological questions and debates, drawing on our wide-ranging collective experiences

of doing research in archives located around the world, and also our extensive involvements in creating new kinds of archives.

Broadly, archival research is concerned with a collection of documents –
texts of different kinds, including but not confined to words on paper, visual
materials or physical objects; and it involves analysing and interpreting these
so as to explore a particular topic or question or concern (Danto, 2008;
Dobson and Ziemann, 2008; Gidley, 2011; Jordanova, 2012; Brundage,
2013). A single document or a collection of items may form the focus, or this
may be part of a denser fabric of archival data that a research investigation
is concerned with. In addition, while often associated with the discipline of
history, many contemporary historians resist the assumption that 'for historical research read archive research', and instead emphasise that in addition
to documents other sources (including oral recordings, photographs, organisational records, census data, leaflets and ephemera...) should come under
inquiry (Jordanova, 2000: 172–98).

As this indicates, a widely held but misconceived assumption is that the
documents that archives hold are always from and about 'the past'. The
complications need to be recognised, for many archives are organised
around contemporary concerns and interests, while of course the contents
of all archives are always read and understood within the present moment
because of the particular concerns that lead researchers to investigate a particular collection or set of documents. In Britain, there is a regularly updated
'Ambridge archive' concerned with characters and plots, actors, producers
and directors associated with a radio soap opera called 'The Archers', with
parallels existing for many other television and radio programmes and films
and their 'stars'. In a very different way, 'big data' constituted by 'mining' or
'scraping' internet sources – say, the contents of Project Gutenburg's book
corpora – can also be continually modified by creating a sub-archive of just
novels, or those of the eighteenth century, or everything by male authors
in a particular genre. As these examples indicate, while some contents of
archives may be 'old' and 'closed' (that is, nothing new is added to them),
others are very much 'new' and 'open' and with continual accretion or mod-
ification a driving force. And given the capabilities provided by digitisation,
some previously old and closed data has become very much new and open.

A result is that the particular approach and methods used in doing archival research need to differ according to the constitution, organisation and
purpose of an archive or collection and the data or contents in question, as
well as because of the researcher's stance and preferred research strategies.
Some of the examples discussed in *The Archive Project*'s chapters concern
long-established collections in major public or university institutions, others
involve researchers as protagonists in the formation and availability of new
archives, and with the older collections having started out in a similar way
to this. Relatedly, a blurred line exists between 'archiving' as an activity
involving finding, classifying and filing archival materials, and 'researching'
as an investigation of the contents of these.

At basis, archival research involves making sense of sources – the traces, what remains of people and events of the past – in a particular kind of location called an archive, which is a repository of some kind for holding and making available collections of things, ranging from institutional and formal edifices to personal collections shared between family or friends. Research is done to address 'I want to know about X or Y' questions, and also indicates the kind of sources and data that are appropriate and sufficient for answering them. These might be questions that people in the past were interested in (for example, could the Indian famines of the nineteenth century have been prevented?) or formulated around present-day concerns (for example, how should LGBT+ history be recovered to ensure a sense of community longevity?). Generally, then, the contents of an archive relate to the past, sometimes the distant past (the letters on wooden tablets written by Roman soldiers at Vindolanda in northern England, perhaps); however, in some circumstances they can be documents which are about 'now' and collected and made available because of their topicality (the papers of recent US presidents concerning their foreign policies, for example).

There are some very different responses to the question of why archival research is important and why discussing and debating it matters. One, the most simple but with profound implications, is that 'the past' is a short-hand for everything that has come before and made us, our lives and the societies we live in, what they are. So understanding even small parts of the past can give us a handle on things in the present and possibly aspects of the future, too. Another, and related, response is that the present and the future are uncontrollable, while the remaining traces of the past, including the near-past that contemporary archiving is concerned with, are finite and can be made at least provisionally known, albeit with many ifs and buts.

Or at least that is the seduction involved, that what is contained in archival places and spaces will indeed be appropriate and sufficient to produce understanding and knowledge. There is another more disconcerting response to why it matters, associated with the work of some of the great theorists of archives and particularly Michel de Certeau (1998). This is that the archive in its canonical form represents, not 'the past' in an amorphous sense, but rather the deaths of all those who lived it, and therefore it invokes or stands for the certainty of our own death too. Herein, engaging with the archive represents a kind of machinery or technology for asserting life against death, giving voice to the past by fixing the meaning of what it inscribes. De Certeau (1998: 5) calls this a 'labour of and against death'; and as he also points out, there are limits to what this labour can produce because the past is ineluctably past.

There are, then, some grand reasons for why archives and research in them matter (life against death), but the lower key and more utilitarian ones (it is imperative that ordinary lives leave traces, and what happened in the past is interesting) are also important, and at their back are fundamental issues concerning the archival sensibility of contemporary times.

Indeed, these levels of meaning are interconnected and come at the same things in different ways: the past has made us, there is a seduction effect, the sources can be tamed and classified, the possibility of knowing hovers, but all knowledge-claims are founded on the ultimately profound unknowability of the past. Consequently, although the seduction still exists, and the labour involved remains propelled by deep curiosity, certainties have to be surrendered in favour of understanding, and archival research engaged with in more open and accountable ways. This is the project and the sensibility that *The Archive Project* is conceived around.

The use of the word 'project' in the title is a mindful choice and gives recognition to the fact that the book has resulted from a collective endeavour and the ideas it explores and debates remain in progress, rather than being signed off and completed. It has a hybridic character as an assemblage somewhere between monograph, edited collection and workbook, with its contents not reducible to one seemless narrative. The title also recognises Walter Benjamin (2002, 2007) as a master of assemblage. Benjamin writes of amassing and classifying detail and, ironically, at the same time also indicates the necessary provisionality of archival research and that its intention to name, tame and to know is destined to fail. As a result, *The Archive Project*'s composing chapters and how they explore questions and issues are written in a way that remains open so readers can engage with them in a variety of ways.

Invoking the idea of a project is apposite for other reasons too. The book's sub-title – *Archival Research in the Social Sciences* – is important here. It is concerned with theory, but in a way that is deeply engaged with the grounded practice of working in – and sometimes creating – particular archives, each with their embedded complexities and frequent vagaries, and then turning this back on to theory, to invest it with the richness of the actualities of grounded archival research practices. Another element of the project is that the examples discussed in its composing chapters show that analysis and interpretation give rise to complex and sometimes unresolvable questions and issues, with the situated and contextual nature of archival research an irreducible feature. The idea of a project has a further resonance too, which is that our approach is based around a particular archival sensibility that gives expression to an integrated set of ideas and a coherent approach to exploring them; that is, a project in the strong sense, advancing a broad methodology.

So who are we? We are an interdisciplinary group of four who came together through a symposium organised at a 2013 British Sociological Association conference in which we gave presentations. We are all located in the social sciences, sociology specifically. However, we are not exclusively of it, with our backgrounds also encompassing political science, law, geography, economics, women's studies, education, philosophy, and feminist interventions in all these. Consequently each of us works across, as well as within, disciplinary formations. And as researchers, we enter an archive, whatever the archive, with great curiosity, intellectual intent, and also armed with grounded knowledges formed in other archives and the wide range of archival research we have between us carried out. These researches have been concerned with different historical and contemporary times, an array of research topics, and archives shaped by divergent governing and disciplining principles. They include national archives, online archives, radical archives, local archives and more, as well as a host of different collections located within these.

As co-authors, we share many ideas about archives, their constitution, organisation and use, and our chapters fit together in we hope useful and interesting ways. There are also some thought-provoking differences of viewpoint, and these too mark how we conceive of, design and carry out archive research. These differences – along with the strong shared basis of ideas that also exists – are discussed later in this chapter, and also the epilogue, to help readers think through their own choices and viewpoints. These differences are sometimes due to our dissimilar archival research experiences, some are grounded in different theoretical, methodological and other influences on us, others result from different working practices and the difficulties and responsibilities of working jointly. However, mainly they stem from the diverse character of the documents, collections, archives and contexts we work in, their situational character, and the consequent need to make informed choices about how to research and analyse them.

The Archive Project conveys a joined up set of ideas about archival research, and makes detailed use of our involvements in a range of archival contexts, then. This first chapter is a collective statement setting out the groundwork of the main body of ideas that inform our overall stance. The chapters following are individually authored, and appear in an order that most helpfully engages with the procedural aspects of archival research, so readers unfamiliar with archival research can gain a strong sense of what is involved. They provide practical examples which illuminate the ideas presented and arguments made, and combine theoretical, methodological and substantive comments on the materials discussed. The final chapter, Chapter 6, overviews the key ideas, debates and methodological topics explored and is also a collective statement drawing together the main aspects of what we have done and the archival sensibility we have brought to this. The details of authorship and information about who wrote what are provided in the prologue, while the epilogue is concerned with synergies, differences and departures.

Mythologies: in other archives

The archival turn is closely associated with an influential set of what have become canonical writings, works that have resonated with successive generations of archival researchers and are now in effect standard reference points. These contain great insights and illuminating ideas of considerable complexity and import; and, while associated with particular publications, the ideas concerned are closely connected with a wider conceptual framework and an *oeuvre* or collected works in which the authors concerned have developed their thinking over time.

Because of their intellectual substance and insightfulness, these archival writings have been excitedly taken up, discussed and then over time referred to in increasingly mythologised ways. By this we mean that, from very different beginnings, reference to them has become almost required – 'What, s/he doesn't reference Derrida! Awful!' – and this is often done ritualistically without really engaging with the complexities involved, indeed sometimes being referenced to support positions that the work in question explicitly disavows. Relatedly, the mythologising process typically involves a readership that focuses on particular comments, sometimes particular short passages repeated over and over, often copied from secondary sources rather than the founding authors themselves. The works in question, then, have taken on a metanomic as well as mythologised character – to say fever, dust, imperial archive, allure, is seemingly to say it all in what is an economy of circulating but attenuated ideas. The point of course is that actually there is much more going on in these writings than what such heavily coded terms are used to reference, as we now discuss.

Derrida and archive fever

This 'more going on' comment is perhaps especially apposite concerning archive fever. Certainly Jacques Derrida's discussion of the archive and the death wish in his continuing debate with Freud caught a nerve, both in French (a 1994 lecture at the Freud Archive in the UK then published in 1995 as *Mal d'Archive: Une Impression Freudienne*), and even more so in the Anglophone world after its appearance in English (in 1997 as *Archive Fever: A Freudian Impression*). As reviewers at the time pointed out, it is less memory and the trace (one trajectory of Derrida's thinking) and more truth, authority and power in the context of psychoanalytic theory (another trajectory, perhaps particularly in his earlier [1972] 'Freud and the scene of writing') that is the propelling concern. But what caught attention subsequently turned out to be neither of these, but its opening comments on archive as power as reinforced by the valorisation of inscription and Derrida's specification of the primary character of the originating meaning of archive-as-arkhĕ, as actualisation of the law.

Reading beyond the opening, there is the exposition of a hefty set of ideas in which Derrida debates his earlier reworkings of Freudian ideas, with Emmanuel Levinas on ethics also lurking, as well as an intertwined thread concerned with memory and writing. These have however been read in many different ways. For us, the core is that there is something to be remembered, and writing or rather inscription (as in Freud's ideas about the mystic writing pad) is central to this, but what this is remains lost, just off frame, and is feverishly sought after. The archive is originatory because inscribed by memory traces, but it is mnemonically faulty, incomplete, or perhaps even wrong. And so the threads of thinking and theorising go back and forth, Derrida and Freud, life and death, the apparent dichotomy between public institutional memory and private 'inner' memory, the trace and fever; and they pass over and through 'the archive', but do not rest or dwell there. However, what has been mythologised can be expressed with some precision: where most people rest and dwell is pages 1 to 23 in the English edition, the 'Note' and 'Exergue'. Putting *Archive Fever* in a lineage, the Derridarian *oeuvre*, it is preceded by (1989 [1982]) *Memoires for Paul de Man* and followed by (2008 [2003]) *Geneses, Genealogies, Genres and Genius: The Secrets of the Archive*. Doing this adds up to something impressive, substantial and compelling, if not always entirely convincing. When not in a reduced form used to depict the archive as a kind of evil empire, then, but placed in its intellectual context, *Archive Fever* contributes importantly to the Derridarian intellectual toolkit, which is as much methodological as theoretical and provides the means for close interrogation of memory, the trace and inscription. No fever, no sweat, but a lot of incisive analysis.

Steedman and Dust

There is a considerable amount of dust in the archival turn, too. Carolyn Steedman's *Dust* is composed by an interlocking set of essays, which draw on her earlier writings about archives and archival research, and also point towards her subsequent related work (for example, Steedman, 2008, 2011, 2015). It is perhaps less a response to Derrida's own work and more to the fever that mythologised readings of *Archive Fever* have produced in followers. The fever is, as she points out, about the historian's romance of communing with the dead, 'the everyday fantastic act of making the dead walk', (Steedman 2008: 5), while in a Derridarian discussion this is an anti-romance.

For Steedman, the archival turn in the humanities and social sciences is related to the quest (also part of the historian's romance) for 'that which will not go away', which is the matter of history, and has in fact been neither lost nor erased but survives in dusty happenstance traces, the flotsam and jetsam of what remains, and can be discovered and found. She points out that dust is Michelet's word, 'I breathed in their dust'; and she is both seduced by the romance and choked by the substance, with her literal comments about a material labour process including her seriously tongue in cheek observations about nineteenth century investigations of the diseases of literary men and the fevers of scholarship precipitated by the infected glue-bindings of books.

Steedman's archive is a literal and material place and the site of intersecting labour processes, the researcher's, the archivist's, those of the people of the past whose traces remain. This is not to say that she abandons an interrogation of Derridarian thinking, to the contrary. The fantasy of a Borges-inspired archive holding the totality of everything past and of being able to make direct contact with the reality of the past hovers behind the comments about romance and quest, as a longing for connection. Her take on this is that it is precisely its absence that feeds imagination and analysis, that scholarly activity of filling the gaps between the traces that remain. It is the very incompleteness that moves understanding forward, and does so in incremental moves because, as she emphasises, there are so few certainties that small new pieces of information might well change previous thinking.

Not all the essays composing *Dust* are in an obviously deconstructionist vein, but come at similar themes in a more ironic or perhaps slyer way. The route to Middlemarch and Steedman's reading of this novel is, for instance, entitled 'without benefit of archive'. However, what departs from, or at least reworks at a more seditious level, Derrida's take on the archive is Steedman's detailed observations of the archive researcher and their, our, 'daily and dog-ged performance of positivism' (153), in which any claim to know is rooted in specific ways of writing and reading the material actualities of an arch-ive and its contents and the resultant ways of shaping the what and the how of these activities, starting with the fact that the researcher is never the intended reader, is always in possession of what are in effect 'stolen' letters, wills, accounts, diaries and so on.

The irony here is that dust has itself become subject to mythologising. Steedman has ironicised the romance of the archive and countered it with a labour process that is externally somewhat tedious and internally greatly rewarding. Deeply ironically, it is the externalities here that have been mythologised, taking on the colours of a new romance of the archive – 'oh, the heady experience of dodgy accommodation and loneliness while away from home' – while the deeply intellectual labour process involved and its corporeal grounding has been bracketed, indeed vanished. The quest and its complex readings and writings that Steedman grapples with are often dissolved by others into plunder that passes as theory. Our quest in this book? To return to Steedman's stimulating ideas about labour process and to rescue the sharp end of the activities involved: writing, thinking, reading, the art and the science of archival research.

Richards, Cohn, Dirks and the imperial archive

The idea of the imperial archive is associated with a triumvirate of rather disparate strands of work rather than one key name, although it has nonetheless been heavily mythologised and its nuances, complexities and grounded inquiries honed down to a powerful resonant phrase: to say 'imperial archive' is enough said. For Thomas Richards (1993), a major contributor here, 'empire' conjures up power, force, central control, and is in significant part a fantasy, as he discusses in *The Imperial Archive*. The reality, he proposes, is rather different. The fantasy is of a metropole, a metropolitan vanguard with grandiose dreams of unity shared with grateful peripheries that willingly take on an imperial identity, its control and not violence and underpinning it, men (and they were men) in metropolitan offices producing letters of instruction and filing responses received, and men in colonial contexts producing surveys, maps, census reports. Its core (with Richards having specifically the British Empire in mind, not also the German, French, Spanish, Belgian, Russian, Japanese or US versions) is knowledge-production, the shuffling of paper which required storage, keeping track of, retrieval and control, and so an archive. But, 'theirs was a paper empire: an empire built on a series of flimsy pretexts that were always becoming texts' (Richards, 1993: 4), for the unity was always specious, the control fantastical, and many cracks existed with resistance seeping through and these had to be covered by paper traces. It is, indeed, precisely the fictive textual aspects that engage Richards, with the workings out of these ideas occurring across chapters in which he provides, not readings, but more strongly rewritings in the emphatic voice, of what a variety of fictional texts have done with such thinking.

The result is a powerful engagement with the idea of the imperial arch-ive in which is it easy to forget Richards' earlier comments that this is in large part a fictive production found in made up stories rather than factual accounts and its ideas do not really translate in those far-flung historical peripheries where imperial control should have existed. Relatedly there is a dominating 'it is so' voice marking his text and so, perhaps not surprisingly, it has been the assertions and seeming certainties rather than the more com-plex underpinnings that have figured large in secondary referencing. The fiction is unseen rather than disregarded, the emphatic voice dominates, the empire *is* a totalising archival project in the mythologised version. Foucault is a presence here. But *contra* Foucault's (1972: 130) view that 'the archive cannot be described in all its totality' because it is the junction of all that is known or knowable, Richards' account of the imperial archive concerns an actual archive with a composing set of institutions (the British Museum, the Royal Society, the Royal Geographical Society, the Foreign Office...). These add up to something rather less than a totalising reality of surveillance and control or 'an entire epistemological complex for representing a comprehen-sive knowledge' (14), for here things are placed but not necessarily found, there are fissures and ruptures rather than absolutism, and there are tears, indeed rips, in the paper.

Foucault's work before (for example, *The Order of Things, Madness and Civilization*) and also after (for example, *Discipline and Punish, The History of Sexuality*) the publication of *The Archaeology of Knowledge* (1972), the work most often referenced by archival researchers, frequently engages with discourse, memory and the archive as a kind of 'library of libraries'. He conceives of the archive under the heading of a system of discursivity, a meta-discursivity indeed, which 'establishes the possibility of what can be said' (Foucault, 1972: 129). However, while these ideas are dealt with abstractly in *The Archaeology of Knowledge*, they are embedded elsewhere in Foucault's work in a very grounded set of procedures for historical inquiry, including in his joint work with Arlette Farge on *lettres de cachet* (Farge and Foucault, 1982) and essays on 'Nietzsche, genealogy, history' (Foucault, 1986) as well as on 'Lives of infamous men' (Foucault, 1994). However, in banishing the 'totality of everything' notion of discursivity, Richards has also removed the Foucault with dusty hands who sat side by side with Arlette Farge, and thus has removed the archival activities of this working pair, something returned to later.

There is also a more grounded account of the imperial archive in its colonial incarnation, inspired and underpinned by the work of Bernard Cohn (1987, 1996) and his concern with the construction of Empire in India as an intellectual and cultural phenomenon occurring through such things as recording observations, mapping areas, carrying out census investigations, as well as the apparatus of armies, garrisons and so on. These are routinised acts of information-gathering helping categorise meaning and enabling surveillance and control, with Cohn's observations of how caste was constructed as well as used positioning this as a key aspect of collecting and typifying information and which led over time to caste as a system being made fixed and rigid.

Influenced by Cohn, and taking as his *leitmotif* Foucault's dictum that history transforms documents into monuments, a recent discussion of archival research in India by Nicholas Dirks in *Autobiography of an Archive* (2015: 27–48; see also Dirks, 1993, 2002) frames this in terms of ethnography, an ethnography of process and reflection, rather than of the 'making monuments' aspects which his later chapters explore. This is a literalist account of working in specific archives and particularly the India Office Library in London, later connecting this with Indian parallels, and signifying a system of governance. His account takes the broad form of a *bildungsroman*, with the naïve beginner first entering, taking detours, experiencing epiphanies, then becoming the confident knowledgeable disposing voice of the person speaking in the text: this pronounces that whatever survives archivally does so in the colonial interest (Dirks, 2015: 47). In Dirks' (2015: 42) comments on this, Foucault is strongly present, for 'Archive research itself invariably proceeds genealogically – record by record, decision by decision, trace by trace – not in the straightforward linear way that most basic histories imply… The archive contains primary sources at the same time it is always a secondary trace of historical discourse'.

As a result, for Dirks, and in a sense in parallel to Richards, this is a system of governmentality inscribed at many levels and in different genres, and its exploration shows its 'peculiar opacity' (Dirks, 2015: 43). This betrays not only its imperial origins but also the contradictions of colonial rule, and reflects governmentality's shift from the political and juridical to social and cultural levels, pushing signs of disruption, dissent and departure into the colonial context. One result, Dirks points out, is that the archival paper trail 'was as contingent, contested and contradictory as life outside the archive' and showed the incapacity of the imperial metropole to take full control (46). The result, stressed elsewhere in Dirks' work, is that, 'the archive not only contains documents but is itself a primary document of history', while at the same time noting that a peculiar characteristic of the colonial archive, that its audience is in the metropole and not just the colony that an archive is situated in (Dirks, 2015: 48). It should be noted here that Dirks treats archives as though synonymous with the state and imperial archives he has worked in, stating that 'The colonial archive was not just the record of the colonial state but also the repository of the sources for an imperial history whose primary public was in the metropole' (Dirks, 2015: 49) and seeing this as adding up to 'the history of archives' in general. Unsurprisingly, this is a view (not a fact) that the contents of *The Archive Project* take issue with, for many, most, archives and collections have much wider and non-state origins and instantiations than this.

The 'everywhere and nowhere' emphasis on genealogy and discourse regarding the imperial archive by Richards is reinforced by using wide-ranging fictions as evidence to address a number of different geographical and political contexts, and which also have at points rather loose connections with the actual imperial archive. These are used to signify what are implied, through the authorial voice used, to be facts about the imperial archive and its workings, rather than what they actually are, works of fiction. There is also slippage between imperial and colonial, as though there are no differences that count. A direct contrast is with Cohn, whose innovative conceptual apparatus, concerned with how categorisation and classification played out in the fabric of everyday relations of ruling, was deeply rooted in Indian and imperial historiography, and who as a consequence never loses sight of the specifics of the particular imperial context he is dealing with. Dirks' approach is rather different. It is certainly grounded in the particularities of India and the form that the imperial project took there. At the same time, he draws on aspects of Foucauldian ideas to emphasise governmentality as it played out in India, and in recent work has also pronounced on 'imperialism and the archive' more widely and generalised what is actually India-specific to other imperial and colonial contexts. However, these other contexts were often very different, not least because imperialism is not necessarily colonialism and vice versa, and certainly settler colonialism elsewhere took very different forms from the Indian experience.

The mythologising process regarding the imperial archive has also focused upon one aspect of a complex body of work, which is as we have indicated composed of some rather different strands of thinking. In this a particular term, the imperial archive, has resonated and been used as though it 'says it all'. What has caught attention is largely the discursive end of this body of work, with the detailed research end of it bracketed and largely vanished from consideration in the secondary literature. This work has drawn on very different evidential bases too: fictions of empire, but also the actualities, of India specifically. In the mythologised version, it is largely assumed that what the term 'the imperial archive' signifies – a fact and an absolute, enacted through force as much as control, propelled from the metropole and enforced in every local imperial and colonial context, with the classifications and efficiencies of the imperial archive of record-keeping at its core – applies everywhere. However, the archetype is over-invested with Britain rather than also including the other imperialisms we noted earlier, and it also ignores the existence of settler colonial contexts, the so-called 'peripheries' where such matters played out differently from India and whose difference it is important to recognise.

Farge and the allure of the archive

Steedman's (2001) *Dust* problematises the romance of the archive and the seduction effect. This mythologised romance was perhaps what led to the English translation of Arlette Farge's *Le goût de l'archive* (1989) as *The Allure of the Archives* (2013). The English title embodies the seduction view of the archival turn, while the more subtle French places emphasis on the taste of the particular, with Farge for instance being engaged by 'traces by the thousand' when 'one morning in the Library of the Arsenal' (2013: viii). Many direct and indirect references to Farge's work in fact appeared in archival turn literature well before the English translation was published; when it was, the book was almost instantly valorised in Anglophone writing because, read in the context of the mythologising processes sketched here, it was dubbed in some reviews an instant classic. What has been picked out in many reviews and references are the aspects that are already part of archival mythologies: the expense and loneliness of archival visits, struggles with unhelpful staff or obtrusive fellow-researchers, also the supposed 'animation' of past people and times, and later the need for 'pulling away' from what has been found. That is, the more personal aspects which are frequently doubly personalised by association with the reviewer's own experiences in proclaiming 'me too' are those emphasised.

However, in spite of responses to Farge's work in terms of allure, nostalgia and romance, there is in fact considerable discussion of the methodological aspects of archival research in her book, including copying materials, deciding on the next box of documents to interrogate, the discovery of more traces of women of the past in some kinds of materials, drawing inferences across multiple sources, as well as an engagement with some substantial aspects of analysis and interpretation. Her consideration of documents, for instance, discusses collection and selection in order to discern patterns and the ways in which these may (or may not) throw light on the topic in hand, as well as the different traps that exist, of thinking that accumulation brings certitude, of over-involvement, and of mistaking our own selections of quotations as though proofs. This is followed by a discussion of what can be done with the inevitable incomplete and fragmented character of what remains and how the people, occasions and – Farge's particular concern – events can be read from these partial representations, and the ethical issues arising.

It is useful to remember here that Farge and Foucault (1982) collaborated in archival work with '*lettres de cachet*', letters signed by the French king enforcing the incarceration of people whose families had asked that they be imprisoned or confined in asylums. In doing so, Farge and Foucault brought skills of inquiry and analysis together, which brings into view the close association between theory and methodology that existed for both. It is also important to point to the clearly indicated specificities that underlie Farge's discussion and which have been largely lost in the mythologising process. The Arsenal is a particular archival place, and what holds true there may be different elsewhere; also Farge is one researcher, and her experiences are not necessarily mirrored by those of others. More substantially, her book is written around her engagement with juridical records, that is, the formal records of one part of the centralised French state (the same kind of records that Dirks also draws on), while the generality of collections in world archives are of very diverse kinds. However, what she refers to as 'brutal' preservation, of the contents of a collection being 'in their raw form' as they had arrived, is familiar to many archival researchers working elsewhere and, rather than evidencing the controlling central imperial state or its sub-sections, these signify the dishevelled untidy faulty apparatus of much organisational record-keeping. While many archives hold state and juridical papers, many more contain the vast array of the papers of local families, small and large businesses, once famous people, and civil society groups at local, regional and national levels. Consequently, what holds true in France, in the Arsenal, for Farge, may not in other places, in other collections, in other archives, for other researchers (as she herself points out).

Mythologising processes and the archival turn

So what are we saying overall about the archival turn in its mythologising aspects? Perhaps some element of mythologising in the sense discussed here – seizing on a small part of a complex set of ideas, exaggerating particular aspects and diminishing or vanishing the rest, ritualistic referencing, working from secondary accounts rather than the source – is almost inevitable in how ideas and theories travel. This process is by no means confined to canonical presences in the archival turn, with some of its features being commented on, for instance, in Edward Said's (1983) identification of the 'travelling' aspects of travelling theory; and by Barta *et al.* (2001) concerning Bakhtin scholarship in a literary context. But nonetheless, and not by intention though as a consequence, the mythologising process has elevated a notion, a surprisingly simple notion, of theory and concepts – fever, dust, the imperial archive, allure – and downplayed or ignored the intellectual and material aspects of archival research which are strong presences in the original discussions of these things. What has resulted is the displacement

CALLED OUT?!

of a rigorous and material engagement with intellectual process and its replacement by reference to ethnography of a kind focused on the researcher 'being there' and the eureka moment of serendipity.

Ethnography is however vastly reduced by being presented as stories of archival researchers 'giving their game away', with the term 'stories' appearing in many titles and with these typically related in a straightforwardly narrative way rather than made subject to inquiry and analysis. The result valorises a confessional moment of telling how it was and 'how virtual, historical, and lived experiences intersect, particularly as researchers extract meaning from sources in locations most associated with isolation and loneliness – the archives' (Kirsch and Rohan, 2008b: 1), albeit with an expanded notion of what and where an archive is and what it collects and holds within it.

But let us be clear here. We have no problem with the idea of stories, and indeed each of us has to one degree or another been involved in exploring and/or facilitating their cultural production and analysis. In this particular context, the problem is that the emphasis is on the researcher in the sense we see as skewered by Steedman, of mythologising 'isolation and loneliness' while a more rigorous understanding of the intellectual labour process in archival research has been side-lined or abandoned. Clues, happy accidents, eureka and serendipity seemingly lead chance encounters to become scholarly research. This is very different from how we see it, as reading, writing, talking, planning, investigation, thoroughness, thought, analysis and so on; that is, the graft involved. However, if there is no method in our grounded sense of intellectual labour, the only thing there can be is serendipity or some version of it, that turning of pages hoping for something to leap out, rather than having a clear plan for organising the finding of things. The weight of the mythological here evacuates the ground of methodology and inquiry.

The founding work discussed above under we hope the provocative heading of 'mythologies' has influenced us too, and in largely shared ways. However, we draw our distance from the secondary mythologising reductions of these outstanding contributions to the archival turn. The archival turn has been rich in ideas, perhaps less so in relating these to the details of archival practices and processes. Our stance is one of recovering the work from the mythology, and in particular recovering the intertwining of theory and methodology from the sloganising, with the intention of following the trace, avoiding romanticising the process involved in favour of unpacking the intellectual labour, recognising the dominant version of the archive but also keeping in sight its many other incarnations, and emphasising that analysis and interpretation require careful attention to the specificities of the remaining traces.

We are in full agreement about this. In addition, there are also some points of creative departure between us, junctures or crossroads where we have all arrived, but then developed different takes on the ideas involved. These concern genealogy and genealogical analysis, heterotopia and heterotopics, configuration and rhythmanalysis, and archival imaginary and archival sensibility. We now briefly discuss what is going on at these crossroads, because gaining a purchase on how we are using these terms will provide readers with an overview of the different ideas and emphases that underpin the four chapters of *The Archive Project* that follow this.

Crossroads

We now discuss some heuristic separations around which it is useful to introduce readers to points of arrival and departure that will play out across the next four chapters. We all find the ideas and concepts discussed important and interesting. These are differences in take, rather than more substantial disagreements; they express shades of opinion and usage rather than sharp disputes; and they exist largely because of the substantive contexts concerned and the methodological purposes and ends to which these ideas are put.

Genealogy and genealogical analysis

Discussions of genealogy and genealogical analysis are core to Chapters 5 and 3 respectively. Genealogy is used in the sense of constructing a discipline or lineage of genealogy, in order to indicate the connections shared with others. It signifies a different genealogy of the archive, a counter-history and also the existence of counter-archives. An archival genealogy moves beyond biographies and ethnographies of the archive (Dirks, 1993, 2002), and beyond archival stories (Burton, 2006), to trace the connections and disconnections between different archives, and archival practices, and the consequences of these for understanding any given archive. Archaeology and genealogy are interrelated strands in Michel Foucault's work that shape its methodological and theoretical direction. As Foucault (1980b: 93) puts it, 'genealogy is the aim of the analysis and archaeology is the material and methodological framework', further adding that 'I never stopped doing archaeology. I never stopped doing genealogy.' But how exactly are archaeology and genealogy interwoven in Foucault's analytics and how do they relate to genealogical analysis?

The weak component of Foucault's archaeological method is his neglect of non-discursive formations and the role of power relations in mobilising transitions between systems of thought, in short, the power/knowledge couplet that is at the heart of his genealogical turn. In this light, genealogy took up the thread where archaeology had left it loose, namely, in accounting for the contingencies and non-linear formations of discursive regimes in the history of ideas and systems of thought. Truth cannot be separated from the procedures of its production. The researcher's task is therefore to criticise, diagnose and demythologise 'truth phenomena' – and archives are the site par excellence for doing this through genealogical analysis. Foucault was an archive addict, although his premature death prevented him from publishing more of his archival work. However, his short lively essay 'Lives of infamous men' (1994) with the memoir of *Herculine Barbin* (1980a) and the *lettres de cachet* (Farge and Foucault, 1982) not only give a glimpse of bio-politics in early modernity but also provide readers with a taste of how Foucault and also Farge compiled, edited, analysed and interpreted their archival documents. As a consequence, they enable us to appreciate the power of genealogical analysis in moving beyond just delineating the history of thought, to pinpoint the detailed processes of its production.

Heterotopia and heterotopics

Heterotopia and heterotopics are analytical presences in Chapters 3 and 2 respectively. The notion of heterotopia in Foucault's work first emerges in *The Order of Things* on a mostly linguistic level of analysis (Foucault, 2000: xviii). Then heterotopia becomes a more spatial and real entity in his essay 'Different spaces'. As juxtaposed to utopias or unreal places, heterotopias are configured as spatial entities of heterogeneous elements that are part of hegemonic spaces, 'but in such a way that they suspend, neutralise, or reverse the set of relations that are designated, reflected, or represented by them' (Foucault, 1998: 177). Heterotopias are ambiguous spaces traversed by antagonistic power relations and saturated by dissonant discourses, and they are 'not something fixed, but a mobile process full of uncertainty, heterogeneity and contradiction'. Conceived as a heterotopia, the archive has the possibility to conform with but also to challenge hegemonic spaces of knowledge production and Foucault used it, the museum and the library as exemplars of his analysis: 'museums and libraries are heterotopias in which time never ceases to pile up' (Foucault, 1998: 182). It is on Foucault's latter reference that Steedman (2011) has drawn to offer her own configuration of the archive as a heterotopia. Thinking in terms of heterotopia opens up for inquiry the existence of peripheral but resonate spaces within which the dominant is disputed and its hegemony undermined.

Not in contrast but in parallel, the idea of heterotopics follows the work of Maurice Blanchot (1982 [1955]) in *The Space of Literature*, a considerable influence on Foucault. Blanchot is concerned particularly with fictions as 'other places' with their own temporalities, protagonists and bit-part players, organisational structures, conventions, modes of engagement, ideas about im/proper behaviour and ethics, and so on. Blanchot's work is particularly helpful for thinking about documents of life such as letters, diaries and autobiographies, for these tread the hazy shifting line between facts and fictions. Letters, for instance, are a representational mode, but at the same time have an ultimate referentiality because of originating in and being dependent upon a 'real world' of people and events. They have strong fictive and heterotopic aspects; indeed, this is perhaps their defining characteristic. But at the same time, the heterotopic aspects of correspondences and wider systems of letter-writing do not necessarily dispute or challenge, other than by mere existence as 'other' to the straightforwardly material aspects of social life, which marks them off from key aspects of Foucault's notion of heterotopia.

Configuration and rhythmanalysis

The terms configuration and rhythmanalysis are drawn on in Chapters 4 and 3 respectively. The concepts of configuration and emplotment are central to Paul Ricoeur's (1984, 2004) work on time and narrative, and are helpful for thinking about archival research both conceptually and in practical 'how to' terms. They form an important part of his discussion of mimesis, which he sees as three-fold (prefiguration, configuration, refiguration) and according to which narrative represents the human world of action. Narrative and time are intertwined and mutually dependent, with narrative the key mode of expression and representation for human lived consciousness. Ricoeur's comments on the archive appear in a number of places (for example, Ricoeur, 1988: 116–17; 2004: 166–81), seeing archives as constituted by documents gathered together, and 'the archiving of things' as a precursor to the 'consulted or constituted archive' (2004: 167). He also asks important questions about the procedures involved in moving 'from collecting documents to writing books' (Ricoeur, 2004: 167, citing de Certeau 1998: 66), deeming it necessary to 'follow the historian into the archives (Ricoeur, 2004: 169) to unpack their research activities so as to understand the knowledge claims they make.

The contrast here is with rhythmanalysis and Henri Lefebvre's methodological suggestions for looking at the rhythms of social spaces and their effects on the subject, including the researcher. For Lefebvre, rhythms are of the world and in the world, they are cyclical repetitions entangled with linear processes, and they are never identical – there is 'always something new and unforeseen emerging from their repetition *rhythm*' (Lefebvre, 2004: 15). He also warns against confusing rhythms with movement or sequence of movements, speed or machines. The meaning of rhythm is obscure and so we need to learn to listen to the rhythms of a house, a street, a neighbourhood, an archive. But what does it mean to think and live rhythm? 'Rhythmanalysis could change our *perspective* on surroundings,' Lefebvre (2004: 17, original emphasis) notes; it makes us aware that there is 'nothing inert in the world, *no things*: very diverse rhythms.' For Lefebvre, then, rhythmanalysis is embedded in the here and now and the importance of listening to the rhythms of movement and activity, and it eventuates in recognising the existence of repetitious patterns, something that Ricoeur downplays. Rhythmanalysis also brings to the fore the catalytic role of the space/time of the archive in opening up analytical paths and insights. It is not *after* the archive that we write history, for the analysis starts while in it.

Archival imaginary and archival sensibility

The archival imaginary and archival sensibility are analytical presences in Chapters 5 and 2 respectively. The idea of an archival imaginary for some signifies a major re-imagining of 'the archive' and as almost synonymous with the archival turn. While the term 'the imaginary' has expositions in the work of Gide and Sartre, it is particularly associated with Jacques Lacan, with its basis the ego in the context of what he terms the 'mirror phase' of psycho-sexual development. The Lacanian psychoanalytic version is rooted in but departs from Freudian ideas about the Oedipal phase, with Lacan inscribing a close association between identification and alienation. More widely, however, the term now circulates in other intellectual contexts with variant meanings. In particular, the term has a different inflection in work within the conceptual domain of archival and associated theory, drawing particularly on Foucauldian ideas about refiguring the archive, but with some work closer to Lacanian ideas of the imaginary (see Hamilton *et al.*, 2002; Petersen, 2002; Matienzo, 2008; Stryker, 2010; Sheringham, 2010).

This line of thought is concerned with challenging, overturning and replacing the archive in its disciplining formulation. In addition, the imaginary has been used in a way that draws together ideas about imagination and the imaginary as a trope standing for the structured constraints that exist in canonical sets of ideas. Michele Le Doeuff's (1989) reconsideration of *The Philosophical Imaginary* is a case in point, and has in turn been taken up in Helen Verran's (1998: 238) use of the trope to situate what is imaginary as 'an element inherent in knowing which, currently, is almost ignored by modern practices and accounts of knowledge' and as 'constitutive of, and constituted by ontic and epistemic communities'. This and other re-workings of the term in the frame of science and technology studies (Jasanoff and Kim, 2015; McNeil *et al.*, 2016) bring the archival imaginary closer to the idea of an archival sensibility.

The idea of an archival sensibility is a conceptual frame that directs and focuses attention in a particular way, with prevailing sensibilities being permeable and changing over time (Boulter, 2011; Valles Martínez, 2011; Wisser, 2011; Tamboukou, 2014b). The current archival sensibility, strongly associated with the archival turn, redirects the attention of archival research in four overlapping ways, as follows.

This contemporary archival sensibility, first, disavows what might be called the bibliographic approach to archival matters and its focus on a valorised notion of collections and their cataloguing and retrieval, in favour of re-thinking ideas about provenance, opening up new routes and new forms of collection, underscoring original order and structures of information, and maintaining the coherence of items within collections, as well as collections themselves, and the contexts marking both. Second, this sensibility rejects seeing 'archival' as a property or characteristic inherent in some kinds of materials rather than others, produced by some kinds of people and groups

somewhat a departure from my own understanding

but not others, and instead seeks to expand what 'an archive' can be without falling into the trap of conceiving this as wide as discourse itself, which it does by placing collecting and collectors centre-stage, rather than collections. Third, it directs attention to the 'black box' of what happens in archives and archival research, both the practicalities involved, and also the 'entanglements of meaning and matter' that constitute the realm of reflexivity, thought and interpretation (Tamboukou, 2014b). And fourth, the current envisioning also reflexively encompasses the idea of a 'post-archival sensibility' that sees the digital as fundamentally remaking 'the document', 'the collection', 'the database' and 'the archive'.

Finally here, can ideas about the archival imaginary and an archival sensibility exist in the same critical plane? We think they can and are different ways of getting at similar things, but of course it will be up to readers to make their own assessments from our different chapters. Consequently we return to this and other differences in the epilogue and consider the ways they play out across our individually authored chapters.

Positioning ourselves: key problematics

There are a number of ideas debated in work on the archival turn that are in process of gaining canonical status as truisms, and which as a result are taking on more settled meaning than earlier. Again, it will be useful for readers to have our shared responses to them briefly set out here, in advance of the different ways they arise and are threaded through the substantive chapters following. A 'problematic' is not a problem, but a topic or question to be explored, along with consonant means to investigate it, and suitable ways of evaluating the results. The things we now discuss raise some key problematics for archival research, concerning which it is important to develop a principled view, as well as recognising that these matters will assume different guises in different archival contexts. Also it should be noted that, although we refer in turn to the epistemological, ontological and methodological problematics, these are of course thoroughly interrelated and are separated here for ease of communication while they are conjoined across our chapters.

Epistemological problematic

Archives and their collections are not totalising, and so are unlike the library coterminous with life itself that Borges fictionalised. Their contents overall (and recognising that particular collections, like those Farge worked on, may be different) are incomplete as well as partial; they hold fragments of traces, representations of representations, and as Steedman (2001: 45) has put it, 'You find nothing in the archive but stories caught half way through.' What then can be known and how? Can knowledge reside in, be derived from, the fragmentary and partial? An influential response has been to reposition archival research in terms of a particular style of ethnography, one that places emphasis on the activities of the researcher in excavating archival stories, both of historical traces, and of the researcher's presence and work.

The epistemological questioning occurring around this has been helpful and interesting, and we largely agree with the tenor of arguments here. However, what we draw a distance from is the tendency to leap to the opposite viewpoint, that if there are not certain facts then everything is just stories and fictions, rather than seeing archival texts as having – as all texts of whatever kind always do – some deployment of fictive devices in their assemblage. We see the tendency here of thinking and pronouncing in binary terms – total facts, or complete fictions – as one of the results of the mythologising process and find it unhelpful once real archives, real collections, real documents, and the immense complexities of these, are brought into frame. Certainly recognising their storied form and content is important when working with documents of the past (and present too). However, our interest is in *their* stories; that is, in the traces and accounts of the people of the past and their lives, and we see the archival researcher as a vehicle for exploring this, rather than being the focus as in some discussions. The result is that across the chapters following we occupy the middle ground and in doing so seek for ways to reclaim the 'half-way through' that Steedman highlights, rather than evacuate or vitiate this.

There are some interesting things to think about here, and questions to which easy answers should be resisted. We recognise the issues in realist approaches to 'facts', but also view reducing the past to stories as unsatisfactory in a number of ways, including concerning the ethical issues involved. In the last resort, readers will take up their own positions, guided especially by what seems fair and reasonable in the particular archival context being addressed.

Ontological problematic

The ontological problematic has a different source from epistemological questions about what can be known and how by using archival traces, as it is instead concerned with 'what is it?' and 'what can be legitimately done with it?' questions. It arises contemporaneously around wide-ranging technological and cultural developments that have impacted and will continue to impact on many aspects of archival research, affecting how we work, and what we work on. For most archival researchers, this starts with the trace itself and with the increasing omnipresence of digital media. It initially surfaced in the form of researchers being denied access to original documents in highly valued collections, and instead required to work with microform or microfilm copies, with their flat surfaces that looked different, felt different, were stripped out of their archival folders, files and boxes, and were difficult to read and make sense of. It has also surfaced, or perhaps erupted, around the re-use of what is called 'secondary data', collected by one set of people for one purpose and later re-used by others for different ones. We are also now in a situation where an archive or a collection can sometimes have nothing other than a digital form – the so-called 'born digital' – with a collection in question starting and ending there, although for most archival researchers this is more often met with over the body and lens of a digital camera.

Digital files and the images they generate are becoming ubiquitous in archival research, both high standard versions licensed by an archive or other repository and, increasingly, the shabbier kinds made by archival researchers ourselves as part of creating our meta-archives of digitised print and manuscript sources. Digital images are more seductive because seemingly more 'real' than either transcriptions or microfilm of documents, because having strong simulacra of presence aspects – they look the same, so long as some features are ignored – such that for some people they become seen as though 'the letters of Thomas Jefferson' or 'Magna Carta' and the thing itself albeit in digitised form.

But of course they are not; and even as simulacra go, digital images are deficient because they lack key properties. Their two-dimensional digital spatial dimensions are very different from the three-dimensional paintings, letters, maps and so on that they are visual representations of; their 'digital images on a flat screen' form of materiality is very different from wood, canvas, paint, ink, parchment or paper; and they lack the recoverable relationality of the archival versions by being stripped from archival context. The loss of the relational aspect is for us something that particularly needs to be acknowledged. As objects in a file structure, each digital image appears to stand on its own, in serried ranks with others. However, the contents of collections and archives never have such anonymity. They do not stand alone, but are rather part of something, being entangled organically with others, for at basis an archive and its collections is a vast set of relational components: relational in the 'real' past lives these are traces of, also relational in archival terms.

There is also, as noted above, the 'born digital' and debates concerning this. While the four of us have rather different takes on its import, we all recognise there are immense materialities underpinning the digital. Examples here are of the programming languages that enable words and images and sounds to take digital form, bringing together the materiality of hardware (machines, screens, keyboards, electronic circuitry, electricity and so forth) and the equally profound materiality of software and coding and programming as well as the software packages and apps that this supports. Focusing on the software, coding and programming aspects, it is important to note that these rest at basis on text and writing – for instance, in the mark-up language TEI used to prepare many written documents for web publication, one line of coding for the opening of a letter looks like this: [*<p><milestone*

unit="lineno" n="1"/>Dear <name type="person" key="36">Reader</ name></p>]. This coding language is obviously – if mysteriously to the unfamiliar – textual in character and it and others like it underpin digital systems of representation, Dear Reader.

There is also another way to think about these matters, which is from the viewpoint of users and the creativity they can bring to exploring and using the enhanced possibilities provided by digitisation, visualisation and companions. Doing so, we fully accept that things discussed above can seem very different and may indeed lead to marked innovations in research processes, conceptual issues, possible outputs of a project and so on.

Overall the points we are making here are simple ones. Clearly, there are important changes afoot. However, seeing the supposedly born digital as somehow *fundamentally* departing from textuality, documents and archiving in the more traditional sense breaks down once the details of what is involved are confronted. But at the same time, there are indeed enhanced possibilities stemming from new developments that need thinking through. And in raising these points, we have no Luddite intentions. Between us, we are enthusiastic users of digital media, if possible take digital photographs to facilitate our out-of-archive work, readily use TEI to mark up text for digital purposes, and have been involved in originating a number of mix-media and electronic-only sources (Feminist Webs, *Olive Schreiner Letters Online*, and the electronic-only journal *Sociological Research Online*). We raise them because the differences noted here do indeed make a difference and need to be thought carefully about. They are not optional in the pantheon of things that need thinking about by archival researchers, however seductive it may be to 'see', for instance, the UK's Doomsday Book of 1086, the American Declaration of Independence, or the last letter that Mary Queen of Scots wrote before her execution, in their digital form. Certainly making digital copies of documents and images can offer solutions to some real problems, like not enough time in an archive to read everything that needs to be read, and not enough money to visit archives and collections across the world. And this can also democratise access to materials previously available only to scholars and students, by bringing things together that are separated in archival space, and asking different kinds of questions about collections and contents. Certainly digitisation *does* help with all these things. But it also brings ontological complexities in its wake, and digital versions should not be mistaken either for the thing itself *or* for simulacra of it – they are something else again.

There are some helpful signposts here. Yes, of course archival researchers should use electronic and digital enthusiastically – and mindfully – whenever appropriate. However, the ontology of digital forms needs some serious attention. And ideas about the 'born digital' should be responded to as claims requiring thoughtful constructive interrogation rather than being facts to be accepted.

Methodological problematic

The context here is the feeling, already alluded to, that the meeting of researcher and archive can be seen in terms of 'an encounter', in the sense of something verging on the conflictual. Archives and collections are not innocent but marked by selections, occlusions, exclusions, partiality, fragmentation, and these pressures impact on what remains, how it is organised, accessed and worked on. In addition, 'the researcher' comes in different sizes, shapes, colours, and such matters as sex, race, age and class also impact on the reception and perception of their presence, as well as their own sense of what is important, interesting, and how it should be pursued. What has developed in consequence is the telling of archive stories in the framework of ethnography. Antoinette Burton's (2006) edited collection, *Archive Stories*, is the archetype here, with the term well on its way to gaining mythologised status within the pantheon of archival turn literature. The contents of *Archive Stories* are supplements or add-ons to a substantial body of archival research and publications focused on a range of historical settings and topics and are most usefully read in this way. However, the methodological problematic inheres in the mythologising process: what in Burton's collection is a good idea and some keen insights about it by its contributors have been taken up by other parties, some of whom do so in such a way as to emphasise and exaggerate one simplified aspect of what is being dealt with.

This has occurred in particular around a different understanding of reflexivity from the one we are drawing on, and is associated with the rise of autoethnography and its emphasis on the thoughts and feelings and presence of the researcher as the topic (Adams *et al.*, 2015). It is the slippage from, 'the researcher is there and this impacts on the research', to 'the research is the impact on the researcher', that gives us pause for thought. Reflexivity here has settled on feelings and presence, while in the tradition we draw on the concern is with the genesis and processes of knowledge production, one aspect of which is that the spatial and material creates conditions for knowing and understanding, with other aspects being those less easily told aspects of intellectual biography concerned with analysis and interpretation. As this indicates, we are certainly not against either ethnography or reflexivity as such, but find the valorisation of feeling and a heroic version of the researcher's subjectivity unhelpful. It is one thing to talk about the unboundaried archive and the researcher's presence, quite another to remain immersed in self, rather than the traces of the lives of the people and events we are supposed to be researching.

Ethically and intellectually, we conclude with some firmness that what matters are the lives and events of people of the past (and the present) and making some kind of sense of these. Relatedly, we see the feelings and experiences of researchers as largely irrelevant except in relation to how understanding and knowledge are produced, and here we think the analytical and interpretive processes involved are certainly important and to be taken critically appreciative note of.

After other archives: situated knowledges and archival practices

Here we briefly indicate the main topics that our individually authored chapters are concerned with and also set out in more detail the aspects of our intellectual biographies which have led us to write our chapters as we have. These statements have something of the character of a credo, being tied to the idea of situated knowledges that has been so powerful a current in thinking about feminist research and feminist methodology (Haraway, 1988; Stanley and Wise, 1983). They provide another key for reading the chapters following, enabling readers to unpack more of the different trajectories that our largely shared ways of thinking about archival research have taken us on. After this outline of our intellectual biographies and interests regarding archival research, and with our earlier interrogation of 'In Other Archives' in mind, we shall then move into the territory of the particular archives and projects we are engaging with in the chapters that follow.

Archival methodology inside the black box: noise in the archive! / Liz Stanley

Chapter 2 originates from teaching students in history and sociology experiencing their first forays into archives, and supervising PhD students and post-doctoral fellows who have not been introduced to practical historical research earlier in their careers. Their dismay on opening the doors of an archive – any kind of archive – has come from them feeling that nothing in the methods of teaching they have previously had (what use a survey, focus groups or interviewing?) has prepared them to make sense of what lies within. It is this that has led me to write something that offers cheerful encouragement and some tried and trusted practical suggestions. These take the form of some basics for surviving in good order, summarised under the heading of 'archigraphics' or 'writing the archive', and they are explored in the framework of a strong archival sensibility. But please, don't treat what's in the chapter as a cookbook: read it, reflect on it and throw it against the wall if it doesn't help!

After starting research on Olive Schreiner's manuscripts in the 1980s (for example, Stanley, 1983, 2002), I thought that because of apartheid it would never be possible to work on things in South African archives. But times change, predictions were wrong, and my first archival encounters in South Africa were in 1995, the first heady year of the young Rainbow Nation. Interested in almost everything and easily side-tracked, my research on Schreiner's manuscripts morphed into the concentration camps of the

South African War, proto-feminist white women's involvement in racialised nationalism in South Africa, and its monuments and memorials (for
example, Stanley, 2008 [2006]; Stanley and Dampier, 2006), eventually
Schreiner's letters (www.oliveschreiner.org; Stanley and Salter, 2014), and
then into Whites Writing Whiteness from the 1770s to the 1970s (www.
whiteswritingwhiteness.ed.ac.uk).

My experience of being confronted by 'the archive', however, came from
neither the imperial archive in the UK nor its off-shoots in South Africa.
It involved an earlier generation of state-licensed South African historians
who had sold their souls for a mess of racial potage and whose activities
mark many records of the South African War (1899–1902) in inscribing
what was *not* to be written about, with their watchword 'this must not be
said'. Their activities? The signs of black folks in 'white' places and spaces
were excised, authentic Boer/Afrikaner names – the right kind of dead –
were ticked, while others were struck through, and the 'correct' ones placed
on memorials (Stanley, 2008: 172–218). So much for these researchers and
their politics/ethics! However, during the really bad years of the apartheid
nationalist state, later generations of archivists took considerable risks to
ensure its controls were by-passed and banned researchers abroad were pro-
visioned with research materials. An example of much importance for my
own research is that without such integrity and bravery from the archival
'establishment', Ruth First and Ann Scott's (1980) ground-breaking *Olive
Schreiner* could not have been written.

This brings the discussion round to ethics, although not the simplistic
kind of an academic reviewer for one of my book manuscripts (Stanley,
2008 [2006]), who wanted the names of people that appear on public monuments across South Africa anonymised as well as those of Lord Kitchener
and Queen Victoria! The more complex position is that in carrying out archival research there is, or should be, a strong sense of a feminist relational
ethics. This is founded on the profound relationality of people and requires
the analysis carried out and the interpretations made to be fully transparent
and accountable. This is a key part of the archival sensibility underpinning
my chapter.

Archival rhythms: narrativity in the archive / Maria Tamboukou

Chapter 3 explores the narrative fabric of archival research, tracing grey
dusty autobiographical documents and following storylines and narrative
personae. But although narrative documents are the sources *par excellence*
of archival research, and as this chapter has already highlighted, the archive
is also a site of fragments. There is always something missing, because not
everything found a place in an archive, because of serendipity, because of
intentional selections and deselections, as well as because of specific rules
of taxonomy and classification that allow some documents of life to be

preserved and others to become obscure and marginalised. Discontinuous and interrupted as they are, narrative fragments create their own rhythms of archival existence and it is on specific spatial and temporal rhythms that my chapter focuses.

In exploring these things, the chapter draws on Henri Lefebvre's (2004) rhythmanalysis of different spaces and different temporalities and considers material and spatial entanglements between the researcher and the archive. This approach is underpinned by a genealogical understanding of history in general and the archive in particular, as discussed above. In this context, the archive is taken as a discursive space, whose boundaries are socio-historically and politically conditioned, but also constantly reconfigured. In raising questions in the history of the present, the chapter also considers some aspects of technological changes and digitisation and effects on the ontology and epistemology of archival research.

The chapter draws on my overall project of writing feminist genealogies, exploring the emergence of the female self in the interface of the private and the public within the social milieux of education, art and work (Tamboukou, 2003, 2010a, 2015b). The archive is central in such an approach to the historical constitution of the female self in modernity: it is its grey documents that I have been excavating over a number of years to unravel folds in women's self-representations, to listen to their silences and to discern possible patterns in their absence from history.

While I consider instances and exemplars from my overall archival research, the particular case studies presented in the chapter derive from my current research of writing the genealogy of the seamstress. This is a life-history research project that traces, collects, archives, analyses and discusses auto/biographical narratives of home-based dressmakers and women working in the garment industry. It spans a range of geographies, histories and disciplinary fields and focuses on the force of narratives in illuminating interrelations between women's labour and its memory, personal, domestic and public spaces, migration histories, political activism, adult education and women workers' forceful interventions in the cultural and intellectual life of the twentieth century. Although this is an extended research project that includes research in archives in France, the USA and the UK, it is specifically my archival work at the New York Public Library that is presented and discussed here, given the limitations and constraints of a single chapter in a volume.

Reading time backwards? Archival research and temporal order / Andrea Salter

Chapter 4 is underpinned by an intellectual and personal concern for how time and temporalities are involved in representing experience and how sense can be made of this. From 2000 to 2004, I worked as a care worker with older people who drew on their memories and spoke of other times, who reflected back on earlier days and made comparisons with the present. Some wrote diaries for research conducted as part of my Master's dissertation, and some took part in serial interviews. They talked about the joys and woes of ageing in terms of its physical effects, and also about making sense of experience when the vista of the past continued to expand, the future to shorten, with connections between points in the temporal landscape becoming dis/connected and re/configured.

Having begun to appreciate the role of space, spatiality and place as an undergraduate, the importance of time and temporalities in making sense of the representation of experience struck me profoundly as a postgraduate and left an intellectual hand-print on my post-doctoral afterlife, helped along the way by subsequent experience of teaching a postgraduate training course on narrative, text and discourse. My chapter, as a product of this, explores time and temporality as structures that researchers can deploy methodologically in conducting archival research.

My main examples are drawn from the doctoral research I conducted at the Mass Observation Archive, Sussex, UK, on its collection of diaries; and in comparison I explore my post-doctoral research experience as part of the Olive Schreiner Letters Project team and involvement in the production of the *Olive Schreiner Letters Online*. Regarding Mass Observation's diaries, the chapter explores the ways in which the different sampling techniques I devised and deployed, including a backwards chronological sampling method, were interpretively productive. This includes looking back from the perspective of the product or products of an archival research project. It also includes other ways in which, alternatively, looking forward from the perspective of the present, or the 'space of experience' to a 'horizon of expectation', can be useful. In raising these matters, the chapter invokes Ricoeur's (1984, 2004) theorising around narrative, time, memory and forgetting, and comments on the implications of attempting to literally 'read time itself backwards' (Ricoeur, 1984: 68).

Overall, I see engaging with time and temporalities as central to archival research, both conceptually and methodologically. I also feel strongly that a methodological approach needs to be appropriate to the materials to be analysed. Temporal methodologies are especially productive when used in the examination of 'documents of life', given their interesting and strong temporal complexities in the representation of experience. Maintaining this congruity between material and method is very important to the strength of the knowledge-claims that can be made regarding the research material. It relates, too, to the ethics of transparency and accountability in archival (and other) research, to pinning down analytical threads and making arguments justifiable.

Weaving an archival imaginary: researching community archives / Niamh Moore

Chapter 5 highlights the process of making an archive as itself a site of research. It focuses on a particular community archive I have been involved

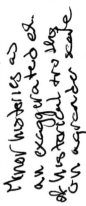

Minor histories as an exaggerated ex of historical true leg on agenda scale

in, Feminist Webs, an archive of feminist youth work in the north-west of England. In writing about a grassroots community archive, I seek to extend archival research encounters beyond formal and official archives, and to encourage more engagement with the extensive and wide-ranging domain of community archives, which offer a rich seam of valuable resources for researchers.

While the approaches developed in other chapters in *The Archive Project* can equally be applied to researching in community archives, I am specifically interested in highlighting the process of creating the archive as a site of research. The *ad hoc* nature of many community archives necessarily draws attention to the process of their production – and this also serves as a reminder that *all* archives are produced under particular conditions that deserve scrutiny. In my chapter, the archive as a site of feminist activism comes to the fore, with the making of the archive being an instance of feminist activism – here feminist youth work in practice – as well as an effort to document hidden histories that might otherwise be lost. The chapter thus continues the feminist archival sensibility of the book while bringing this approach to feminism itself as a topic of research.

The chapter emerges out of my previous work in oral history and particularly participatory community history projects. This has frequently involved sharing skills in research methods, such as oral history and an involvement in creating community archives. Community oral history and community history serve as important reminders that research also happens outwith the formal bounds, and thus the phenomenon of community archiving can be understood as a site of vernacular research as well as a form of cultural participation. In this way, the long history of community archiving, as well as community-based oral history research, offers a commentary on the reluctance of many social scientists to engage in archival research and to archive their own research data (Moore, 2007b). However, rather than reifying distinctions between professional archives, community history and academic research, I take up the concept of 'boundary object' developed by Susan Leigh Star to highlight the way community archives can be understood as shared spaces that exist between and in relation to other sites – here professional archival practices, youth work, feminist history and academic research. The community archive is, then, a flexible entity which moves between more and less formal practices – which may be archival practices, academic research practices, participatory youth work or feminist activism, depending on which site is foregrounded at any one time. These mutable 'boundary infrastructures' allow us to understand community archiving, not as an inadequate professional archive, but rather as an archive tailored to its location. This reworking of the boundary object to reconceptualise the practice of community archiving offers useful resources, particularly to those who wish to focus on the construction of such archives. At the same time, I also hope to encourage researchers to consider independent and community archives as possible sites of research materials for understanding social change.

Into our own archives...

We hope these brief intellectual biographies, together with the earlier discussion of the archival turn, its mythologising aspects, our intellectual crossroads, and comments on where we stand in relation to the great problematics currently facing archival research, will provide a good sense of 'where we're coming from', and how we position ourselves regarding the key ideas and writings influencing archival research. We now move into the territory of our individual chapters, which offer four different but mutually supportive ways in which our ideas about archival research can be put into practice. These convey the crucial methodological aspects of doing archival research as they shape up in the context of the different kinds of archives and collections that are discussed. Read on!

Interlude

Chapter 1 has set the scene and we now move into our individually authored chapters, which offer four different but cumulative and mutually supportive ways in which our ideas about archival research can be put into practice. These convey the crucial methodological aspects of doing archival research as they shape up in the context of the different kinds of archives and collections that are discussed.

Chapter 2 introduces a number of grounded investigative practices involved in carrying out archival research and how these inform and are informed by conceptual, theoretical and methodological ideas. Its core concern is, when the door is opened and the researcher walks into an archive – any archive of no matter how grand or how humdrum a kind – then what can be done to make sense of the traces remaining. It explores this using a number of research exemplars. In doing so, it foregrounds the archival researcher as an active presence in getting to grips with the configurations of archives and collections and in making selections for close analysis. Its framework builds on Michel de Certeau's emphasis on how the grounded practices involved discipline and shape knowledge, and shows how different investigative strategies can be deployed to support analysis and interpretation.

2 Archival methodology inside the black box

Noise in the archive!

Liz Stanley

Archival research: opening the black box

Is an archive a particular kind of place, a collection of connected items, a system of classification imbued with power relations, or something else again? What is it that people do, when they're doing archival research? Is there a particular archival methodology, or is this actually the same as reading books in a library? In what ways can the small parts of a collection – individual letters, photographs or other items – be related to a whole thing and to the wider context these traces of the past were part of? How can collections, sometimes huge in size, be made sense of and used to explore specific research questions? What does good archival research look like and what distinguishes it from the not so good?

These questions are explored by examining the detailed practices involved in archival research and how they inform and are informed by conceptual, theoretical and methodological ideas. Such questions are returned to in the chapter's conclusion and some responses provided, including how the approach here can be used to carry out projects that are different from it. They also beg some additional questions, such as 'what is an archive?' 'what is a document?' and 'who gets to say?' (Craven, 2008; Levy, 2011; Eichhorn, 2013). The answers include that it all depends on the ideas framework within which these questions are asked. Beyond this, the intangibility of what remains, *the traces* (a term used by both Marc Bloch [1954] and Jacques Derrida [1974]) of the remains of times past, have as their remnants some *documents*, with their content (which can exist in many formats) concerned with events and situations, with some of these becoming *records*, in the sense of being part of the contents held in *collections*, which are located and managed in *an archive* of some kind or another. However, at a deeper level, an archive is in a fundamental sense about neither history nor the past: it is an edifice or institution located in the present, with accompanying activities surrounding it that hinge on how what we call 'the past' and its present-day traces are understood. Researching archives and collections and documents from the historical past occurs in this present-time context. But what exactly is it that archival researchers *do*?

It is still rare to find discussions of what archival research actually entails, which is why this book has been written. In the early 1990s, for instance, Michael Hill (1993) commented that archival research was a 'black box', with reading historical documents mentioned but without other activities being discussed, and criticised this silence and the failure to engage with what people actually do. What has been hidden is what Michel de Certeau (1998) in *The Writing of History* called the 'historiographical operation'. This is composed by the specific activities involved, which are strongly shaped by the conventions prescribed and proscribed in methodology writings (Gidley, 2011; King, 2011; Brundage, 2013), by more reflective accounts of archival research (*History of the Human Sciences*, 1998, 1999; Steedman, 2001; Burton, 2006; Featherstone, 2006; Merewether, 2006; Stoler, 2009; Farge, 2013 [1989]; *Comparative Critical Studies*, 2011; Brockmeier, 2015), and also by the particular features of the documents or other data an archival researcher works on. Reading, in particular the researcher re-reading along the archival grain and against it (Stoler, 2009; and on re-reading, Dampier, 2008) continues to be emphasised in much influential literature on archival work, with other activities still largely bracketed (cf. Richards, 1993; Trouillot, 1995; Lalu, 2009), including indeed other ways of reading (Best and Marcus, 2009; Klein, 2013).

As Michel-Rolph Trouillot (1995: 26) has helpfully indicated, archival silences are structured at four crucial junctures: 'The moment of fact creation (the making of *sources*); the moment of fact assembly (the making of *archives*); the moment of fact retrieval (the making of *narratives*); and the moment of retrospective significance (the making of *history*) in the final instance.' As a result, the idea of the black box continues to resound, for example being used by Maria Tamboukou (2010c) in discussing the still prevalent failure to detail the actual research practices involved and how these might fit together. Of course there are distinguished exceptions to the convention of 'silence in the archive', including de Certeau's ground-breaking *The Possession at Loudon* (2000) as well as *The Writing of History* (1998), Carolyn Steedman's (2001) discussion of the 'dust' of archival minutiae and its relationship to how the past is written about, and the contributors to Antoinette Burton's (2006) edited *Archive Stories* in advancing an ethnography of archival presence. But these are exceptional and what remains lacking is a literature that ties together methodology with theory with the details of practice – the black box still needs to be opened, the silence broken, a light shone on what happens inside, and the noise involved listened to.

The effect of 'silence in the archive', unintended, has been the puzzlement of many beginning archival researchers, who read heady ideas about archive fever, the imperial archive, serendipitous findings and eureka moments that remake a field, but are unable to square this with what they find themselves actually doing during their encounters with an archive and its often bewildering array of collections. There's so much of it! And much is mundane and tedious! What on earth to do with it? How and where to start?

The expositions of 'first do this, then do that' found in beginning texts – such as, compile a bibliography, make a list of collections, identify specific things to find out, contact archivists, work on what was identified then go home – contain some sensible suggestions, but often advise an overly narrow approach, including reading just what you came for and then leaving, compared with the broader ideas set out here.

Usually, the importance is stressed of starting by attentively reading the existing literature on a topic, to identify gaps or unsatisfactory closures, and so to formulate better research questions. This is of course important. But for de Certeau, inside the black box other things are going on, which are the detailed activities that are only rarely spoken let alone written about. For him, the prevailing silence concerns *writing*, seen as fundamental to the historiographical operation. It consists of the different kinds of *rewriting* that are carried out, in scribbling notes, making quotes from secondary sources, transcribing documents; and also of different kinds of *writing 'proper'*, in bookreviewing, making conference presentations, drafting and writing chapters, articles and books. As this list indicates, writing comes first, last and also through the middle of the research involved – it isn't just a late add-on with a publication or report or thesis/dissertation in mind. Thus while commonsensically it might be thought that archival research is organised around reading, in practice this is actually writing, with the researcher actively engaged with secondary sources and primary (archival) documents by rewriting aspects of these in their notes, summaries, transcribed quotations and so on. The result is that the archival researcher creates a parallel archive of their own, discussed later as 'an archive of the other archive'.

Writing is seen by de Certeau as the fundamental technology for understanding (that is, for being attentive to an accurate view of the content and organisation of documentary sources), for disciplining (that is, recognising that prevailing academic or other conventions will impact on what is seen as important or not, what is written and how), and also as constitutive of analysis and interpretation (that is, it is not just a way of recording but rather the key means by which analysis, interpretation and resulting knowledge-claims are produced). What de Certeau is emphasising here is that, as soon as pen is put to paper or finger to keyboard, the selections and interpretations made by the researcher enter the frame and do not leave again. This is, however, neither the proclamation of bias nor the contention that the past does not exist because cooked up in the researcher's mind. All research, no matter how 'scientific', involves a point of view, for researchers are living and breathing people; and the documents or other remaining traces provide ample evidence of the activities and realities of people who lived in those temporal realms we call 'the past' and which stretch from just a short while ago, back to prehistoric times.

The framework for this chapter is provided by de Certeau's emphasis on the actual practices forming the historiographical operation and their role in understanding, disciplining and being constitutive of knowledge, including the ways that rewriting and writing are involved and interface with re-reading. It explores the details of carrying out archival research around some research-based examples. And in doing so, de Certeau's ideas about rewriting and writing as the fulcrum for other components of the historiographical operation are developed. As he points out, good research should be responsive to the particularities of the research context and what the data is, as well as what it says, and so no fixed rules or single right way to do archival research is presented here. De Certeau's ideas provide a handy framework, not a straight-jacket prohibiting thoughtful responsiveness and flexibility, and consequently different strategies for analysing varied kinds of archival data will also be noted.

However, before embarking on this, it is perhaps helpful to emphasise that, yes of course I am aware of conceptual and theoretical debates about 'the archive' and have written about such matters elsewhere – but when it comes down to it, there are still the things, the archival stuff, the traces that remain, to be made sense of. It is 'making sense' and 'the stuff' that is focused on in this chapter.

Researchers at work: archigraphics

In discussing the grounded practices of archival research, my long-term engagement with different archives worldwide, and also in building and publishing a number of new digital archives, is drawn on (Stanley, 1984, 1988, 1995a, 1995b, 2008 [2006]; Stanley and Dampier, 2006, 2012; and for new meta-archives, *Olive Schreiner Letters Online*; Whites Writing Whiteness). The discussion opens the black box, scrutinises the activity going on inside and the noisy practices involved, and explores these under the heading of 'archigraphics'. This term – writing the archive – summarises the range of interconnected activities involved in rewriting, writing and their iterative relationship with different kinds of reading, including re-reading and surface reading, both explored later in the chapter. Its different components structure discussion in this section of the chapter and are:

- Starting in good order: rewriting, the archive of the other archive, and the now/past.
- Getting the measure: mapping the heterotopic geographies of a collection.
- Documentary analysis: context1, pre-text, text and intertext, post-text, context2.
- Working it out: interpretation and the ultimately referential character of the past.

These ideas and headings might seem rather abstract – what about the emphasis on noisy grounded practices promised earlier? However, when used to explore the nitty-gritty aspects of archival research, as they are here, they provide helpful ways of getting to grips with the activities involved. They are put to use around my ongoing research on the Forbes Family papers, combined with connected research on other collections and archives, for as noted above, different kinds of data can necessitate different methodological strategies.

This research is part of a wider funded project, Whites Writing Whiteness, concerned with how the racial order of South Africa was re/configured over the period from the 1770s to the 1970s. Whiteness is the focus because of the powerful and almost definitional association between South Africa and what was for a lengthy time its highly structured racial order – later termed apartheid – which was emergent at the start of this period, and in its transitional or even terminal stages at its end. The project has a Qualitative Longitudinal Research (also known as QLR) methodological approach, with its conceptual framework provided by a broad interpretation of the work of Norbert Elias (2008, 2012, 2013) in thinking through how social change takes place (for more information, see www.whiteswritingwhiteness.ed.ac.uk).

Archival research always takes place in a context that is social and political as well as ideational. South Africa, the context for much of my work over the last twenty years, has quite a complicated system of archives, as with other countries. The National Archives of South Africa are composed of archival depositories in each of the formerly independent states (Natal, the Cape, Transvaal and Orange Free State) that entered the Union of South Africa in 1910, as well as a national depository. There are also manuscripts and archives departments in most universities; national English- and Afrikaans-language literary museums with archival collections; and many independent archives, of the churches, Parliament and so on. Many, not just the National and province-level State Archives, rely to different extents on state funding. And some are much better organised and run than others. In the post-1994 dispensation, when full democracy was instituted and a majority government gained political control, ensuring the good survival of records of the past, including the political past, has not been high among the many priorities the government has faced; alongside this, equality policies at local levels have often led to skills shortages; and both have attendant effects regarding how collections are managed 'on the ground' as researchers engage with them. Unpicking the past and interrogating how events unfolded such that racial segregation and apartheid came into being has consequently taken on urgency. For instance, various records of the South African War and its concentration camps I worked on earlier (for example, Stanley, 2008) have been subsequently damaged or lost or stolen. The result is that South African researchers have become greatly concerned about what many see as a crumbling system (Hamilton, 2013a, 2013b; and for the wider view, Hamilton *et al.*, 2002). This background needs to be kept in mind in what follows, and it is paralleled in many other places too, as neo-liberal funding policies bite in the former imperial metropoles.

The Forbes collection is located in the National Archives in Pretoria. Its contents run from 1850 to 1930. Contributed to by many people – close family, related households, kin in Britain and other settler colonies, business partners, lawyers and bankers, government officials, neighbours and friends and 'archived' by family members – these papers are important for investigating the changing activities and views of ordinary white people in South Africa, from the early days of colonisation to the rise of the increasingly racialised form of nationalism and segregation which later eventuated in apartheid. The Forbes were traders and hunters, turned farmers, expanding into agri-business, sheep and stock farming, horse breeding, prospecting, mining and share-dealing. The collection's contents include many thousands of letters, diary entries, legal documents, notes, tallies and inventories, accounts, maps, wills and more. These concern the unfolding lives of the interconnected Forbes, Purcocks and McCorkindale households and the people they had dealings with, including the black people who worked for them as domestic servants, farm workers, shepherds, herders and messengers (Stanley, 2015a, 2015b). The size, diversity and comprehensiveness of the collection make it a helpful core example around which to discuss the practicalities of archival research.

There are of course different ways in which the black box of archival research can be opened up. In this chapter, the ideas and activities clustering under the archigraphics heading are explored using a number of exemplars. These are not meant to be 'exemplary' in the sense of ideal, but are useful examples for explaining ideas by showing archigraphics at work. The discussion following consequently does not provide a 'how to' primer or a set of instructions, but rather explores examples which throw light on archival experiences. This is not a rule-book, then, but suggestions for engaging with what actually happens inside the black box of archival research. The exemplars discussed are provided in the text for ease of reference. In addition, examples that are more briefly referred to, and also the exemplars, will be found at https://sites.google.com/site/thebookarchiveproject/noise-in-the-archive-chapter-2.

Starting in good order: rewriting, the archive of the other archive, and the now/past

How does an archival research project start? Surely, this is with reading what other people have written about the topic! But why then is rewriting seen as so important by de Certeau and others?

Rewriting involves writing notes, making verbatim quotes, listing references and compiling bibliographies, copying articles and book chapters, keeping records and making notes of the contents of an archive collection, digitally photographing documents, all connected with the idea or topic being researched. These things are done in every research project. Reading, in the form of reading against the grain, along the grain and surface reading (all discussed later), is of course also involved – but there's even more rewriting of what is read, in order to remember, distil and make sense of it. Together, these compilations of rewritings add up to the researcher's meta-archive (for a canonical example, and also a cautionary tale of how accumulation can inhibit synthesis, see Benjamin, 2002, 2007). It can be usefully called 'an archive of the other archive' because it is focused around a question or topic to be addressed primarily by archival means, with these rewritings gathered as a support and stimulus in doing so. And having a research question or questions or a topic around which this assemblage occurs is taken as the bedrock in what follows – best start with something in mind around which to organise!

Sometimes the contents of a researcher's archive of the other archive will be small and fragmentary (scrappy notes, references to chase up, 'to do' lists) and sometimes formal and extensive (computer files recording archival documents looked at and verbatim extracts from these, oral interview recordings and transcriptions, stored digital images, drafts of possible chapters or articles). And as this suggests, rewriting shades into writing in the formal sense, such as producing seminar and conference papers, and writing articles and books intended for public presentation and publication, with these too part of the particular archive of the other archive that a researcher – me, you – assembles. All archival research involves the creation of an archive of the other archive; and whatever the scale and content of the researcher's meta-archive, some general questions and issues arise and are discussed later.

Alongside the ideas of 'rewriting' and compiling 'an archive of the other archive', the companion term of the 'now/past' draws attention to the fact that an archive researcher's account of the past also results from present-day intellectual and disciplinary concerns, not only from documents of the past. What is produced from a research project – a publication or report or dissertation/thesis – has a hybrid character concerning its temporal structure. That is, it has aspects of both now and then, rather than straightforwardly representing the past and nothing but. For instance, how key events in, say, South African history concerning apartheid are perceived and understood now, about two decades after the country's 1994 political transition and transfer of state power, is very different from just three or four decades ago, say in the late 1970s following the 1960 Sharpeville then the 1976 Soweto massacres (Beinart, 2001). The 'now' view of these matters, and the 'then' one, make use of largely the same evidential sources, but these are interpreted differently because the context – here the specific time-period in which the interpretation is made – makes a difference to how meaning is attributed to the sources.

'The past', then, is neither stable nor over and done with (for thoughtful interrogations, see Derrida, 1982, 2003). Understandings of its events and their meaning change according to the concerns and ways of thinking that prevail in the present. And because time does not stand still, successive layers of often very different, not just incremental, interpretations can be found.

Like rewriting and the production of an archive of the other archive, the now/past is always a feature of archival research. It is a product of the fact that living breathing people do research on the past, not machines, and it is inescapable because people are always products of their times, not separate from them. Recognising this consequently indicates the need for caution and making modest specific knowledge-claims about the past (de Certeau's (2000) account of prevailing beliefs concerning demonic possession in seventeenth-century Loudon and its 'teratology of truth' is illuminating on this).

To begin at the beginning: how does archival research actually start and what is the role of archigraphics in this? Feeling intrigued, irritated or puzzled by something is often a factor. My editing Victorian maid-of-all-work Hannah Cullwick's diaries for publication (Stanley, 1984), for instance, began with a newspaper item about Arthur Munby, the upper class gent Cullwick eventually married, which mentioned his relationship with a diary-writing servant. No computers or online finding aids back then, so I went to my local library, the Manchester Central Reference Library (see also Chapter 3 on the New York Public Library), and found some background information. Immediately I decided I wanted to work on these diaries and was indeed on a train to Cambridge and the Wren Library, where they are archived, the next morning. Research on the Forbes collection, by contrast, had different points of origin that slowly combined, much like another early project, on the 1930s and 40s radical research organisation Mass Observation (Stanley, 1995a; and see Chapter 4 regarding Mass Observation).

With the Whites Writing Whiteness project in mind, I visited numerous South African archives looking for relevant collections. I came across the Forbes papers, which I 'scoped' and then also 'mapped' (both archigraphical activities discussed later) and was fascinated by. As part of preliminary reading, I came across discussions of the Forbes that were slightly irritating because they confused different members of the family (the Forbes clan were major recyclers of family names) and so got some information wrong. Having to find relevant collections, fascination, and irritation with published work, were the propelling factors here.

A number of black box activities have been mentioned which it will be helpful to pick out for further discussion: rewriting and its relationship to reading; surveying what exists (published, also unpublished archival sources) by using catalogues and registers; scoping; and mapping.

For many people and at all stages of academic work, note-taking and reading go hand in hand, including in highlighting sentences, writing notes with referencing information at the top, pencilling comments on to a copy of a book, article or chapter. My preference is for this latter, as it avoids later mistaking any passages quoted as my own; and the more interesting something is, the more copious my pencilled comments. A page from de Certeau's *The Writing of History* that I found particularly interesting, for instance, bristles with short half-sentences about his argument (provided at https://sites.google.com/site/thebookarchiveproject/noise-in-the-archive-chapter-2), while elsewhere my notes are more reflective or questioning. When these notes on de Certeau were made, I was just starting the Whites Writing Whiteness project and reading at volume, with the rewriting involved not a summary but a selection of what seemed most important. Rewriting is always the selection of things that at the time of writing have charged relevance for us and it involves interpretation. Rewriting, like reading, is an immensely temporal activity.

Another example concerns a mainstay of textbook recommendations: produce a bibliography of the secondary literature. More than just keeping references, rewriting here requires reflection on perceived high and low points in what is read and can also indicate things to be returned to and possible gaps. The exemplar here is an annotated bibliography I produced about missionaries for the Whites Writing Whiteness website (provided at www.whiteswritingwhiteness.ed.ac.uk and go to Publications, then Reading Lists). While I would now not agree with all its assessments, rewriting in making these annotations was helpful in shaping my initial thinking. My knowledge base has increased subsequently thanks in large part to the many kinds of rewriting I carried out.

The idea of rewriting has wider remit still, extending into activities carried out when working in an archive which are not 'reading' in the usual sense, but working out what to do. Perhaps obviously, surveying the territory is extremely important in this. The most usual finding aids are catalogues (although often these do not cover manuscript collections, just printed sources) and inventories. This initial surveying also includes making use of online sources. For instance, my work on the Rhodes Papers in the Bodleian Library at the University of Oxford used its online catalogues and downloaded what was useful; located relevant secondary sources in books and journals; and also searched the UK's National Register of Archives which, in addition, lists the large Access to Archives (A2A) collections, including relevant ones elsewhere in the world. But none of these sources is infinite! There are boundaries within which each works, and also inevitable gaps. Consequently surveying the territory should include making full use of the different 'finding aids' that will be physically found in whatever archive is being worked in, for these aid thinking laterally as well as literally about the topic in hand and help add other relevant material to that already known about. Among these, finding aids will usually include inventories for larger collections.

An inventory is a list of contents and an important piece of kit for archive researchers as well as archivists (Wisser, 2011). Inventories may be brief and schematic in recording just the main sections of a collection (for example, personal papers, divided into letters and cards, diaries, engagement books and so on; and business or political papers, also divided into sub-sections), although sometimes they fully itemise contents. This is so for the very large Findlay Family collection in the Cullen Library manuscript collections, for example (see www.historicalpapers.wits.ac.za/?inventory/U/collections&c=A1199/I/56820). Inventories often but not always exist for 'classified' collections, that is, those that have been worked through by an archivist before being made available to researchers. This might be taken to mean that an archivist has organised the contents of collections, although actually this is much less common a practice than supposed, and collections now usually arrive in the shape and order that researchers encounter them, although perhaps orchestrated by family archivists or by the inheritors of letters and other documents, with the policy generally to preserve the order at purchase or donation (Craven, 2008; McKemmish *et al.*, 2005; Wisser, 2011). This was the case with the Findlay papers, which were organised and inventorised by family member Joan Findlay. Moreover, archival research-ers generally treat inventories as working documents, rather than guides, for they are read and frequently re-read and have an iterative relationship with working on a collection's contents. Discussing two different styles of inventories shows how rewriting is involved in this.

The first concerns the Forbes collection. The exemplar here is its inven-tory, dated 1957. It consists of an index, a two-page overview of the Forbes family, and a thirteen-page list of composing sections which is the inventory proper. Annotations in an archival hand have been written at some earlier point on both the introduction and the inventory proper, correcting mis-takes and adding new information, including prohibitions on use at the time of writing under a South African Archive Act (now superseded). I have made many photocopies of the Forbes inventory over the years of working on the collection, with annotations in pencil on successive copies by me and any co-researcher as part of our archival working practices. One of its pages, for instance, shows we have used it to record work done, or not done, to act as an *aide-memoire* noting information, to add to or sometimes correct original information, to estimate how many letters and other documents are involved, and to gauge broadly the time needed to complete various work not yet done (provided at https://sites.google.com/site/thebookarchivepro-ject/noise-in-the-archive-chapter-2). This is messy, it rewrites in the sense of overwriting information thought correct in 1957 as well as subsequently, and it does not always take trouble to overwrite itself and leaves some earl-ier and later rewritings side by side. It is also extremely useful.

The second example here is an inventory of the full kind, concerning the Pringle Collection in the Cory Library, Grahamstown. It is twenty-three pages long; and although every individual document has not been itemised, every dated letter or other item covering a set of composing materials has been, so it is considerably more detailed than the Forbes example. One of its pages shows signs of my detailed check of its contents (provided at https://sites.google.com/site/thebookarchiveproject/noise-in-the-archive-chapter-2). Working through each item and ticking these off against the listing showed that the inventory was 'sort of' correct. Rewriting involved here concerned this 'sort of' and was not made on the inventory itself, but in a fieldwork

is an inventory similar to
the online catalogue?

notebook (always open alongside my computer) which recorded on 2 July 2014 that:

> The collection is misnamed for there is more of Mrs Hockly & her daughter Harriet Townsend, who married Wm Dods Pringle as his 2nd wife. The main sections of the collection as I think it hangs together are –
> Folders 1–13 W Dods P 1820s to late 1860s+, letters, land, other business, legal stuff incl his conveyencing, also cases as he's litigious; covers the K war but 'race' otherwise an absence, is just white folks
> Folders 14–15 Eliz Hockly nee Moore
> Folders 16, 18–23, 25–32 Harriet Townsend nee Hockly later Pringle
> Folder 17 Ellen Hart, 1st wife
> Folder 24 Quirk, Cork property & rents???
> Folders 33–38 scrap paper, writing desk, newspapers etc, misc stuff
> Mainly, the coll = the remains of a business run by HT after the death of 1st husband, Edward. Pringle elements more bitty, but v. interesting letters.
>
> (LS, Research notebook, 2 July 2014. Provided
> at https://sites.google.com/site/thebookarchiveproject/
> noise-in-the-archive-chapter-2)

Another entry shows the important role a research notebook can play in supporting rewriting in the broad sense of reconsidering and revising what is known. In early 2013 while in the Cory Library working on another collection, Gold Fields Consolidated, I was struck out of the blue by the connections existing between people who might mistakenly seem to belong to different networks and time-periods because materials by them are in separate collections. I broke off what I was doing and made a rough diagram of some connections across people, organisations and time-periods (provided at https://sites.google.com/site/thebookarchiveproject/noise-in-the-archive-chapter-2). This has been developed subsequently and the current version helps guide which collections are worked on, with this first sketch having great significance for me because it symbolises a breakthrough moment in considering how my research on different collections might be joined up.

The last kind of rewriting for discussion occurs when immersed in an archival project while also having ideas from the academic literature at the back of the mind, with the example here regarding the Forbes research. The Forbes collection is humungous: there are around 5,000 letters and about three times as many other documents in it. It involves a large number of letter-writers and a complicated set of interpersonal and economic links in which family, household, kin relationships, related households, agri-farming and other business ventures were closely intertwined, interconnecting people in the Transvaal where the Forbes had their base, Natal, Swaziland, the Cape, Scotland, England and at points South Australia. What to call this complex entity? This is no trivial matter, for the terms used will to a large extent set the parameters of analysis.

The terms family, household and domus (the latter term is from Emmanuel Le Roy Ladurie's [1980] work on a mediaeval parallel) do not stretch far enough in covering all the elements involved, and even Norbert Elias's (2008, 2012) concept of a figuration (a social entity – a dance, the naval profession, a family – which persists over time, although its original members drop out, leave, die), although in some ways more satisfactory, still falls short. On one level, the name does not matter so long as the complexities and their ramifications are recognised. On another, the lack of a suitable term signifies an analytical hiatus. An attempt to pin down 'what it is' resulted in a diagram depicting the changes over time while recognising that some structuring persisted (provided at https://sites.google.com/site/thebookarchiveproject/ noise-in-the-archive-chapter-2). This connects closely with rewriting, indeed this diagram is itself an act of rewriting. It brings together ideas from working on the Forbes collection overall, with ideas from the academic literature about family and household structure, to find the latter not entirely helpful when faced with the complexities of the former. This 'what is it' question is something I have also explored in 'writing proper' (for example, Stanley, 2015a, 2015b) but have still not yet found a fully satisfactory way of conceiving what the Forbes were about. However, these attempts were 'good enough' at the times written, which says something helpful about writing more generally, that it is always of its time, may be later superseded, and should be seen as a marker of thinking at a particular point.

Most archives hold many collections, sometimes numbering thousands. When someone arrives to do research, they usually know about at least something they are interested in, which they have found out about through reading, by online searches or using the archive's website and any online catalogues, and sometimes by word of mouth. But how to discover what else might be of interest is often a puzzle, for such searches often come up with titles – for example, Gold Fields Consolidated – rather than detailed inventories, or if the latter exist they are of 'important' collections (politicians, military personnel, major organisations, leading literary figures, and mainly male), which may not be those of most interest. Most archives provide physical catalogues and also inventories. The watchword is, 'use them' in spite of the limitations, and read as many as possible. Perusing them will frequently throw up something of interest, such as a name recognised or a topic that is connected, and with perseverance and luck, such as finding a list of an archive's collections with brief descriptions (a meta-inventory, usually referred to as an accessions handbook or similar), a checklist of other collections of possible interest can be assembled. But what to do then? Scope!

Most researchers have a finite time allocated for an archive visit. It is best always to over-estimate, so that plunging into and staying within the confines of just one thing already known about can be guarded against, and to ensure there is time for additional items to be found and worked through. Scoping is important here, with the Voss Collection in the South African National Archives having been scoped in an afternoon's break from working on the Forbes papers. In the list of accessions, it is briefly noted as a family collection (why I was interested in it) and consisted of seven boxes of papers with no inventory. A handy rule of thumb in scoping a collection is, if there are four boxes or fewer, then skim the contents of all; if there are five or more, then skim the first, last and middle boxes; and if the collection is very large, then add more boxes incrementally. 'Skim' here means a quick scan of all contents, turning the pages to get a broad sense of what kinds of things are in each box and what is going on in them and briefly noting high points. Scoping and skimming are companion terms, then.

What resulted from this was that a broad idea of the Voss collection as a whole – with its central figure a natural scientist with 1950s and 60s letters and papers – was gained, and brief notes were made about each box (provided at https://sites.google.com/site/thebookarchiveproject/noise-in-the-archive-chapter-2). The shape of the collection became clear, although the knowledge gained about specific content was limited. However, it was sufficient to show it contained letters spanning a lengthy time-period, although not in large numbers, and that the Vosses were part of the educated Afrikaner urban elite and represented a different network of people from those I had come across previously. I concluded that at a later stage the Voss collection should have its contents, particularly its letters, worked on in depth.

A similar scoping procedure was adopted in initial encounters with the Forbes collection, with a first scope showing how rich and fascinating the collection was and that it should certainly be a focus for detailed research. Because of its large size, another scoping exercise was done, this time including more boxes from the total of forty-one, and skimming the contents with 'race' matters particularly in mind. Carrying out these two scopings meant I gained a good grounded understanding of the collection fairly quickly in spite of its size, and this provided me with a helpful and substantial knowledge base for the work that followed.

Work on the Pringle inventory, discussed earlier, also involved a version of scoping. However, skimming the whole of this six large box and bulging thirty-eight folder collection was carried out here, because although the inventory is detailed, the contents seemed odd and rather chaotic. What doing this showed was that Pringle is not 'a' collection, but composed of some different sets of things gathered under one title, and with the logical order of these broken at a number of points by items from other parts of it. As a result, this exercise on the Pringle collection took longer than usual (a day, rather than around three hours) because it required more attention to specific content, and so shaded into what was referred to earlier as mapping, which is discussed in the next section.

Rewriting has practical significance for the nitty-gritty of archival research and is as much involved in overviewing boxes and collections through scoping as it is in note-taking or writing annotations. The now/past is also a strong aspect of everything discussed so far, because some degree of analysis and interpretation occurs around the interface between the documents of the past and the researcher's practical work in making sense of them. Some helpful pointers that arise are as follows.

First, it is important for beginning researchers to recognise that rewriting is a fundamental part of working in archives and to appreciate that from early stages they will be engaged with analysis and interpretation, not just in the report or article or dissertation/thesis produced at the conclusion. Although research methodology tends to be taught and written about in a rather linear way, 'writing' should be understood as a broad continuum and involves activities that start at the outset of a project. These early stages, including scribbles of notes and references, are important in honing key practical as well as analytical and interpretational skills and for doing 'writing proper' later on down the line.

Second, as well as recognising the importance of rewriting, an eye also needs to be kept on and ways found of foregrounding the original archival materials – the stuff, the trace – around which such rewritings occur, so there is always a way of gauging the character of the selections and interpretations researchers make. This will help interpretation to remain 'defensible', in the sense that an evidential base can always be pointed to.

Third, some people dive into an archive with the equivalent of a short shopping list – they know exactly which document/s they want, because they've read about them in other people's work – but they are not to be emulated! This is because they will remain within the limits of their knowledge or lack of it. The point, however, is to increase the knowledge base concerning a research topic, so it is important not to stick to what the secondary literature says, but to survey the territory, scope collections, and to use catalogues and inventories to find other relevant materials. Take some mild risks, exceed a narrow definition of what needs to be done, and enjoy!

There are ways of taming scoping as an archival practice and making it a painless and even a pleasurable process. I have outlined a simple procedure for this here, and it can be customised to suit other people's preferred style of working and used for very different projects. Using the procedure takes practice because scoping is a skill, needs to be learned on the job, and underpins successful detailed archival research. Think of it as a bit like learning to swim or cook: practice brings competence.

Getting the measure: mapping the heterotopic geographies of a collection

A collection, or an interconnected group of documents in a collection, and howsoever 'collection' is defined, will have a particular configuration of space/time and depict the world in typical ways. This constitutes what Michel Foucault (1967, 1975; see also Hetherington, 1997) has termed a 'heterotopia', influenced by Maurice Blanchot writing on fictional worlds. Discussion here follows Blanchot (1982 [1955]) regarding the 'worlds' created in novels and other representational fictions, and is rather different from how Foucault's idea is used in Chapter 3. Here the idea of heterotopics indicates that what results in these fictionalised 'worlds' is a written version of the world with its own geography for situating people, places and events. This is a representational order with a complicated less than coterminous relationship with the rest of lived experience. Relatedly, every letter- or other document-writer will have customary ways of configuring the representational order depicted in their writing (photography, interview and so on). They are likely to do so differently when using different forms or genres (letters, diaries, memoirs...), for these have their own conventions regarding what is represented and how. In addition, these 'how' and 'what' aspects are likely to change somewhat when writing to or addressing different people or groups.

All documentary materials have such heterotopic aspects. Wills, for instance, locate a named set of people in relation to property of a material and often spatial kind around a disjunctural conception of time, being documents made in life but 'activated' only by the deaths of their authors, and concerned with objects in place and their re-allocation to other people. Diaries, maps, share certificates, accounts and photographs also have – somewhat different – heterotopic characteristics too. 'A collection' and its contents, then, require unpacking, for the conventions governing how facts are seen and claims about them evaluated will differ for each kind or genre of archival materials, and these heterotopic aspects have considerable importance in shaping the interpretational work of researchers.

Archival research tends to be time-consuming – there are numerous archives and vast numbers of collections, many are huge, and a large number will have relevance for a particular research project – and as a consequence it is easy to become lost in an archive and relatedly to feel it is impossible to get to grips with. Mapping to the rescue!

Surveying the territory and scoping collections helps in taming these feelings. But it is also useful to build on them by developing another archigraphical skill, that of 'mapping' a collection. This is a more detailed activity than scoping, but still not a full-on investigation of content in precise detail. However, it does provide a helpful way of getting the measure of content, with scoping more about the structure and how something 'works' as a collection. So what does mapping mean in practice? The exemplar this is discussed in connection with is the Paton Papers, part of the Kimberley Africana Library collections.

In mapping a collection, it helps to start with some practical but important questions (rather than theoretical or conceptual ones). Examples are:

1. How is a collection organised, what is included and excluded and how are its boundaries configured?
2. What are its main contents concerned with, its overall themes and concerns? And can guesstimates be made of any glaring absences?
3. What would it be helpful to record now, at first acquaintance with a collection, concerning its organisation, overall content and particular aspects (for instance, by writing notes in notebook or computer file or perhaps making an entry in a database)?
4. Should digital photographs of any documents be made, if this is permitted by the archive concerned? If so, of what – and why?
5. Are the contents either in whole or part relevant to your particular research topic? If they are important enough to later carry out more detailed work, what should this consist of?

The collection these questions are explored around contains the papers of a well-known Kimberley man, a jack-of-all-trades and entrepreneurial farmer turned diamond mine owner, George Paton. Paton was a close associate of the imperialist politician and entrepreneur Cecil Rhodes, and with Rhodes was one of the MPs for the Barkly West constituency in the Cape Parliament. There are sixteen archive boxes of his papers, and a rather schematic inventory that fails to convey that most of the collection resides under one of its later, rather schematic, headings (provided at https://sites.google.com/site/thebookarchiveproject/noise-in-the-archive-chapter-2).

In around seven focused hours of concentrated work on the Paton collection (no breaks, no lunch, no chats, forget breathing and the toilet) I was able to answer the above questions, make working notes in a notebook, write four pages of structured notes in a Word file, digitally photograph the inventory and a few interesting items with the Whites Writing Whiteness project in mind, and decide whether further work on the collection might be carried out. Mapping the collection involved the following activities, which are transferable to mapping other collections:

Read the inventory thoroughly, then again. When an inventory exists, it tells the researcher about the shape of a collection as this was perceived by an archivist who, when it was compiled, was also in process of making sense of it. So revisit and rewrite the inventory where appropriate as mapping proceeds (and see above regarding the Pringle and Forbes inventories).

Call up (for example, make a request to an archivist, usually done on a special form) some materials – an archive box or folder, depending on how it has been curated – from each of the main sections of the collection as signalled by the inventory. This may look something like, personal and family letters, company papers, notebooks, letter-books. Skim-read through a file or box of documents from each section, to get a sense of overall content and then make short *aide-memoire* notes about each box or file examined.

Call up the box/es holding the earliest dated items, and skim-read through the contents to get a broad sense of what they're concerned with and make brief *aide-memoire* notes on this.   1st ①

- Ditto the latest dated items in the collection.   middle ③
- Ditto a box in the middle.

last ⑥

If a collection is composed of five boxes or fewer work just with these. If larger, add equidistant boxes as appropriate to collection size. The point is to overview a good spread of documents across the collection as a whole, so resist diving in just to look for something specific! Looking for just the specific might seem a good shortcut, but it will lead to things of importance being missed, and also this specific item won't be understood properly unless a sense of the whole it is situated among is gained.

Decide provisionally what are the most interesting aspects of the contents examined. Regarding the Paton collection, this was the early less controlled phase of diamond mining, and the Newlands Diamond Mining Company that Paton established and which later failed because of what he saw as a shareholders' plot, something I was intrigued by.

Call up more of the items seen as particularly interesting, and read them more carefully. Also now make more notes, and more detailed notes, about these interesting things.   one at a time system

Fairly late in the time allocated for mapping, decide which items to digitally photograph (if this is permitted) and resist snapping the whole lot! Doing so will just defer the problem of figuring things out and is a beginner's mistake that takes much recovering from. Regarding the Paton collection, I photographed the inventory, a scattering of letters about land purchases because this often entailed the disappropriation and removal of black people, some items mentioning the early Diggers Revolution against the emergence of conglomerate mine-owning, and about the Newlands Company shareholders. Before this, I made a file structure on my computer with these headings, so each small set of digital images was downloaded where they could be easily found again.

Search the catalogue for anything else relevant, in this case on Paton and the Newlands Company, and keep anything found for follow-up.

Leave at least fifteen minutes at the end to go over notebook jottings etc., during which time of reflection any additional points thought of can be added.

Having done this, answers to the questions outlined above which resulted from the Paton mapping exercise are:

1. I gained a good overview of the collection, including both its boundaries and also the detail that lies beneath the spare headings in its very schematic inventory.
2. The collection's main themes were pinpointed and briefly noted.

3. Brief notes were made in a notebook as I went along. I also recorded in a computer file some notes on items read, together with meta-data (archive and collection reference, date, writer, named recipient, address etc.) for referencing purposes (NB: I used a database for this, but a Word file would work just as well). At the end of the day, I wrote an overviewing document in a Word file.
4. Then I took digital photographs of the inventory and of about fifteen documents I found interesting, as explained above.
5. I concluded that the Paton collection was interesting, but not directly relevant to my wider research because there were too few letters covering only a fairly short period of time for it to be part of Whites Writing Whiteness. But it would be a good source for someone interested in Kimberley, diamond and gold, and (failed) Randlords, the richest and most powerful owners of diamond and gold mines in South Africa.

Finding these things out, compiling a handy set of notes and records, and copying a few interesting documents, took one day's work. It was a day I considered well spent, and still do. Although the Paton collection is not massive, it is quite large, and this mapping exercise shows just how much, with a simple straightforward plan, can be done in a day's work. Other archive researchers have told me they don't have time to do anything like this, they just flip through hoping something juicy will leap out (aka serendipity – see Chapter 1). This seems a waste – for in not much more time, I gained an understanding of how the Paton collection works, what its contents are and the highlights of these, how Paton and his associates connect up with other interests of mine specifically concerning Cecil Rhodes, and found some items directly relevant to Whites Writing Whiteness that I wouldn't otherwise have known about.

How does carrying out a mapping exercise give a window on to the heterotopic aspects of collections and sets of documents, referred to earlier as an important point of interest? Mapping has the important pay-off of increasing awareness of the contents of a collection, of how the different contributors figure, with the location of people and activities in time and place coming into view. My mapping exercise on the Forbes collection pointed up core aspects of the everyday life focus of Forbes letter-writing (Stanley, 2015a). It also raised the relationship of the different parts of the collection to each other, specifically of the Forbes diaries to the rest. Entries in the diaries, unlike other genres represented in the collection, have a strict temporally bounded character, 'a day' written about in the moment, which throws into relief their geographies in situating places, people and activities in a condensed way.

This can be shown regarding another exemplar, a diary-entry written by David Forbes senior. What to do, when it comes to analysing in detail individual records or documents? Surface reading!

The method of analysis employed here, and also in scrutinising in detail a number of other documents later in this chapter, is 'surface reading' (Best and Marcus, 2009; Klein, 2013). This is not skim-reading, referred to earlier. It is a way of re-reading texts in precise detail, attending closely to the words on the textual surface in their surrounding context and also any deletions, insertions, scribbles, marginalia, silences. Rather than using hindsight and in particular political hindsight, as the more familiar idea of re-reading does (Dampier, 2008), surface reading reads with the grain of what is written, the better to understand the mechanics of how it 'works' as a piece of writing, as a trace or document.

From 1882, the Forbes wrote farming diaries, a recognised form in the South African context, used to record things such as sheep-dipping, herd sizes, hours worked by farm labour, and measurements of cloud, wind, temperatures and rainfall. The Forbes diaries were being scoped as this chapter was written. From thirty-five years of diary-writing, the 6 January 1903 entry was selected randomly because it was the entry arrived at when this section of the chapter was being written. With mistakes and omissions as in the original, it is:

> Kitty, Madge and I rode up to Athole Blockhouse. Jim has about 30 Natives washing the cattle for tick fever. We went out to see some cattle and got wet before we got back to the tent. We got home after the thunderstorm was past and got no rain on the way
>
> Kobaraz finished ploughing behind the house but made a bad job of it
>
> Duke Breslers mare was sent to him yesterday but it came back to day and the boy who took the mare to him brought back I believe a blackguard letter to Dave about the cattle he brought from Standerton and of which he (Bresler stole 8 young cows or full grown heifers 1 Bull and 1 ox he now claims 10 oxen for bringing the cattle down – Although Dave borrowed him from the Govt and he got his pay all the time
>
> Rain .35
>
> The small Kafir girls planted out a lot of lettuce
>
> Van Booyen came claiming the small cart he says he borrowed it from Norman who wants it back or £8 – we found it near the big field – one wheel smashed
>
> (6 January 1903, Diary, Forbes NAD. Provided at
> https://sites.google.com/site/thebookarchiveproject/
> noise-in-the-archive-chapter-2)

This diary-entry starts with place, and as a Blockhouse (a turret built by the military during the South African War of 1899–1902) is mentioned, a separate entity called Athole is also implicit. It is not clear why the cattle were being seen, but what is written demonstrates a division of labour – 'Kitty, Madge and I' rode up to see, while Jim 'has about 30 Natives', and these latter are the people doing the actual work with the cattle. Also such was the import of weather that 'no rain' on the way back was recorded. There are no clues in this first paragraph about who these people are or their relationship to each other, apart from the arrangement of people around the different activities, in the place called the Blockhouse.

Behind the house (implicitly, Athole) is arable farm land, and ploughing it has been done by someone, implicitly male, with a 'Native' name. The longer third paragraph concerns a dispute about payments involving Duke Bresler and what is seen as an unjust request, both in itself, and also became via Dave, the government had already paid him. It is clear who the '30 Natives' and Kobaraz are in this landscape from the activities they engage in, and ditto Duke Bresler. However, neither Jim nor Dave, nor 'Kitty, Madge and I' is explained; implicitly they form a group, people familiarly referred to with 'white' names. The others, including Van Booyen in the last paragraph, do things in the landscape, while Jim, Dave, Kitty, Madge 'and I' are primarily figural presences.

Rainfall appears in a paragraph of its own. It is picked out, regarding both that it had happened and its quantity. For farmers at high summer in the south-eastern Transvaal, the occurrence of storms and rains was extremely important. This also seems to provide the context for lettuces being planted by 'small Kafir girls' (on complexities and issues in racialised terminology in Forbes' usage, see Stanley, 2015a). Again, this records other people doing things, with where the planting was done unspecified. With other elliptical comments, this indicates a familiar reader, someone who would know what such references were to, perhaps its writer, David Forbes senior, at some future point. The last paragraph in the entry records a caller, although who Van Booyen was is not explained. As with Bresler, what is written here concerns disagreement or controversy, about a cart on the farm, payment for its use, and damage to a wheel. 'We' is the Forbes, although finding the cart, given the rest of the diary-entry, may have been done by the workers on the farm, and the passage has the feel of an *aide-memoire* included to record the claim, as no discussion or resolution is noted.

The M.E. Pringle diaries in the collections of the Cory Library, Grahamstown, can be compared here. These are also farming diaries, but exist 'on their own', not as part of a surviving wider entity of writing as with the Forbes diaries. There are forty such diaries, written between 1911 and 1960. There are similar things recorded, but unlike with the Forbes diaries there is no other reference point, and therefore their relationship to other ways of recording the 'same' matters cannot be established. The Forbes diaries, mainly by David and his wife Kate but not about them in a personal sense, can however be considered in the context of many other Forbes writings. These concern the 'same' people – but different things are recorded in the different genres, as shown by different documents from a single date (discussed in Stanley, 2015a). The diary-entries by David Forbes foreground heterotopic aspects of people in places doing activities; the 'scribbling' documents (notes, tallies, lists and so on) in the collection record what and how much, concerning time, people, animals and money; and the epistolary ones are bound up in dialogical exchanges with correspondents. Succinctly, the diaries, scribbles and letters may seem to be about the same thing, but represent this in very different terms.

Rewriting is of course also involved in mapping a collection. My transcription of the Forbes 6 January 1903 diary-entry, for instance, involves analysis and some interpretation, rather than being a one-to-one rendition, for this latter would be the diary-entry itself. Mapping in such a way as to work out the configuration of a collection in dialogue with, rather than just following, any inventory that exists, as with the Paton collection, is rewriting of a significant kind and takes it clearly onto the borders shared with analysis and interpretation. This in turn points to the now/past aspects: it is a researcher with the mind-set of 'now' who engages with, selects, decides, concludes and analyses; and the concerns with the early days of mining, the connections with Rhodes, the shape of a day and its geography of place, people, events and time, are significances in that mind-set, not that of George Paton or David Forbes.

Some pointers from this discussion of the practices involved in the archigraphics skill of mapping and its companion activity of surface reading are:

First, mapping should cover all aspects of a collection. It is important not to pick and choose, because this will result in a false impression of the whole and consequently a misreading of its particular parts. For instance, David Forbes' 6 January 1903 diary-entry analysed in isolation from the wider collection would produce a very particular view of the Forbes, their daily activities and relationships with others. However, considering it in context enables its typical and also atypical features to be seen.

Second, mapping is akin to sampling – it makes choices randomly using the simple sampling frame of picking the first, the last, the middle, and where appropriate equidistantly placed others. It prevents selectivity at too early a stage, and it encourages and supports broad-based understanding.

Third, mapping places a greater degree of emphasis on the content of documents than scoping, although in the context of a collection's structuring aspects. It points up that the heterotopic aspects of collections and also individual documents – their configuration of place, space, people, events, time, feelings and meanings – significantly shape these.

Fourth, mapping requires close attention to the structure and content of particular documents and how these are configured, with the analytical skill of surface reading important here. It shows, among other things, that for particular writers or speakers or organisations, there are aspects that are typical and characterise their particular way of representing the social world. Also embedded here are ways of presenting 'the facts' and adjudicating disputes about these (as with the diary-entry's account of the Duke Bresler and Van Booyen incidents), things which add up to the viewpoint being represented and which it is important that the researcher has some comprehension of, because of the impact on interpretation of what the facts are and for whom.

Documentary analysis: context1, pre-text, text and intertext, post-text, context2

The analysis of archival documents involves taking a text apart, examining how different aspects of its structure and content 'work', and combines re-reading with the attentive analytical focus of surface reading. Documents, whatever their kind or type, and whether written or oral or visual, do not 'speak for themselves' but were produced purposively, from a particular viewpoint or position, and their author/s had particular purposes in mind (which may or may not come to fruition). Being able to analyse this is another important feature of an archival researcher's toolkit. In explaining this, the background is first explained, then the ideas involved are put to work in analysing an exemplar. But first a note of caution: there is no notion here that documents or other texts can – or should – be analysed 'objectively' as though with an empty mind. Empty minds find little that is worthwhile. As Marc Bloch (1954: 64) puts it, even 'the most accommodating [documents] will speak only when they are properly questioned'; therefore it is important to recognise that, as he goes on to comment, 'every historical research supposes the inquiry has a direction at the very first step. In the beginning, there must be the guiding spirit'.

Archival source materials, whether oral interviews or visual images or written documents or material objects, all have artful character. They are always produced from a particular viewpoint. Consequently different sources are likely to contain different versions of events and even 'the facts'. Such clashes are likely to be encountered at some point during archival research and will obviously impact on what can be known and with what degree of certainty by researchers. There are more subtle ways too that such artfulness becomes apparent, regarding the form or shape of a source, which often influences how meaning is discerned, including through how its reader or audience is located and its authorial 'voice' positioned (or ostensibly removed). Relatedly, how documents cite and use other sources – that is, their intertextual character – also needs to be part of the analysis, for these references indicate the wider frame of relevance and 'where they're coming from' in an ideas sense. Connected to this, archival sources, the traces remaining, do not exist in a vacuum but were produced in and take their larger meaning from their originating contexts, so understanding this broader context needs to be part of analytical concerns.

Letters are documents of life – they are not researcher-generated but exist as a part of ordinary social life (Plummer, 2001; Stanley, 2013). Also, they put across a particular message in a particular voice, and intend (but do not necessarily produce) a particular desired effect on their reader/s. Consequently they need to be treated in an inquiring and analytical way. There are different kinds of documentary analysis, with the approach adopted here using 're-reading' combined with 'surface reading'. This involves reading in an analytical way against, as well as along, the grain of how its writer has structured and intends a letter or other document to be read; and in doing so, attending closely to the surface of the text and its deletions, insertions, marginalia and so forth (for examples and discussions, see Dampier, 2008; Stoler, 2009; Best and Marcus, 2009). The framework for doing this involves focusing in turn on context; pre-text; the text and its meta-data, content and structure and any intertexts; post-text; and the new context that subsequently arises. It can best be explained by working through analysis of a document as an exemplar:

> Offices of the Swazie Nation
>   Swazieland Feby 8th 1893
>   This is to certify that David Forbes Esq of Athole New Scotland is the registered holder of an undivided 3 / 8 (three-eight) interest in and to a certain grant for unreadable ^grazing^ farming, timber and other rights on certain portion of Swaziland known as the Mananga Grant and the title thereto is clear and unencumbered in the Registry Books of the Swazi Nation
>   Wm Penfold
>   for Theo: Shepstone
>   Res Adviser & Agent
>   Swazie Nation
>   (William Penfold for Theophilus Shepstone jnr, 8 February
>   1893, Swaziland; Forbes Collection, NAD Pretoria. Provided
>   at https://sites.google.com/site/thebookarchiveproject/
>   noise-in-the-archive-chapter-2)

Context1

The broad context in which this 1893 document was written involved the 'scramble for Africa', European colonisation, the discovery of diamonds and gold and other minerals, and the creation and exploitation of black labour, with significant literatures on these. The specific context concerns the period 1886 to the later 1890s, when there was a 'concessions rush' in Swaziland and white prospectors and miners competed for access to land believed rich in minerals, including tin and coal as well as gold. The Swazi king Mbandzeni was overwhelmed and made land grants headlong and haphazardly. After he died in 1889, his mother the Queen-Regent, Tibati Nkambule, and the Swazi Council of indunas/chiefs employed Theophilus (known as Oppie) Shepstone junior as a Resident Agent, with part of Shepstone's role to ensure concessions were systematically managed. William Penfold was Shepstone's deputy and secretary. On one level agents of the Swazi rulers, in practice Shepstone and Penfold pursued economic self-interest and were disliked by (some) other whites for their veniality and incompetence, and also because farmers among them saw their stock-grazing concessions being usurped by minerals claims.

[handwritten marginalia: Broad in world @ time ↓ in country ↓ local]

Pre-text

The immediate circumstance producing the Shepstone document was the anticipation of a new rich mineral discovery, and the role in this of various members of the Forbes family, including David Forbes senior, his brother James Forbes senior and David's sons Dave junior and Jim junior. David senior was at this time primarily a commercial farmer in south-eastern Transvaal, close to Swaziland, and James senior was a prospector involved with others who either shared or were in competition for the concessionary interests being then advanced for Swazi recognition. As well as the Swazi elite, the Resident Agent had to deal with a (white) Legislative Council of mainly prospectors and miners, as well as many concessionaries including farmers with competing interests, with the document one of many examples in which Shepstone constructed the semblance of legalistic order in a situation where his motives and practices were (rightly) suspected on all sides.

Text and intertext

Meta-data

The meta-data of research records is provided by information about 'who, when, where from, archive location', and also 'to whom, where to', and is crucial for ensuring specific documents can be easily retrieved from potentially many thousands. The Shepstone document begs questions about some meta-data. First, which David Forbes, father or son, is invoked? This is ambiguous. Second, while on the surface an official certification with a seal, the document also has some 'letterness' features: an address it was written from, a date it was written on, signatories, and also 'address' in the sense of being directed to a (unspecified) person or persons about the matters certified.

Content

Whites Writing Whiteness research records an overview of narrative content for a 1 in 5 random sample of all letters or other documents read. More detail is recorded for documents which are particularly interesting, of which this Shepstone example is one. It has strong official overtones, with a printed heading and concluding with an official sign-off and seal. Also it is presented as in itself a certification of, if not ownership, then the 'holding' of land in a 'certain area' for specified purposes. However, for anyone 'in the know', as David Forbes (both father and son) certainly was, the increasingly fraught relationships between the Resident Agent and the 'Swazi nation', the Agent and different groups of concessionaries, the concessionaries and the Swazi ruling elite, would have been apparent. Also the document's authority is referenced to the Registry Books, indicating that its certification depends on what these entities contain.

Structure

The 'voice' the document is written in is an authoritative one; it certifies and does so presumptively on behalf of 'the Nation'. Authorial location is removed ('it is certified', no person does this). However, it ends with signatures that are not 'the Nation', but Penfold (who is he? this is not stated, indicating an in-group readership who would know this) signing on behalf of Resident Agent Shepstone. The reader is positioned to receive the document, not respond to it, but there are also signs, like not stating Penfold's position, that readership has been a factor in the organisation and tone of the document. Other aspects of this come to attention through re-reading, for close attention shows that the claims to certificatory authority rest on two externalities: the implied synonymity between the Swazi Nation and the Resident Agent, and intertextual references to the Mananga Grant and to the implied boss text of the Registry Books.

Post-text

It is only rarely that the direct impact of historical (or indeed contemporary) documents can be gauged (although see Stanley and Dampier, 2012). However, many archive collections are organised in temporal order, and anyway a database or Virtual Research Environment (a bespoke online platform for data management and for aiding data analysis) can easily sort records by date, so 'what came next' can often be traced even if the direct impact of a document cannot be known.

Regarding the Shepstone document, other letters in the Forbes collection provide quite detailed information about the course of events. The dissatisfactions of the Swazi ruling elite with the Shepstone Residency increased, because of its double-dealing and corruption. The 'young Queen', Labotsibeni, the mother of Bhunu, king-to-be but still a minor, gained political control. Shepstone was removed from office, with a tussle over 'the Books' resulting in these being audited by the book-keeper of a firm employed by the Swazis. Also, with the support of Dave Forbes junior, the Swazi rulers sent a delegation to Britain requesting assistance in resisting attempts by the Transvaal government to take over Swaziland. Other Forbes letters relate to these matters and show the 'one thing amidst another' character of unfolding events.

Regarding the direct concern of the document, the part-concession for some rights (but not others) within the Mananga Grant, this had behind it the deceased king Mbandzeni's concessions of land many times over to different people for the same or contradictory purposes. Being close to the Swazi rulers and advising against this policy, the Forbes then gave way and obtained a number of concessions themselves. Later, many such interests were contested by contending interests and were not legally sustainable. In the case of a concession to Dave junior for grazing and timber in the area of

Forbes Reef (which might be that specified in the document), for example, the coal mine's later owners established that these surface rights were null and void.

Context2

Social life is always *in media res*, in process, and the flow of wider events affecting Swaziland continued, as well as the small part of them alluded to under the 'Post-text' heading. A London Convention of 1894 gave way to Transvaal designs on Swaziland as a source of cheap labour by assigning it a 'protectorate' role. However, in 1910 and against the demands of the incoming Union of South Africa government formed that year, the Protectorates of Basutoland [Lesotho], Bechuanaland [Botswana] and Swaziland retained their independence. The Forbes' Transvaal farming and Swazi mining and other interests became more diversified, including after the death of David Forbes senior in 1905.

This analysis of the 1893 Shepstone document has used a simple but effective reading frame involving re-reading and surface reading to highlight both its content and its structure, and also the context which gave rise to it and in which its ramifications played out. It has strong heterotopic aspects concerning its disposition of people, divided interests, land, a nation, and its Resident Agent; and these are referred to in an apparently removed 'voice', for 'This' certifies in a removed abstract way, rather than the document's signatory. There is also more going on than in the bare words on the page, and an attentive re-reading shows the complexities of the authority that is seemingly able to certify the three-eights land claim, but which depends on the Swazi Nation as the origin and source of this. In addition, the legitimacy of the claim depends upon the invoked authority of the Registry Books, both a boss text, one that governs subsidiary ones, and an intertextual reference indicating this is proof of 'clear and unencumbered' title to the three-eighths claim, but with later events showing Shepstone had in fact cooked the books. Reference to context provides much information about the situation giving rise to this and similar documents concerning Swaziland land and minerals concessions and considerably adds to re-reading the document itself.

Some useful pointers to draw from using this analytical toolkit regarding the exemplar of the Shepstone document are:

First, keep it simple! There are, as noted, different ways to analyse documents. The version used here is a simple but handy reading frame – based on the idea of surface reading introduced earlier – that focuses on how letters, diaries, photographs, official pronouncements and so on 'work'. It is organised around recognising that documents, all kinds of documents, have strong temporal aspects in the sense of a before, during and after to their writing and intended impact. This framework and its toolkit are transferable; that is, they can be used to analyse different kinds of documents, including visual, oral and material ones as well as the textual variety.

Second, be analytically even-handed! A major benefit of using such a reading frame is that it makes analysing documents both thorough and streamlined and gives points of comparison across documents. The David Forbes diary-entry, for instance, could be analysed using this framework, as could the next exemplar for discussion, an 1894 letter by David Forbes, and this would enable comparison of the heterotopic aspects of all three, the different ways that authorial 'voice' appears in them, the different ways in which they situate the reader and so on.

Third, don't focus just on content and ignore the rest! Whatever kind of approach or reading frame is used, it is important to design this to take into account the context that has led to a document coming into existence; the context the document itself refers to (either directly or indirectly); and also the context which prevails after it has been produced and used or sent and which helps the researcher in knowing 'what happened next'.

Working it out: interpretation and the ultimately referential character of the past

If analysis involves taking a document or documents apart, then interpretation requires putting the components back together, but in a new way that provides an explanation of meaning, including often by connecting it with a bigger picture. This can be through 'internal' means, by relating it to connected archival documents or other relevant materials; through 'external' means, by relating it to known or claimed facts about some relevant part of the past; through 'theoretical' means, by relating it to ideas and theories in the connected academic literature; or indeed all three. In an important sense, interpretation and its wider meaning-making is the whole point of archival investigations, although it is salutary to remember this cannot occur without the earlier stages of finding out and analysis being carried out.

Tacitly, most researchers recognise that the traces remaining are evidence of things that actually happened and ultimately tell of events and people of the past. Archigraphics is not agnostic on the representation/referentiality question and the irreducible things that happened. The past is not a given, its resurrection is impossible, and achieving certainty in making claims about it occurs fairly infrequently, for history is never sure and the traces that remain always fall short, as de Certeau (2000: 1–9) usefully reminds readers. There is no naive realism involved in the exposition of archigraphics as a methodology in this chapter, then, and the referential fallacy that we can 'know the past' with certitude is rejected. At the same time, a distance is also drawn from the stance of perceiving historical records as fictions and stories (for influential examples, see Richards, 1993; Burton, 2006; Stoler, 2009; Lalu, 2009), because this unsatisfactorily brackets or even dismisses the ultimate referentiality of sources that account for the things that actually happened.

It is ethically and politically important to keep in mind that 'the past' is shorthand for recognising that people before us lived, enjoyed, suffered and died, and this matters. As Paul Ricoeur (1988: 118) insists, 'As soon as an idea of a debt to the dead, the people of flesh and blood to whom something really happened in the past, stops giving documentary research its highest end, history loses its meaning'. The interpretational position of archigraphics consequently is also an ethical one and it rejects seeing the past in binary realist v. fictional terms. Instead, it recognises the ultimate irreducibility of the past and the reality of the things that happened, but also that the remaining archival traces are representational in character and raise profound questions about the socially constructed and contested character of knowledge-claims about it. This dualist stance is a thread running through the discussion of documents in this chapter, the working practices used in making sense of them, and the interpretations based on it.

The broad context of social change in South Africa drives the point home, for the people, activities and events in the exemplars in this chapter, including the Pringles, Findlays, Patons, Vosses and Forbes, were part of the social, economic and political processes which produced segregation and apartheid. What they were like, what they did, who was involved in this and how, is not just a matter of musty old bits of paper, and anyway these are an essential part of figuring out how it happened, how the largely mundane matters they represent led to the particular social formation of apartheid coming about and later being dismantled. Attending to the detailed specifics of this process and the lumpy-bumpy way that change eventuated is important.

One aspect of this concerns words and terms which now have a heavily racialised and negative meaning in the South African context, but which mainly originated very differently. Whites Writing Whiteness is investigating this by recording their use in letters from the 1770s through to the 1970s. These time-travelling terms include Kaffir, boy, native, maid and the 'n word', with the latter imported via American miners around the discovery of diamonds in Kimberley. A letter by David Forbes senior to Dave junior on 20 August 1894 provides the exemplar around which the practices involved in interpretation are now explored:

Athole Newscotland August 20th – 1894
Dear Dave
We have not heard from you for some weeks but I suppose you went to Delagoa and I expect Jim will be there as soon as this letter...
We dont hear any Swazi news I think the Swazies have been told that they have to go under the Transvaal and if they dont I expect the Transvaal will be told they can do as they like in the matter they will have a free hand like Rhodes...

"Maneban" was at Vins some days back and ~~wa~~ Vin was taking him up to Grobbleaar. I hear the Government want[s] to see him – I suppose he can give them a good deal of information

... all the Native tribes are being taken over by some power ~~of~~ or other they are considered to be in the way of civilization its rather rough on the niggers but he is a low rascal Jackall is here just now and has told Nellie that a fellow named "Jack" who has come from their kraal at Williams is a sheep stealer and that he has carried sheep up to their kraal all the way from here and made Williams boy help him to catch them and asked? Vronjeens wife to help him but she refused. Jackall also says get rid of? Vronjeen as he is bad and that his mother is the worst of the lot. I will get that boy over and see what I can get out of him. I would like to convict him if possible but in any case he must clear out but I believe the most of the Kafirs are a bad lot Swazis are born thieves and liars -

...We dont hear much commando news...Erskine was here last night and says that one of the commandos got surrounded by the kafirs and the General wired to Pretoria that he could not assist them...

...I hear that Magato is to be left alone he pays his taxes but will not go into a location so perhaps he will be left alone till it is more convenient.

...I believe you are still blamed for interfering in Swazi matters there are still letters in the Barberton papers but no names are mentioned. Erskine said that the boers blame you...

All send kind love to self and Jim

Your affte Father

David Forbes

(DF senior to DF junior, 20 August 1894 Forbes NAD.
Provided at https://sites.google.com/site/thebookarchiveproject/
noise-in-the-archive-chapter-2)

David senior's original letter is very long and a shortened version is provided here, with ellipses indicating passages editorially shortened (with the complete letter provided at https://sites.google.com/site/thebookarchive-project/noise-in-the-archive-chapter-2). For space reasons, the letter is not analysed in detail, although outside these pages it has been because detailed analysis is essential to interpretation. It is also worth noting that a beginner's mistake is to collapse analysis into interpretation, and thus to interpret without first giving detailed attention to the heterotopics and 'mechanics' of a text concerning how it intends a particular reading, and so this should be avoided.

The purpose of David's letter overall was to convey various news to his son Dave, absent from Athole in what is now Lourenço Marques, on the southeast coast of Mozambique. The context involved Swazi/Transvaal tensions, the Transvaal itching to annex Swaziland, a local man – Maneban (and note his name being diminished by appearing in quote marks) – providing what is implicitly the British government with information about this and, later in the letter, a Transvaal commando troop active in the area. Such matters were of particular concern to Dave junior for reasons the letter alludes to, in 'interfering in Swazi matters' by acting as an unaligned adviser to the Swazi elite and a trusted translator for them with both Transvaal and British officialdom.

In what initially seems a sympathetic way, the letter comments that it is 'all the Native tribes' and not just the Swazis that are being 'taken over' and this is 'rather rough', so it is all the more shocking when this is followed by 'rough on the niggers' and 'he is a low rascal'. The change of tone and emphasis continues with the tale told about sheep-stealing evidencing this 'rascalry', with its bottom-line the sweeping conclusions drawn that 'most of the Kafirs are a bad lot' and 'Swazis are born thieves and liars'. There is another change of gear in the rest of the letter, concerned with the Transvaal commando, Magato, as clearly a powerful man, and feelings locally about Dave's 'interfering'. But how should David senior's letter be interpreted, what are its most important features, and what about the 'n word'?

First, for both David senior and Dave, the possible Transvaal takeover was a long-term concern, and on various occasions Dave especially made attempts to influence the British presence to oppose this. Together with his fluent Tswana and friendship with many of the Swazi elite, this led to Dave being seen by local Boer people as opposing Transvaal interests (which adversely affected the Forbes' economic and farming activities). The comments about these matters therefore reference both the wider political context and the local political–economic one. Second, Dave had significant economic interests in the Athole Estate and at this time especially its sheep, so sheep-stealing by someone employed by and living on Athole land would be of great concern to him, as would its resolution in the culprit's 'clearing out'. Third, the use of negative racialised words and negatively glossing racial comments often appear in Dave's own letters and he is a particular user of the 'n word'. However, his close association with the Swazi elite, his trusted role, and his championing of Swazi interests even though a Transvaal citizen, caution against any easy attribution of unrelieved racism to him. And fourth, for David senior this is the only time when such things appear in his letters or diary-writing. His use of contemptuous words and descriptions here is so atypical that it seems shocking as well as surprising, and for this reason I have characterised it as 'an outburst', rather than as with Dave junior, par for the course. And of course, they were written specifically when he was writing to Dave.

As these points suggest, there is (ordinarily) more than one way of interpreting letters or other documents, because they are composed by different structural elements that may have different concerns and intentions, and also because meaning is not 'a thing' that can be directly pointed to, but is pieced together (including by the original reader, of course) by reading in an inquiring way across these elements and in relation to a wider context of knowledge. These interpretive comments are supported both from re-reading the letter using a reading frame with its analytical aids, and also by using what can be called 'externalist' (first comment) and 'internalist' (second, third and fourth comments) comparisons, as with the Forbes diary-entry discussed earlier. The internalist comparisons provide an evidential basis for drawing some conclusions about racialisation and David Forbes senior's letter – it is an atypical outburst, made to someone who often negatively racialised people but in a complicated way, and there were particular concerns making the context unusually fraught for him – with this resting on the archigraphical practices of scoping, mapping and using a reading frame for analysing documents in depth.

Some wider interpretational matters arise from David Forbes senior's 1894 letter that, while taking particular shape in the Whites Writing Whiteness and Forbes context, have more general relevance. Pointers regarding these are as follows:

First, 'the thing itself' and referentiality matters: the data that archival researchers work with are (generally) not 'the thing itself', but representations of this, traces that are fragmentary and emanate from particular viewpoints. The referential fallacy of straightforwardly concluding 'it was so' from any document needs to be avoided, while also still recognising that there was a past in which real things happened and the remaining documents or other traces reference this albeit in complicated ways.

Second, identifying the topic is complex: social life does not come in discrete chunks labelled 'gender', 'class', 'whiteness', 'the scramble for Africa' and so on. The word 'whiteness' does not appear anywhere in David Forbes' letter and has to be interpreted by reference to the people characterised and the activities commented on. Also while an analysis of the specifics of the letter supports an investigation of whiteness, as one piece of evidence, this is not the totality of what is required, which necessitates working on letters at volume and over time, rather than cherry-picking one-off examples which may – or in this case may not – be typical.

Third, working out what it means is hard work: interpretation is an iterative procedure involving going back and forth between conceptual, methodological, analytical and interpretational matters and working out links and connections across the relevant traces until something making sense of all of them eventuates. Good defensible interpretation requires analysis. It also requires having a feel or a 'nose' for what is interpretationally interesting. However, this is not magic or a special gift, but results from close familiarity with the archival sources, carrying out detailed analyses of specific documents, and working across things to discern the wider picture. This archigraphical skill, like the others discussed in this chapter, is honed by being repeatedly used and mistakes learned from.

Fourth, the traces are always elusive and the sources always partial. By no means can everything that happened be found in archives or documents.

However, the major factor producing the fragmentary and incomplete character of what remains derives, not from exclusions operated by 'the archive' as an institution, but instead from the happenstance of what is recorded and what isn't, who keeps (or hoards) and passes on and who doesn't, all the vagaries of ordinary life and its flotsam and jetsam.

A reminder of this flotsam and jetsam character of the traces and their partiality can be found in the Schreiner-Hemming Collection in the University of Cape Town's Manuscripts and Archives. Among its many letters, a small number are by a woman, elderly when they were written, who was the daughter of freed Mozambique slaves and who had earlier in her life become 'Nannie', as she signs her letters, to the then-children of the Hemming family. These letters are important because of the rarity of a highly literate African woman writing in the 1900s and they convey a particular picture of their writer: her pension had decreased, house rents increased, and the letters convey much anxiety about her future. The picture conveyed is, however, rather misleading, because relating to just one period in this woman's life.

A clue to this was gained initially through an 'internalist' comparison – a photograph (provided at https://sites.google.com/site/thebookarchiveproject/noise-in-the-archive-chapter-2), tucked away with others in an ancillary part of the collection, gives a very different impression. Taken in an earlier period, it shows a resolute, indeed commanding, youthful Nannie in a Good Templars uniform and insignia, together with a white woman. Seeing this led to some 'externalist' checks being made, in tracing the uniform and what the organisational ranks of the women were, and Nannie's later high-profile public activities as a social reformer. Sister Nannie, as she became known in her public work, was Anna Tempo. The photograph shows her as a senior figure in the Good Templars temperance organisation, with the unnamed white woman holding a rank below hers. Their poses in the photograph reflect Anna's superordinate and the other woman's subordinate organisational ranks, with 'race' both there and absent. There is a fascinating story to be told about Anna's public work, including the hostels for unmarried women she ran as well as her other reform work. However, telling this in more detail would require a separate strand of research, for relevant traces are not located in this collection or others. The traces remaining are a few newspaper stories, hints in letters about other things, an obituary, a house, a street name, a photograph.

This is a cautionary tale with general relevance for archival research. Much has been written about archives and the governing power they exert over knowledge. There is another story to tell, just as important. Most of everything that happened in everyday life is forgotten or lost because never recorded; some people are just too busy getting on with it, or have little truck with the written word in any of its guises; and if traces remain, as they do for Anna Tempo, they are more often than not found elsewhere. What is presently in archives can and should most certainly be expanded and made to 'speak' about disenfranchised and outsider groups and people. Some examples, including those concerning Anna Tempo, have been explored in this chapter. However, the 'voice' or register in which this is done needs to be modest and provisional, for what can be said is necessarily partial, and the traces remaining, like Anna's letters, may be misleading.

Extreme archiving? Archigraphics, contra fever and the rest

Discussion here starts by returning to the questions set out at the start of this chapter, to provide some brief responses. It then reflects on a number of additional aspects of the methodological approach presented.

First, archives and the collections they hold are particular kinds of entities, and they are many and varied both in contents and in an ontological sense. They are creations of the present and imbricated with present-time concerns and understandings. They have their own rules and regulations, but there *is* a distinct methodological approach to archival research that can be assembled, formed by some key working practices for engaging in and with them.

Second, archival research is different in some fundamental respects from 'just reading', because rewriting and writing are crucial to it. And this point has been developed around exploring archigraphics and its core components.

Third, this takes skills that previous generations of archival researchers have had to learn on their own while in an archive and working under its prevailing rule of silence. However, it is more helpful to have the noisy practices involved spelled out and the transferable skills involved indicated. This chapter does so by discussing activities that enable a good grasp to be gained of both the details and the general structural features of collections and archives.

Fourth, working through the exemplars has shown how the components of archigraphics can be put to work. They have been presented in an incremental way, they all involve transferable skills, and they can be used to carry out different kinds of research projects from start to finish.

Fifth, not on the agenda earlier but very much on it at this juncture, the practices involved in the different kinds of reading deployed are important in getting to grips with the textual politics of documentary sources. Emphasising the fundamentals of writing under the heading of archigraphics certainly doesn't mean neglecting reading, but rather situating it within the archigraphics framework.

And sixth, a truism of archival research is – or should be – that what you do should depend on what you have and are working with. It all depends on the stuff! That is, the useful methods for exploring, making sense and analysing and interpreting archival collections and their contents that have been explored here should be modulated, extended and otherwise fine-tuned to the situated specifics of whatever research context someone is working in.

Not elaborated earlier but important in reflecting back on discussion here: the approach discussed has a kind of rhythm to it – the quickness of the practices composing archigraphics can provide great richness of data *and* depth of analysis and interpretation; what is quick and what gains depth, then, do not need to be seen as in opposition. Relatedly, there are a number of points in the discussion where the comment has been – stop, think and pause for thought and reflection, including scribbling notes about such reflections on activities in a notebook or on computer file. Archival working rhythms (discussed in Chapter 3), then, are precisely rhythmic: they have their rises and falls, upbeats and downbeats.

In fun, and with project colleagues and graduate students I've worked with over the years, we have referred to the activities discussed in this chapter as 'extreme archiving' and on a par with extreme sports such as mountaineering, abseiling and so on. The grain of truth here is that working in such a focused way and concentrating attention on the nitty-gritty of the research process is not as usual as it should be. Perhaps because of that 'good heavens, what to do with it all?' response noted at the start of the chapter, many people seen in archives observably work in a very fragmented way, a couple of hours here and there, many breaks, and without a definite plan for finding out. So 'extreme archiving' is at basis having a focused plan of action and carrying it out.

toxic?

The points I've discussed add up to the particular archival sensibility that informs this chapter. It is underpinned by a guiding sense of what archives 'are' in an ontological sense, some strategies for working on their contents, and a keen focused attentiveness to details of the documents and other texts they contain and how to interrogate them. The chapter has been conceived as a rejoinder to some presently influential ways of thinking about archives and archival research, doing so in ways that readers will hopefully find useful and interesting. It has not been concerned with archive fever, nor its counterpart of dust, nor the romance of taste and allure, and nor has it inscribed a shift from archive-as-source to archive-as-subject either (Derrida, 1995; Steedman, 2001; Farge, 2013 [1989]; Stoler, 2009). It has also not carried out an ethnography of archival presence, for its emphasis is on the contents and not the researcher; and nor does it seek to remake the archival imaginary, for it wants something more responsive and nuanced than yet another 'position'. Its concern instead is with archival sensibility (Foucault, 1975; Burton, 2006; Sheringham, 2010).

So what is this chapter and its archival sensibility about? It has been concerned with making the practices of archival research and the terms of engagement for working with documents and collections visible and audible – the sight and the noise of working in archives. In particular, it has explored in detail how these can be used and the transferable skills involved, thereby enabling other people to make sense of the confusing plenitude that is archival research. This involves archigraphics, the term used to cover rewriting and writing and their attendant working practices of scoping, mapping, surface reading, analysis and interpretation, which are the things making up the core activities going on inside the black box of archival research. It has also stressed the importance of contextual specifics and the need to be responsive to these. As a result, starting with some key questions and a black box, where this chapter has ended is with a set of transferable working practices that will enable the archival researcher to craft the now/past in more open, visible, defensible and also more accountable ways.

Go for it!

Acknowledgements

My thanks to the ESRC for funding the Professorial Research Fellowship that has supported the Whites Writing Whiteness research drawn on in this chapter (ES J022977/1).

Archival sources

Forbes Family Papers, National Archives of South Africa, Pretoria.
Findlay Family Papers, Cullen Library, Johannesburg.
Gold Fields of South Africa Ltd, Cory Library, Grahamstown.
Mass Observation Library, University of Sussex, Brighton.
A.J. Munby Collection (Hannah Cullwick), Wren Library, University of Cambridge.
Paton Collection, Kimberley Africana Library, Kimberley.
Pringle Family Collection, Cory Library, Grahamstown.
M.E. Pringle Collection, Cory Library, Grahamstown.
Rhodes Papers, Bodleian Library, Oxford.
Schreiner-Hemming Collection, Manuscripts & Archives, University of Cape Town.
Voss Collection, National Archives of South Africa, Pretoria.

Interlude

In Chapter 2, some core archival research skills have been introduced around detailed discussion of a number of exemplars, showing how methods can be put into practice, and by doing so opening the black box to show what happens in the nitty-gritty of archival research. In addition to practices and strategies, archival research can be thought about by standing back from the busy detail to conceptualise how such activities are located in a broad framework.

[handwritten margin note: writing of history?]

Chapter 2's framework is concerned with the historiographical operation. Chapter 3 operationalises a narrative framework and focuses on activities and ideas around how genealogical questions and spatio-temporal rhythms impact on archival research, pointing up particular storylines and narrative personae and analytical insights, and also how such matters are written about. Although the specific analytical concerns and focuses of Chapters 1 and 2 may seem at first sight rather different, their broad approaches are largely consonant at ontological, epistemological and methodological levels. This includes viewing the researcher as an active presence in making sense of the traces remaining, in shaping selections, and in using analytical ideas to produce theoretical and other interpretations.

3 Archival rhythms

Narrativity in the archive

Maria Tamboukou

Encounters and entanglements in the archive

How many ways are there to engage with archival research and how have digital and other new media changed the way we do it? How important are the questions we bring into the archive and what are their possibilities and limitations? How do we deal with eruptions and unexpected encounters in an archive? What does it mean 'to feel' narratives in the archive and what is the role of spatio-temporal rhythms? How can we understand the researcher and the archive as an entanglement rather than as separate and independent entities?

In exploring these questions, this chapter draws on my research in the Archives and Manuscript Division of the New York Public Library. This involved me working with documents of women trade unionists in the garment industry in the first half of the twentieth century, and more particularly with the papers of Rose Pesotta (1896–1965) and Fannia Cohn (1885–1962), two of the very few women vice-presidents in the history of a predominantly women's union, the International Ladies Garment Workers Union (ILGWU). Despite their importance in the history of the American Labour movement, they have received little attention in the relevant literature with the notable exceptions of Elaine Leeder's (1993) biographical study of Pesotta and Ricki Cohen-Myers' (1976) PhD thesis on Cohn. Among the many themes that have arisen from my research and which have informed a range of conference papers, methodology workshops and journal articles (Tamboukou, 2013a, 2014a, 2014c, 2015a), in this chapter I explore the paths of a narrative sensibility within the archive, something which informs all my work on this project.

In particular, the chapter focuses on how genealogical questions and spatio-temporal rhythms have an impact on how researchers orient ourselves within the archive, how we follow specific storylines, narrative personae and analytical insights, and how we write about them. It is striking from my archival research at the NYPL that, although working in the same institution for two consecutive summers, my experience was very different from one to the other, not only in terms of the surrounding space but also regarding the nature of the archival documents: 'real' papers in 2011, micro-film versions in 2012. As I will show, there were things to gain and things to lose from both, which calls into question simplistic divisions between old and new ways of doing archival research and shows the complexity and sometimes unpredictability. In addressing these questions, the chapter unfolds in three sections: imagining the archive, working in the thickness of archival research, and the return from the archive.

Imagining the archive

The questions we carry with us into an archive are important because they will have shaped the preparatory work we have done for the research, which is both theoretical and practical. As archival researchers, we mostly work within limited periods of time and on relatively low budgets, so careful preparation is as important as the actual research. It is the time before the researcher arrives at the archive that I want to consider here, by raising a seemingly simple question: when does archival work begin? Looking back at my journeys in a number of archives in the UK, France and the USA where I have conducted research over the past twenty years, one of the patterns I can discern is that of multiple beginnings. Following a research question and immersing ourselves in the relevant literature is of course a recurrent mode of tracking and identifying archival sources, but it is only one of many. Sometimes beginnings emerge while we already work in an archive and we encounter a line of writing, a document, a person or a source that we want to trace further. But even when such new beginnings emerge in the middle of a process, they still demand planning and preparation to be realised as concrete archival projects. Although deriving from my own experience of doing archival research, this understanding is transferable to different contexts and can be helpful for a great variety of archival research circumstances.

Archival research is a process that is conceived as part of a wider research project, but which develops its own life, puts forward its own demands and requires specific responses to the questions and problems it raises. The latter are both intellectual and material and always interrelated as such. The material conditions of possibility for archival research always include intricate space/time arrangements, both local and global. Take for example my NYPL project on the papers of women trade unionists. This started through my reading of autobiographical documents of seamstresses in the first half of the twentieth century; Rose Pesotta emerged as an intriguing figure in this body of literature, and this is how I decided to follow her in the archive. The only way I could have access to her papers was physically to visit the NYPL; but in order to secure funding, I had to make sure that her papers were not available in any digitised or other form that would be accessible in different and possibly cheaper ways. The fact that the library had a detailed catalogue of her papers (NYPL/RPP/MSS2390) was immensely helpful: this gave me a very good idea of the extent and overall size of the collection, which helped calculate the study-leave time I needed to ask for, and also guided practical but essential arrangements, such as travel expenses, as well as accommodation and subsistence costs. In this light, the online resources of the NYPL were a gift: they helped my research in ways that would not have been possible twenty years earlier when I made my first trip to an archive. This was in 1994 when I visited the Modern Records Centre at the University of Warwick to read Clara Collet's diary (Tamboukou, 2003). I remember phoning the archive beforehand to make sure that a copy of the diary was indeed there. I knew that the original was with Jane Miller, Collet's great niece (Miller, 1990), who I had talked to in relation to my PhD project on women teachers' technologies of the self (Tamboukou, 2003). The archivist told me that they had no such diary, but a week later I received a letter from her, apologising for having 'misguided' me and confirming that a copy of the diary was indeed there. All I would have to do now would be to type 'Clara Collet' in a Google search and a lot of information would be at the tips of my fingers (for example, MRC/CCP). As this suggests, locating inventory aids, where they exist, is a very important step for any type of archival research.

But once in the archive new beginnings emerge, around people, documents and sources that had not been thought about when designing the research. In my case with Pesotta's papers, two new projects erupted from the archive: a) the importance of women workers' education, a theme that made me return to the NYPL the following year to work with Fannia Cohn's papers; and b) Pesotta's epistolary friendship with Emma Goldman through her involvement in the anarchist labour movement, something that sent me to Emma Goldman's papers at Berkeley the following year as well (Tamboukou, 2013b). It goes without saying that new space/time preparations and funding applications had to be initiated, but this is the nature as well as the excitement of new and multiple beginnings.

What also came out of these archival projects is the importance of considering migration in the gendered history of the labour movement. While both Pesotta and Cohn were Jewish immigrants who fled the Russian pogroms at the end of the nineteenth century, Italian women immigrants in New York also emerged as an important group to be considered (Guglielmo, 2010). In looking for archival sources for this thematic strand of my research, I came across oral interviews with women garment workers and more specifically the collection, 'Italian Immigrant Women in New York City's Garment Industry Oral Histories, 1976–1978', in the Sophia Smith Collection (SSC/IIW/MS556). While contacting the archivists of Smith College, however, I found that they could send me digitised copies of the oral interviews I was looking for, which have now been added to the archive of my overall research project of writing a feminist genealogy of the seamstress (Tamboukou, 2015d), my version of the 'archive of the other archive' discussed in Chapter 2. The possibilities of working with 'real papers', with microfilm or with digitised versions of documents in archival research has received much discussion (for example, Nicholson, 2013; Berry, 2012; Rogers, 2008). It is the use of microfilm I want to discuss next, placing it in the wider context of 'the digital turn'.

Archives and microfilms

> 26/6/2012: First day in the archive: I have woken up feeling slightly jet-lagged but not quite ... I carry a small beige box full of [microfilm] reels in my hands while going down the stairs of the New York Public Library. How long ago has it been since I have worked with reels? I suddenly remember my PhD and lonely days at the Queen Mary and Westfield college archives in Mile End, reading the unpublished papers of its founder, Constance Maynard – which by the way have now all been digitised (QM/CMP). But this is different: I am not alone anymore. The basement of the NYPL is buzzing. I try to start, with hesitation and remorse. I so much preferred my experience of the 2011 summer, when I was working with Rose Pesotta's 'real papers' in the secluded area of the second floor manuscripts division of this same library... As I find a machine that both works and is somehow in a quiet corner, I realise that I can see the Empire State Building through the window I am sitting next to. It feels as I am at the heart of the city where thousands of women worked and fought for their rights and as I start reading the first reel I feel that something is happening to me and my work...

This is an entry from my research diary from mid 2012, when I returned to the NYPL archives to look at Fannia Cohn's papers, funded through a British Academy small grant. Although I knew that Cohn's papers were available in thirteen reels of microfilm (*ZZ-35052), I had thought that working with the actual papers would have still been an option, which it was not. I only had the chance to touch and smell Cohn's boxes when I worked with her photographs on just one day during the whole month I worked at the NYPL archives. Instead I found myself disappointedly carrying a small box full of microfilm reels to the basement of the library, leaving the lovely section of the manuscripts division on the second floor to those lucky researchers whose documents had not been turned into the cold microfilms that I was going to work with for a whole month. Everything was different in July 2012, then, even the weather was unbearably hot in relation to 2011, or so it had felt...

But after overcoming the first shock and learning or rather remembering the ropes of using the microfilm reels, avoiding broken or unfocused machines and securing places to sit that were quieter than others, new possibilities emerged. Apart from the obvious fact that the reels give the researcher the opportunity to magnify texts and thus read difficult handwriting or black and thick typewriter fonts, what came as a nice surprise was that I had much more freedom with using documents from across the collection: they were in the form of films and therefore not sacred any more, so I could 'do more things' with them. Take Cohn's 'Correspondence', for example, which together with her 'Writings' are the biggest sections of her papers, comprising eight boxes out of thirteen. They have been classified as 'Letters received' (Boxes 1, 2, and 4) and 'Letters sent' (Boxes 4 and 5) in the initial collection (NYPL/FCP/MSS588). If I were to work with the Boxes, I had first of all to read the 'received' files before I could ask for the 'sent' ones – the order could be reversed of course – and I could never have more than two Boxes in front of me. Things were different with the microfilm reels, however. I could move fast forward or backwards, find the sequence of a letter immediately and see how the argument had developed, twisted or changed. I could also more easily search for a particular sender or addressee who seemed to be relevant to an epistolary conversation or debate and thus put together missing pieces of epistolary puzzles. This freedom of surfing the microfilms gave me a better understanding of the stories that were unfolded in these documents, the issues that were at stake, as well as the role of the different 'dramatis personae' in them (www.oliveschreiner.org/dramatis_personae). Let us consider a moving letter that Theresa Wolfson (1897–1972), a labour economist and professor at Brooklyn's college, sent to Cohn on 6 May 1922:

> As I came to the desk to write my letter, my eye fell upon the letter you were writing- and my attention was riveted to one word – 'lonely'. That word followed me – I felt it so deeply – and your extreme loneliness that I read the few lines – and for this I hope you will forgive me! Why should I misunderstand your loneliness – your feeling of unhappiness? [...] It is only when one knocks, and knocks, and knocks – that one can perceive the real 'you' and how many people are there ready to knock when souls can be had for the asking? And even when you and I are talking on a perfect basis of friendship – your work, yourself as a part of your work, creeps in and you are no longer yourself – but what you would be – what you would like your work to be!
>
> (FCP/NYPL/MSS588/Cor/LR)

Among the many themes that struck me when I first read this letter was the question of how Wolfson could have had such close access to her friend's desk and why she wrote this letter from Cleveland, when she could have talked to her about it in New York, where they worked together. Eventually I wrote a paper about this epistolary exchange in terms of the relational stage of recognition that opens up between the two letter-writers (Tamboukou, 2014c). But what I want to highlight here is the way I worked while still in the archive to configure this relationship: by moving fast forward to 'Letters sent', I could retrieve Cohn's response, written only nine days later, on 15 May 1922:

... Do you wonder that working under such conditions for an ideal that is dear to one's heart, one can never sufficiently detach oneself from one's work, and willingly or unwillingly he is forced to become part of it... there are those amongst the few, who possess deep feelings and who refuse to accept things as they find them... they are rather complex, and it is only 'when one knocks and knocks and knocks' that one can break through one's real self.

(FCP/NYPL/MSS588/Cor/LS)

By having immediate access to Cohn's response, I was able to put their epistolary conversation in context. But also having parallel access to the other parts of the catalogue and particularly her 'Writings' (Boxes 6–8), as well as the 'ILGWU documents' (Boxes 9–12), I was able to trace the space/time conditions of this epistolary exchange: Wolfson was staying in the same hotel room with Cohn in Cleveland, where they had both gone to attend the ILGWU Cleveland convention, which took place 1–12 May 1922. This is how Wolfson had inadvertently read her friend's letter; Cohn left Cleveland before the end of the convention, but Wolfson stayed on and felt the need to write to her friend about failures in their communication.

I have used this epistolary exchange as an example, to show how the microfilm form has supported what I later discuss as the narrative fabric of archival research. Although deriving from my own research, this is certainly not a unique or unrepeatable case: researchers in the digital humanities have already written about the possibilities that are opened up by digital collections, particularly in relation to the 'contextual mass' and the multiple connections they can facilitate between and among texts, authors and documents (for example, Flanders, 2014). Cold as they were, the microfilm reels opened wider vistas in the documents and their context, and did so while I was still in the archive and therefore able to re-read documents, revisit details that had initially gone unnoticed, see their relation with other documents in the same or different catalogue series, or photocopy important letters of a particular epistolary encounter. Indeed, the fact that all the machines were connected to a printer gave me the opportunity to have a photocopy of whatever letter or document I was interested in immediately, without the need to fill in forms and have to wait for a month until the digital copies could land in my inbox, as had been the case the previous year.

It should be noted that, according to the NYPL regulations, you have to present your photocopies when leaving the archive to make sure that you have not gone over the limit of what researchers are allowed to photocopy; but this is also because you need the receipt to claim the cost from your funder, if you have one. The immediate access to and possession of photocopies significantly changed and enhanced the things that I could do when the archive was closed: having more time with the documents opened up possibilities for contextual information to fill in missing gaps of my understanding and orientation and ultimately it changed the rhythms of my working in the thickness of the archive, a theme I discuss in the next section of the chapter.

Having an overview of the entire collection literally in my hands, I could also more easily discern Cohn's epistolary strategies and tactics, feel something of the mood she was in when writing, and last but not least I could see the patterns of silences arising from the gaps between and interstices of her letters and other writings. I do not want to say that this understanding of the archive was an effect of using the microfilms; as I will discuss in the last section of the chapter, all of the things discussed above are included in the analytical and interpretational practices at play during 'the return from the archive' (Farge, 1989). What the microfilms gave me, however, was an immediate feeling that such interpretations could further unfold; in a way they provided shortcuts for my understanding and initiated the shaping of some of my analytical paths and directions. Here the question was not so much how to 'do things quickly', and more how to 'do things in time', for my stay in New York was limited and expensive and returning would be difficult.

What I want to show by looking back at my experiences of working with different types of documents in the same archive for two successive years is the growing multi-modality of archival research, which calls for more openness towards the effects of the digital turn. Working with microfilms is just one way – and a rather old one – of thinking about a wide range of theoretical, epistemological, methodological and ethical issues that the digital turn has brought forward. As Adrian Cunningham has rightly noted, we need to be more attentive to the differences between concepts such as 'digital curation', 'digital archives' and 'digital libraries', since 'the phrase digital archive has been misused and even hijacked, and that this misuse obscures fundamental issues associated with the capture and long-term management of archival resources' (Cunningham, 2008: 530). One thing is certain: the need to recognise the fact that archival documents are transposed not only when they are filmed, photographed or digitised but also when they are transcribed. 'With an electronic scan... I can read words that I would not be able to see,' Carolyn Steedman (2011: 327) has commented about her digital experiences, and in doing so she has also acknowledged the epistemological questions that arise from such 'technologies of retrieval'. These are wider questions we raise and discuss throughout the book (see in particular Chapters 1 and 4 and the epilogue), since they are relevant for a wide spectrum of archival research in the humanities and the social sciences.

Digitised, filmed or photographed documents should not therefore be considered as surrogates of the originals, but as kinds of documents in their own right that impose and indeed demand situated and tailored methodological approaches, as well as different analytical and interpretational strategies and tactics. The digital archive has radically shifted our understanding of 'what an archive is' to a realisation of 'what an archive can become'. Understanding the specificities of the digital turn provides transferable skills that can be applied in many cases and very diverse contexts. What I want to highlight in concluding this section is that digital archives are here to stay and archival researchers need to learn how to work with them, as well as how to include them as important components in the assemblage of our archival practices. In this sense the digital turn has not only changed what it means to do archival research but has also greatly influenced the epistemologies and ontologies that underpin archival projects.

Working in the thickness of archival research: space/time/matter rhythms

In the previous section I have discussed the imaginary phase of archival research when researchers plan and prepare a visit to an archive, and have also looked at some aspects of the digital turn as one node of the multi-modal nature of archival research. Drawing on my experience of doing research at the NYPL archives, I have considered positive and negative effects of unexpected encounters in the archive. Indeed, no matter how well we have prepared, once we find ourselves in an archive, we have to adapt to new conditions and contexts, synchronise ourselves with its space/time rhythms, and in this way become organically entangled in it. It should be remembered here that archives and libraries are power/knowledge institutions and like other organisations impose strict time/space restrictions and regulations. They all have different opening hours, usually complex systems of ordering and delivering documents on your desk, restrictions about how many files or boxes it is permitted to have in front of you, as well as diverse arrangements about photocopying, photographing or otherwise reproducing archival documents. Over the years I have worked in archives, I have understood that allowing myself time to get to know these rules and adapt to different archive systems, as well as to the diverse rules and regulations prevailing, is as important as finding, reading or transcribing documents. In this light, 'start slowly' would be my suggestion for researchers visiting an archive for the first time. But as the research proceeds, we also have to take into consideration that speediness and slowness should be considered in their interrelation, for archival research is a question of rhythm, and it is the depth of the understandings that result that we are primarily interested in.

What is also important to bear in mind is that researchers must not upset the archivists they will need to work with. The archive is their workplace, while we researchers will only temporarily reside there: we are therefore welcome guests, but guests who need to know how to behave appropriately. Moreover archivists have different personalities and expectations, and practices that seemed fine to one archivist on Monday morning might not go down well with their colleague in charge on Tuesday afternoon. In this light, a researcher cannot just storm an archive and do things instantly from the beginning, no matter how experienced, well-published or academically famous they are. In this connection, there were cautionary stories about 'prestigious' although unnamed academics told in a paper entitled 'How researchers can frustrate the work of archivists', given at a conference on *Failure in the Archives* in October 2014 in London (https://failureint-hearchives.wordpress.com/2014/09/02/conference-programme/).

It is also worth remembering that a researcher's relationship with archivists may continue well after the researcher leaves the archive in question. They are the people we may need to contact for additional or missing information, or if more photocopies are needed, for instance. It is these archivists who will also facilitate permission to reproduce and for other copyright processes when the stage of publishing research outputs is reached. Archivists are thus importantly involved in the whole research process and acknowledging their contribution should be part of archival research ethics more widely, a topic returned to in Chapter 6.

In raising these concerns, my point is that the materiality and sociality of the archive is crucial for the entire research process and that as researchers we should not separate the physical, social and intellectual dimensions of the archival research we carry out. But what does it mean to become organically involved in an archive? I address this question by drawing on Henri Lefebvre's (2004) ideas about the 'rhythmanalysis' of different spaces in relation to what I have called the 'heterotemporalities' of archival research (Tamboukou, 2011).

Finding the rhythms of 'other spaces'

'What we live are rhythms, rhythms experienced subjectively,' Lefebvre wrote in his major work, *The Production of Space* (1991: 206). But it was only at the end of his academic life, when perhaps he had more time to indulge his love for music (being a pianist as well as an intellectual and activist) that he wrote a small book on *Rhythmanalysis*. The book was published in French after his death in 1992. However, it took twelve years to be translated in English, being published in 2004, which explains perhaps why this approach has yet to be taken up more fully in methodological discussions in the social sciences. The fact that Lefebvre's three-volume *Critique of Everyday Life* – wherein *Rhythmanalysis* appears in context – was only published in its full form in 2014 throws further light on the neglect of this approach.

In following Lefebvre's method of rhythmanalysis, already briefly presented in Chapter 1, I shall consider space/time rhythms as constitutive of archival practices and therefore of the knowledges that can derive from archival research. An archive is a dynamic space traversed and indeed constituted by multiple rhythms and is thus open to new ideas and encounters. Moreover, an archive is not restricted within buildings or other architectural arrangements, majestic though some of them might be. Conceived as an entanglement of space/time rhythms, the archive extends into the world, both in terms of its immediate locality as well as with reference to its global position in colonial histories, as influentially discussed by Ann Stoler (2009).

This is where my situated position as a sociologist in the archive has been at its best, since I have considered myself as an ethnographer and in a classic ethnographic way I have gone beyond the archive. This does not mean that in 'going beyond' I have downplayed the importance of the archival stuff, the things that need to be pointed to as crucial in advancing knowledge and understanding. Rather, my point is to emphasise that we cannot separate material and intellectual processes in configuring and mapping archival worlds. This stance of holding on to the importance of the archival stuff and not merely downgrading them to a backcloth of other research approaches, such as ethnographic fieldwork, is important and we return to it throughout the book and particularly in the last chapter.

I have written elsewhere about my visits to all the addresses that Gwen John (1876–1939), an expatriate Welsh artist in Paris, wrote letters from to her *maitre*, lover and mentor Auguste Rodin, as well as about the effects that these spatial encounters had upon the direction of my research and my overall understanding of John's extravagant narratives (Tamboukou, 2010b, 2011). During the two summers of my research in the NYPL, I followed the rhythms of New York, a city that was the hub of the US garment industry in the first half of the twentieth century. Living in the 'fashion district' of middle Manhattan and walking up and down streets still full of garment workshops was thus a spatial experience that was entangled in the daily rhythms of my archival understanding. Indeed, spatial and temporal serendipities had an unexpected impact on my research. When I first went to New York in summer 2011, I chose my accommodation in the 'fashion district': it was within walking distance from the NYPL and it felt comfortable as I had not lived in New York before. It was quite accidentally that my visit in 2011 coincided with the centenary commemoration of the *Triangle Fire,* one of the most tragic events in the history of the garment industry in the USA, when 146 young immigrant women garment workers died while trying to escape the burning building wherein they were locked (Stein, 1962). Reading women's immediate impressions of this event in their letters was thus a moving experience framed within different temporalities: 'I suppose you are still waiting for the letter of which I spoke to you in my card of last week yet. I could not write, I could not do anything for the last two or three weeks, the Triangle tragedy had a terrible affect upon me,' Pauline Newman (1887–1986) wrote to her friend Rose Schneiderman (1882–1972) on 12 April 1911, just a month after the disaster (RSP/TAM/18). For Cohn, the Triangle Fire was not just a shock, but also a turning point in her life, as she wrote in an autobiographical letter to a friend much later in her life, on 8 May 1953:

It was the Triangle Fire that decided my life's course. This tragedy influenced then my decision to join the labor movement. I faintly remember joining the protest demonstration on the East Side against this tragedy, but I cannot recollect the streets where we marched.

(FCP/NYPL/MSS588/Cor/LS)

Reading these letters a hundred years later in the heart of a city that staged a series of mnemonic practices to remember these events, and also reflecting upon women's current position in the world of work, had a significant impact upon my own affective understanding in the archive (www.wnyc.org/story/118644-100-years-later-remembering-triangle-shirtwaist-factory-fire/). Dipesh Chakrabarty (2000:113) has argued that a relation of contemporaneity allows historical time to unfold and disrupts 'the empty, secular and homogeneous time of history'. In this light, leaping into *Triangle Fire* times and places became a condition of possibility for a genealogical understanding of the hardships of women garment workers' lives. I read Pauline Newman's letters in the archives of the Tamiment Library, which is literally round the corner from the Triangle Fire Building, after having visited the exhibition that the students of New York University had co-curated as part of the commemoration events (www.nyu.edu/greyart/exhibits/shirtwaist/shirtwaisthome.html). This opened up a third space of understanding where 'time present and time past collapsed' (Dinshaw, 2007: 121). Indeed, by reading letters written in different times – just after the event, as well as forty years later – by women who had witnessed it, and who had also worked to make it part of the history of political struggles around women's labour, made me feel like a body immersed in multiple and heterogeneous times. It was here that the Foucauldian genealogical framework of my archival research made it possible for all these different times to be held together, a way of re-imagining the past as the only way of revisiting it: 'one "fictions" history on the basis of a political reality that makes it true, one "fictions" a politics not yet in existence on the basis of a historical truth,' Foucault (1980b: 193) has influentially written.

In 2012, I chose to live in Brooklyn as it was cheaper and I felt more comfortable moving around the city in my second summer there. But Brooklyn was also the place where Pesotta as well as most of the Jewish seamstresses lived. Retracing their steps and daily journeys from home to work thus created a different affective space for their writings to be read and understood. Let me provide an example from my reading of Pesotta's 'fictional diary'; it gives an almost breathless image of the garment industry working rhythms, which the alarm clock seemed to be ticking incessantly day after day:

> *Monday, 7 A.M.* The alarm clock rings…. Riding in the subway, there is enough time to look over the Want section. In the proletarian Rits (The Automat cafeteria in the Garment Centre) I meet friends. Many are out of work … usually this is our busy season, but now it seems there will be no busy season for us… A friend and I answer an advertisement. The employer without any questions gives us two machines – he seems to be rushed… the place is nice and airy and the workers seem to be more human… We work the whole day. The employer is anxious that we stay to work overtime – everybody works overtime – we stay…

Tuesday, 7 A.M. I do not wait for the alarm clock to wake me. Am up early to get to work on time... We stroll along the Garment Avenue meeting friends still in search of work... In the newly found shop again... The workers throw hostile glances towards our section... a bad sign... we work till noon. My work finished, I take it over to the counter; there is nothing more for me- no more work! We decide to spend the rest of the afternoon at the library.

Wednesday, 7 A.M. Again the cursed alarm clock, the newspaper Help Wanted section, the "Ritz" – a new job. This time it is a dark and gloomy joint... At noon in the market, shall inquire among friends if anyone has heard of a job... Gertrude comes soon. She has found a new job where another worker is needed. She has already spoken to the employer about me – we can go up this afternoon.

Thursday, Ditto A.M. Work, Work, Work, I must go to work... My garment finished, about ten o'clock in the morning, I must leave... It is raining, I shall seek shelter at the office of the union. At the office someone has a job for me, but he seems to be reluctant, telling me that it is a tough job. The employer is a lady and everyone seems to hesitate about going to work for a LADY-BOSS.

Friday, 7 A.M. Luckily it is the last day of the week. The strain is nerve wracking! The whole night I have dreamed about garment mannequins... I am called to the mannequin – something does not fit. [...] It seems whatever was good yesterday is extremely wrong today. My prejudice against the LADY is growing... The day is coming to an end. I am exhausted... I shall quit now, this very minute.

(RPP/NYPL/MSS2390/Writings, emphases in the text).

The garment industry was indeed organised along specific and intense spatio-temporal rhythms that women workers had to learn how to synchronise with on a daily, weekly, monthly, seasonal and annual basis. In writing this fictionalised diary, which clearly draws on remembered real-life experiences, Pesotta was able to condense the rhythms of working life in a few pages and thus to freeze the continuously passing moments of being-in-the-world-of-work. Although dates are among the usual temporal frames through which we remember, it is rhythms that structure the memory of work of the diary above. Remembering time is not easy and is always inextricably linked to particular spaces. Since temporality and spatiality are always entangled in memory, the New York garment district as it appears in the diary extracts above becomes the memory frame within which bodies, places, objects and events are presented and emotions and affects are expressed. It also becomes a frame within which we, as readers of the diary, can imagine what is remembered and written about.

It is at this point that my own rhythms of living in New York were entangled with echoes or distant vibrations of Pesotta's diary rhythms. Living in Brooklyn I could feel Pesotta's frustration in the morning subway: most probably we were travelling along the same line to go to Manhattan's fashion district. Moreover, during the summer of 2012, the NYPL had an interesting exhibition about 'Lunch Hour in NYC': it was while visiting this exhibition (during my own lunch hour) that I learnt about the New Yorkers' excitement of 'the automat cafeterias' that Pesotta wrote about in the Monday entry of her diary above. Both my experience of the exhibition as well as my reading of Pesotta's diary changed by actually realising that 'lunch' acquired its modern identity in New York as a means to accommodate the long working hours of a relatively new metropolis. Lunch was therefore an effect of industrialisation that merged bodily, industrial and urban rhythms in a daily practice that we take for granted today (http://exhibitions.nypl. org/lunchhour/exhibits/show/lunchhour).

so interesting

Thus, during my research at the NYPL archives, my actuality as a researcher was becoming a blurring sensation of past and present images, spaces and times. This co-existence of different spatialities, temporalities and urban rhythms influenced my understanding, as well as my theoretical and methodological orientations within the archive. It was an understanding that I could not have experienced sitting at my desk in London and simply working with digitised versions of documents. To return to the debate around the digital turn, the materiality of the archive does matter, while digitisation changes not only the form and content of archival collections but also the ways we read and understand archival documents, and last but not least it drastically changes the ways we do archival research and 'feel the archive' (Tamboukou, 2015b).

In drawing on my understanding of Pesotta's diary rhythms, I also want to highlight that archival methods are often combined with other approaches such as ethnographic fieldwork. In this light, attention to the physicality of the research is not only a rich source of inspiration and ideas but also necessary in terms of how to make better sense of our sources and their complex interrelation. Attention to 'rhythmanalysis' places the researcher in the middle of his/ her sense-data, thus challenging the distinction between subjects and objects of research, the world as it is and the world as we perceive it. As I have written elsewhere, archival research can be considered in parallel with the epistemological restrictions and limitations of any scientific experiment conducted within a laboratory, including acknowledging that the way an archival project is set up will affect its outcomes and findings (Tamboukou, 2014b). It is while living/ thinking in between other spaces and different temporalities and in the realm of the sociological imagination that ideas have emerged, themes have been followed, ideas have been coined, and also 'narrative personae' – that is, archival people, both real (as they did live) and imaginary (in terms of my internal conversations with them) – have come into life, as I discuss next.

A feminist genealogist in the archive

The researcher goes to an archive with certain questions in mind, since 'the documents do not speak unless someone asks them to verify, that is, to make true, some hypothesis', as Paul Ricoeur (2004: 177) has aptly noted. As I suggested in the first section of this chapter, there is no doubt that our research questions initially orient us within the archive, and they are necessary in how we prepare, plan and organise our research, including the selections from the archive we will explore. The question of how to gender the memory of work was central to my research in the NYPL archives and shaped my initial theoretical departures, as well as my methodological strategies. Following the genealogical quest of problematising the present, I wanted to excavate the conditions for needlework to emerge as the feminine 'labour problem' *par excellence* of the nineteenth and twentieth centuries: how has the seamstress been marginalised in the social and political movements in modernity? And why is women's work still a riddle even among feminist theorisations and debates? These were the genealogical questions that I took with me into the archive.

But instead of seeing history as a continuous development of an ideal schema, genealogy is oriented to discontinuities. Throughout the genealogical exploration, there are frequent disruptions, uneven and haphazard processes of dispersion, that call into question the supposed linear evolution of history. In this context of reversal, the present is not theorised as the result of a meaningful development, but rather as an event, a random result of the interweaving of relations of power and domination. Genealogy as a method of analysis searches in the maze of dispersed events to trace discontinuities, recurrences and play, where traditional historiography sees continuous development, progress and seriousness. Women's work in the garment industry is a paradigmatic case of uneven historical developments and its study seriously deviates from the canon of analysing the industrial formations in modernity.

Archival research is thus catalytic for the emergence of the event, indeed it is in itself an event, an eruption that may radically shift our habitual ways of reasoning and understanding, as Arlette Farge (2013) has remarked. What erupted as an event in my NYPL research was the richness of women workers' cultural lives. I was there to excavate their involvement in the socio-political movements of modernity, but among their agonistic labour literature I found novels, poems, essays in literary criticism, and theatrical plays (Tamboukou, 2013a, 2015a). These unexpected encounters made me return to the NYPL for a second year and had a huge impact on my research interests and 'objects of inquiry'. Indeed, the events that erupt in the process of doing archival research often radically change our practices, our prior knowledges, as well as the objects of our inquiry.

This is why pointing to 'the archival stuff', following it and attending to its specificities, is so important, as we flag up throughout this book. In further understanding the contingencies in the way 'the present' has come to be what it is, researchers need to be inspired to think about other possible ways of being that have not been actualised, and which can become possibilities for the future. As a direct way of facing the past, archival research makes researchers more intensely conscious of how past, present and future co-exist and the part this plays in how we understand and make sense of the social.

But, given the eruptive nature of the archive, what exactly is happening when we fly away from the grounds of our initial understanding? Alfred North Whitehead has offered a lovely metaphor for flying and understanding: 'the true method of discovery is like the flight of an aeroplane. It starts from the ground of particular observation; it makes a flight in the thin air of imaginative generalisation; and it again lands for renewed observation rented acute by rational interpretation' (Whitehead, 1985: 5). Interestingly, Whitehead talks about 'the thin air of imaginative generalisation', which in the case of the archive is always juxtaposed to the thickness of archival research as a laboratory of memory. The study of memory reveals a thickness, in the sense that it possesses a depth not penetrable directly by consciousness. What we are dealing with, then, is a rhythmical movement between the thickness of memory and the thinness of imagination within the specific space/time continuum of the archival research we are entangled in, our research experiment, which in my case regarding analysing narratives I have called 'narrative phenomenon' (Tamboukou, 2014b).

Thus, while working with women trade unionists' papers at the NYPL archives, I was at the same time looking at the histories of the US labour movement and at the gendered power relations, discourses, ideologies and practices that had created conditions of possibility for such archival documents to be created. Surprisingly enough, I did not have to worry about external institutional selections and deselections, for the simple reason that it was Cohn and Pesotta themselves who had carefully selected the papers they bequeathed to the NYPL archives. In this sense, their archives were considered in the light of wider autobiographical discursive limitations and constraints as influentially theorised by Stanley (1992) among others (see also Smith and Watson, 1998). Of course such 'archival technologies of the self', as I have called them (Tamboukou, 2014a), come as no surprise: both women were aware that they had to look after their legacy (see also Chapter 5). This is after all the concern of many single women, whose memory may be lost because there is nobody to enact mnemonic and commemoration practices after they die.

What is important for social researchers to remember when working in archives is that archives are institutions of power/knowledge relations and formations, an acknowledgement that should mobilise a critical approach to the knowledges and memories they hold and offer (*History of the Human Sciences*, 1998, 1999). However, archives are more than that; it is their labile and open spaces, as well as the counter-discourses and counter-narratives that their dusty documents carry with them, that a researcher who is interested in 'othering' the history of the present can trace and explore. What emerged from my research in the NYPL was Farge's and Foucault's taste of the archive, *le goût de l'archive*: the archive became a heterotopic place of archaeological excavation, a site of genealogical deconstruction, and most importantly, a laboratory of memory (and forgetting). It is therefore in deploying genealogical strategies that I have worked in the archive, looking at women workers' narratives as Foucauldian 'grey dusty documents' (Tamboukou, 2011). These documents have re-enacted marginalised voices and subjugated knowledges from the archives of the memory of work: they have textualised the conditions of women workers' lives and have mapped material and discursive entanglements between workspaces and personal spaces. In so doing they have foregrounded the intimate, intense and often invisible ways through which women workers lived their workspaces, populated them with ideas, beliefs and everyday practices, and also imagined them differently. As already noted, it is because the archive is not a monolithic space that different histories can emerge while we excavate it. It is in this light that the archive has been conceptualised as a heterotopia, a spatial notion in Foucauldian analytics, as already introduced in Chapter 1, and I have drawn on in my work with archival documents (Tamboukou, 2000, 2012). Genealogical investigation in the heterotopic spaces of the archive is a site for counter-memories to emerge and for mnemonic practices to be revealed and deconstructed, wherever our research area or field is located. But how are these diverse experiences, different spaces and heterogeneous times brought together? This is what I discuss in the next section of the chapter.

The return from the archive, or the narrative fabric of archival research

As researchers we become entangled in a web of archival stories, irrespective of whether we do narrative analysis or not with the documents we find in archives. In considering stories in the archive, we are of course mindful of Steedman's provocative warning that 'archives contain practically nothing, just disconnected fragments of documents and lists, collected for purposes forgotten or not to be known' (Steedman, 2001: 18). Archival research is indeed a process of finding fragments and working with discontinuities. It is here, however, that narrativity becomes a way of assembling disparate and sometimes disconnected pieces and fragments into a design that has a meaning. In thus considering the narrative fabric of archival work, I want to look at two classical narratological themes, characters and plots, and see how they have been deployed in archival research, but also how they can be transposed in my post-narratological approach.

One of the things that struck me from the very beginning of reading the 'Letters received' section of Fannia Cohn's papers were the letters of Evelyn Preston it contained. These were warm, kind and very different in style from all the other letters that Cohn was receiving in the same period. After reading three of these letters, I had already decided that I could not wait until I finished the whole 'Letters received' section. Instead I moved to the next microfilm reel of 'Letters sent' and carefully searched for Cohn's response to them. In doing this, I wanted to trace a body of correspondence that might throw a different light on Cohn's dry administrative life as it appeared in the archive. I did this by reassembling the temporal order of the documents, a meticulous work that could only be done after the archives had closed (see also Chapter 4 on deploying different temporal orders). The fact that these different and disparate letters were already photocopied and stored in the beautiful plastic files I had bought from the library shop filled me with joy as I left the NYPL archive each day. The importance of women's friendship as a support network consequently emerged as a crucial storyline in my analysis, and its unexpected twists and configurations created conditions of possibility for a more complex understanding of Cohn's life.

Evelyn Preston was a wealthy and well-educated young woman with a passionate interest in the labour movement. She was 23 years old when she met the 37-year-old Cohn and despite or maybe because of their age difference they developed a warm friendship and spent time together, going to dinners, the theatre and even swimming on Coney Island: 'I am looking forward to having you chauffeur me around in your four cylinder Buick ...', Cohn wrote to Preston on 21 September 1923 (FCP/NYPL/MSS588/Cor/LS). By that time Preston had left New York to follow a Master's Degree in labour history and Economics at the University of Wisconsin, their friendship had become mostly an epistolary one, but still very important for Cohn. Moreover, the collection of letters between Cohn and Preston were very different both in content and in form from the letters between Cohn and Wolfson, some examples of which have been discussed in the first section of the chapter. As I have written elsewhere, the Cohn-Preston correspondence highlights issues around cross-class encounters in the gendered histories of the labour movement, but they also put forward complex interrelations between ethics, aesthetics and politics (Tamboukou, 2015a). They certainly paint a different image of Cohn, revealing her love for art, her care for young women's development, as well as the way she deeply valued the gift of friendship. As Cohn wrote to Preston on 2 January 1923:

> I am a great believer in friendship... I never could over-estimate its value provided it is based on real understanding and confidence. Every person is eager to have a human being close to him. We cannot share with everyone around us some of our innermost feelings. And nothing is so helpful to deepening our minds and clarifying our thoughts as exchange of views with our friends... We can get the best out of our friends if we can make an effort.
>
> (FCP/NYPL/MSS588/Cor/LS)

Cohn thus appears as a different person when writing to Preston than when writing to Wolfson, let alone when writing to the International Ladies' Garment Workers' Union (ILGWU) president or other friends and collaborators. There is a rich body of literature revolving around the epistolary I/you relationship, including the variety of the subject positions that correspondents take up, inhabit and move along (Altman, 1982; Stanley, 2004; Stanley and Salter, 2014; Tamboukou, 2010b, 2014d). What I want to highlight in relation to archival research, however, is that Cohn's different epistolary personae have created a new way of ordering her letters in the 'other archive' of my research. The new ordering followed the mode of significant correspondents: 'Evelyn Preston letters', 'Theresa Wolfson letters', 'Marion Philips letters', 'Charles Beard's letters' (Tamboukou, 2014c). After mapping the letters across significant correspondents, I created a second level of ordering, this time drawing on periodisation: the 1921–1922 letters, the years when significant changes in workers' education occurred, so it was important to have an overview of the synchronicity of Cohn's correspondence (Tamboukou, 2014b, 2014d). The lived rhythms discussed earlier were thus transposed to a reconstruction of temporal and ordering rhythms in the archive.

The importance of 'significant correspondents' as a way of ordering also made connections with my experience of working with Pesotta's letters in the NYPL. Apart from the fact that these were 'real documents' that demanded different 'real time' rhythms, Pesotta's papers included a wide range of diaries, as well as a rich collection of creative writings. Three surprises thus erupted from Pesotta's papers that had an impact both on the ordering of the researcher's 'other archive' but also on the analysis.

Her diaries were very different in style, form and content – some of them were very private and revealing, others business-like agendas. However, revealing as some of her diaries were, it was neither in her diaries nor her letters that insight was provided into her inner world, but in her creative writings. And it was not in the letters that she sent, but in the letters that she received that we can discern something about her emotions and feelings. Pesotta is actually the first woman in my experience of working with letters on love, gender and agonistic politics (Tamboukou, 2013b, 2013c; 2014d) where I have mostly read the other side of the correspondence – her lover's letters, not hers. After reading these letters, I felt for the first time the need to consider the question of 'men in love'.

What I want to highlight here is the difficulty of grappling with 'the return from the archive'. There are many issues to consider about 'the return'. There is the question of how to manage the welter of archival data that the researcher comes back with. There is the problem of how to reconnect with the world left behind while in the archive, while retaining the memories, affective bonds and imaginary travels that were experienced while in the archives. And also there is the small detail of writing, of creating the publications that were promised to funders but are also important to the academic self you hopefully still inhabit. This is where the importance of narrative sensibility emerges: stories are traces of human existence and human actions, Hannah Arendt (1998) has famously suggested; without stories there is no history, it is through stories that we are entangled in the web of human relations. Drawing on the Arendtian take on narratives, I suggest that it is through narrativisation that we create meaning in archival research. There are of course interesting debates around the force, power and even domination of narratives, including Hayden White's (1987) critique of the content of the form that I want to consider here in making the argument for a narrative sensibility in archival research.

In exploring 'the content of the form' of narrative discourse in historical thought, White has influentially suggested that 'narrative, far from being merely a form of discourse that can be filled with different contents, real or imaginary as the case may be, already possesses a content prior to any given actualisation of it in speech or writing' (White, 1987: xi). Narrative in this conceptualisation imposes its form on modes of historical analysis and understanding. Although I agree with White that content and form are inextricably entangled, I cannot see their interrelation simply as limiting and restrictive. In analysing Rosa Luxemburg's letters to her lover and comrade Leo Jogiches, I have argued that 'the epistolary form dramatises and gives specificity to the relationship between politics and love' (Tamboukou, 2013c: 52). In extending this line of argument I therefore suggest that narrative offers new modalities of re-assembling the archive in line with the research questions, theoretical frameworks and epistemological orientations of the research. Discontinuous and interrupted as they are, narrative fragments create their own rhythms of archival existence and it is specific spatial and temporal rhythms that the genealogical investigation follows and focuses on. Narrative sensibility means that the analysis starts when we are still in the archive, and here I am in disagreement with Steedman, who has argued that 'historical knowledge is always produced *after* the archive (2011: 323, original emphasis). While in the archive and during our attempt to manage the bulk of material we encounter, we start following rough paths of storylines that usually revolve around grey archival figures, something I have come to configure as 'the narrative personae of my research' (Tamboukou, 2010a, 2014e), a concept that I want to explicate in the context of the archive.

As already noted, narration in Arendt's thought creates conditions of possibility for uniqueness, plurality and communication to be enacted within the sphere of the political. Read in this light, the seamstresses' archival documents open up a performative scene, a dialogic space wherein the writer of the document and the researcher as reader meet, interact and negotiate meaning about subjects and their world. The archive of the seamstresses' documents thus becomes a site of mediation and communication enabling the emergence of a multiplicity of meanings and traces of truth interwoven together in the narrative fabric of archival research. Moreover, far from being essentialised, pinned down in a fixed subject position, or encased within the constraints and limitations of the archival documents, the seamstresses become 'narrative personae',

90   *Maria Tamboukou*

figures who respond to the theoretical questions and concerns of the researcher without losing the actuality of their 'words and deeds'. In configuring the seamstresses as 'narrative personae', I have followed Deleuze and Guattari's (1994) notion of the 'conceptual personae' in philosophy. 'Philosophy constantly brings conceptual personae to life' (62), Deleuze and Guattari have suggested, and the Socrates in Plato, the Dionysus in Nietzsche, the Idiot in Descartes, are their exemplars of the best-known conceptual personae in the history of philosophy. The philosopher speaks through her/his conceptual persona, keeping a critical distance from what is being said and from the subject of enunciation. This is a third person – the conceptual persona, not the philosopher – that says 'I', since there is always a multiplicity of enunciations and subjects in the work of philosophy.

But although the initial idea of the narrative persona comes from Deleuze and Guattari, it is in Arendt's work that the concept has been narratively grounded. As Arendt (1990: 106) notes in *On Revolution*, the roots of 'the persona' are to be found in ancient drama wherein it has a twofold function: first, as a mask disguising the actor in theatre; and second, as a device that, although disguising, would allow the voice of the actor to sound through. If we follow the historicity of the concept, however, in Roman times the persona passes from the theatre to the legal realm and means a legal personality, a right-and-duty bearing person, a Roman citizen, not any natural person. So there is the drama persona and the legal persona. In this context, the notion of the narrative persona in my work is a conceptual figure, who acts and whose story we can follow in the pursuit of meaning and understanding. But the fact that we follow the story of the narrative persona does not necessarily mean that this story represents the essence or character of who these people 'really' were. This is not to deny that they were real persons, but to denote the limitations of their – and indeed anybody's – stories to convey the essence of who their author is. As Arendt has aptly put it, 'nothing entitles us to assume that [man] has a nature or essence in the same sense as other things' (Arendt, 1998: 10). But the lack of essence does not necessarily lead to 'the death of the subject', be it in Barthian or Foucauldian terms. Foucault (1988) himself returned to the subject, in considering ethics as a genealogical axis alongside truth and power. While rejecting essence, Arendt theorises human existence, 'life itself, natality and mortality, worldliness, plurality and the earth' (Arendt, 1998: 11), and here again she emphasises the fact that we are not reducible to the conditions of human existence. Instead of a unified and autonomous subject, there are instead nomadic passages and subject positions that the narrative personae of my inquiries take up and move between, while inscribing personal and political stories. It is through their stories that certain concepts, ideas and events can be expressed, rehearsed and dramatised, so that their enactment can create a scene for dialogic exchanges, communication, understanding and action.

Further considered within the legal dimension of the Roman tradition in Arendt's analysis, the narrative persona takes up a position in discourse and assumes her rights as a legal subject. This positioning does not essentialise her either; it rather creates a person with whom one can be in dialogue, but also to whom one is responsible: 'a right-and-duty bearing person, created by the law and which appears before the law', as Arendt (1990: 107) has pithily remarked. The seamstresses of my archival research thus become personae through their narratives: as a feminist narrative researcher, I am accountable to them, having taken up the responsibility of presenting their stories as an Arendtian design that has a meaning. The latter is open to interpretation and negotiation between you as audience/readers, myself as an author and narrative researcher, and my narrative personae. Although dead for many years, they are still alive, active and very much among us as their 'words and deeds' still shape feminist histories in the making and therefore the archives of the future.

As researchers in the archive, we are thus surrounded by the narrative personae emerging from the archival documents we work with. We listen to their voices and also talk to them as we read their documents; their ideas give us some orientations; we have arguments with them and yes, we need to acknowledge it, we like some of them and dislike others. It is actually while struggling to make sense of 'what is wrong' with some of them that questions and problems arise that have an effect on our analysis and understanding: Why was it that Pesotta seemed so gloomy in her diaries? Why was she crying almost every night? Why could she not sleep? Her diaries did not give any answers, I had to read her letters of the same period to start making sense of some of the problems she was grappling with and even then I could not always agree with some of her ideas and attitudes to life. 'Stop doing that, girl,' I kept telling her as if she could hear me; and reading a box of her papers later, I could turn to her /myself and say, 'well, I can see your point now' or 'I told you not to.' As I write this chapter, I am still in conversation with the narrative personae of my research and I do not think that this conversation will ever conclude. 'Never the last word,' Molly Andrews (2013) has emphatically written about the process of revisiting life histories as well as the narratives of our analyses and interpretations.

While in the archive we are thus entangled in the web of human relations that include both the living and the dead. Even though I have had access to Pesotta's amorous correspondence, I know there are things I will never write about. It wouldn't be right, no matter how many copyright clearances or how much time would have elapsed since her death. My research ethics and even more myself as a researcher have been moulded through my relation with Pesotta, even though she has been dead for sixty years. As Steedman has aptly noted, 'there has been little attempt to theorise the place of the dead and death in the human and social sciences' despite the fact that 'contemplation of and interaction with the dead was a foundational activity for history' (Steedman, 2011: 327). Taking up the challenge of our non-interaction with the dead, I am therefore proclaiming myself accountable to Pesotta, not only because she has been configured as a narrative persona bearing rights, as already explained, but also because she is inextricably interwoven with my own self as a researcher. As Stanley has succinctly put it, we need to consider the specificities of 'ontological ethics' in documents of life research (Stanley, 2013: 27). Drawing on Simone de Beauvoir, Stanley has persuasively argued for a relational notion of the self, 'a self-and-other' which constitutes the premises of ontological ethics. Archival research is indeed a milieu where ontological ethics should play a crucial role, a proposition that is returned to in the last chapter of this book.

Feeling narratives in the archive: some conclusions

In this chapter I have created a plane for diverse theoretical approaches to illuminate my archival research practices: Lefebvre's spatio-temporal approach of rhythmanalysis was underpinned by Foucault's genealogical analytics, while an Arendtian-based narrative sensibility was my proposition for reassembling and making sense of the texts, discourses and figures emerging from archival documents. Although these theoretical and methodological approaches revolve around my research in the NYPL archives, they also arose in doing archival research over the last twenty years in other archives in the UK and around the world. These include the Queen Mary and Westfield College Archives, University of London and the Modern Records Centre at the University of Warwick (Tamboukou, 2003), the Rodin Museum Archives in Paris, the National Library of Wales Archives, the British Library Manuscripts, the Harry Ransom Humanities Research Centre at the University of Texas at Austin and the Massachusetts College of Arts Archives in Boston (Tamboukou, 2010a), the archives of the Tamiment Library, Collection at New York University, the Emma Goldman's Papers Project at the University of California at Berkeley (Tamboukou, 2013b) and the Bibliothèque Historique de la ville de Paris (Tamboukou, 2014b, 2015b, 2015c, 2015d). The diversity of these archival spaces and places shows that such approaches and practices are transferable and can indeed be used in different research and disciplinary contexts. As already noted, each archival case had its own specificities with emerging questions and problems to be addressed and solved, but together they create an assemblage of methodological approaches and moves that I have tried to unpack in addressing the questions raised at the beginning of this chapter and to which I now return.

As will be obvious from the archives discussed in this chapter, I have mostly worked in what could be considered as 'traditional archives', that is, collections of archival documents in libraries, universities and museums, although I have also worked with digitised documents as well as microfilms. There are many more diverse archives discussed throughout this book, but even regarding the traditional archival places and spaces, different approaches can be deployed. This multiplicity of modes of doing archival research relates to the interdisciplinary nature of the archive as a research milieu, and also to the radical changes that the digital turn has brought in what used to be a place/paper/bound research approach often covered with many layers of dust and even more layers of power/knowledge relations and discourses. What I have tried to show throughout this chapter, however, is that space, time and matter are crucial not only in our understanding of how an archive becomes but also in how the researcher and the archive create an assemblage that fuses divisions and separations between the subjects and objects of the research. They also help problematise a range of dualisms, such as mind/body, texts/readers, reason/experience, memory/imagination, reality/representation. In short, this changes the world as it is and the world as we perceive it. (See also Chapter 4 on the idea and practice of cultural assemblage in relation to digital archival projects.)

Confronting the archive as an assemblage of documents, institutional practices, power/knowledge relations as well as space/time/matter rhythms, has epistemological, methodological and ethical implications for doing archival research. Such a conceptualisation goes beyond the conditions and limitations of the exemplars unpacked in this chapter, and opens up new paths in the field of archival research in the social sciences and humanities. In drawing on my experience of working at the New York Public Library with the papers of women trade unionists in the garment industry, I have shown the more general applications of this approach. Also, throughout the chapter I have emphasised that archival research is always a situated process with emerging questions, problems and issues, and these need to be addressed and dealt with in an ongoing way. This multi-modality of engaging with and raising questions about the archive in itself creates an archive of methodological approaches that can be drawn upon, by always bending 'previous rules' and charting new paths. In this sense, archival research charts trails for research, invites new researchers to follow some of them but also to open up new paths while immersing themselves in the specificities of their own inquiries and archival circumstances.

In perceiving the archive as a process, a becoming, I have highlighted the importance of the research questions we bring to the archive, and also the limitations of our prior understandings and conceptualisations. I have argued that we should be bold enough to deal with the openness of archival research, to welcome and indeed embrace unexpected encounters, and to be willing to abandon some of our habitual ways of theorising and understanding. Here the archive has been conceived not only as a process but also as an event, marking discontinuities and ruptures in our modes of analysis and interpretation. In doing this, I have looked at how genealogical questions and spatio-temporal rhythms have an impact on how researchers orient ourselves within the archive, how we follow specific storylines, narrative personae and analytical insights, and how we write about these.

In configuring the archive as both a process and an event, I have also highlighted the importance of narrative sensibility. Analysis always starts while we are still in an archive, in what Whitehead has called 'the middle of the pack, where there is pushing, shoving and mutual constraint' (Stengers, 2011: 448). This is where the narrative fabric of the archive is being interwoven with our subsequent analysis and the writing of our research outputs. In considering narrative sensibility in the archive, I have followed lines of Whitehead's theorisation of feelings as crucial in the constitution of reality as well as in our understanding (Tamboukou, 2015b). As Whitehead influentially argued, 'there is nothing in the real world which is merely an inert fact. Every reality is there for feeling: it promotes feeling; and it is felt' (1985: 310).

Here it goes without saying that the richness of the archival worlds that researchers engage with over the years will never be represented in an encompassing way in our writings, no matter how nuanced our observations, how robust our analysis or how eloquent our writing style are. But what we can try for as researchers is to open up windows to the worlds of archives and invite others to visit them. It is by sharing our impressions that we can perhaps gain some further grasp of the social worlds we are trying to understand. Despite the institutional constraints and limitations, archival research is a world of activity enabling the expression and flow of feelings; it further facilitates the flight of imaginative experience, shapes new modes of thought and ultimately initiates creative processes in how we can understand ourselves and the world we emerge from.

What I therefore hope readers will gain from this chapter is an understanding of archival research as an entanglement of intellectual and material practices with multiple points of emergence, some unforeseen destinations, as well as a wide variation of flows and rhythms. In this light, being-in-the-archive is both a journey and an adventure that needs a map and a compass, but it will certainly also open up its own paths. I hope that some of the analytical trails and methodological moves suggested in this chapter will be helpful in orienting researchers in their archival journeys to come.

Acknowledgements

I am grateful to the British Academy for funding my archival research with Fannia Mary Cohn's papers (SG112079) and to the University of East London for funding my research with Rose Pesotta's papers.

Archival sources

Archives Marie-Louise Bouglé, Fonds Jeanne Bouvier, Bibliothèque Historique de la ville de Paris (BHVP/AMB/FJB) http://bibliotheques-specialisees. paris.fr/catalogue/recherche-simple.dot?query=Marie-Louise+Bougle [Accessed 4 July 2015].

Constance Maynard Papers. Queen Mary University of London Archives (QM/CMP) www.library.qmul.ac.uk/archives/digital/constance_maynard [Accessed 4 July 2015].

Clara Collet Papers, Modern Records Centre, University of Warwick (MRC/CCP) http://dscalm.warwick.ac.uk/DServe/dserve.exe?dsqIni=Dserve.ini&dsqApp=Archive&dsqDb=Catalog&dsqCmd=NaviTree.tcl&dsqField=RefNo&dsqItem=COL#HERE [Accessed 4 July 2015].

Dora Carrington correspondence with Lytton Strachey. British Library, Manuscripts: (BL/DC/MS3687) www.bl.uk/reshelp/findhelprestype/manuscripts/msscollect/manuscripts [Accessed 4 July 2015].

Dora Carrington Collection, Gerald Brenan Papers. Harry Ransom Humanities Research Centre, the University of Texas at Austin: (HRC/DCC, GBP), http://norman.hrc.utexas.edu/fasearch/findingAid.cfm?eadid=00023 [Accessed 4 July 2015]. http://norman.hrc.utexas.edu/fasearch/findingAid.cfm?eadid=00017 [Accessed 4 July 2015].

Emma Goldman's Papers, University of California, Berkeley. (UCB/EGP), www.lib.berkeley.edu/goldman/ [Accessed 4 July 2015].

Fannia M. Cohn papers. Manuscripts and Archives Division. The New York Public Library. Astor, Lenox, and Tilden Foundations. (NYPL/FCP/MSS588), http://archives.nypl.org/mss/588#overview [Accessed 4 July 2015].

Gwen John MSS, National Library of Wales (NLW/GJMSS), www.archiveswales.org.uk/anw/get_collection.php?coll_id=250 [Accessed 4 July 2015].

Italian Immigrant Women in New York City's Garment Industry, Oral Histories, 1976–1978, Sophia Smith Collection, Smith College, Northampton, Mass. (SSC/IIW/MS 556) http://asteria.fivecolleges.edu/findaids/sophiasmith/mnsss440.html [Accessed 4 July 2015].

Mary Gwendolen John Boxes, Rodin Museum Archives (MGJ/MR) www.musee-rodin.fr/en/collections/archives [Accessed 4 July 2015].

Mary Titcomb, Massachusetts College of Art Archives (MassArt), http://inside.massart.edu/Library/Collections/Archives.html [Accessed 4 July 2015].

Pauline Newman papers. Arthur and Elizabeth Schlesinger Library on the History of Women in America. (SL/PNP/MC 324; M-44) http://oasis.lib.harvard.edu/oasis/deliver/~sch00018 [Accessed 4 July 2015].

Rose Pesotta papers. Manuscripts and Archives Division. The New York Public Library. Astor, Lenox, and Tilden Foundations (NYPL/RPP/MSS2390) http://archives.nypl.org/mss/2390 [Accessed 4 July 2015].

Rose Schneiderman Papers. The Tamiment Library and Robert F. Wagner Labor Archives Collection (RSP/TAM/18) http://dlib.nyu.edu/findingaids/html/tamwag/tam_018/ [Accessed 4 July 2015].

Interlude

In Chapter 3, the narrative fabric of archival research has been pointed to, with stories always already 'there' and requiring analysis, including in the narrativity which provides archival researchers with the means to assemble the fragments remaining. Archival research is a situated process and has its own spatio-temporal rhythms, as well as needing to be attentive to those inscribed in the sources or traces worked with, and Chapter 3 has explored how archival entanglements unfold and what is done with them analytically by the researcher.

Chapter 4 is concerned with the intertwining of narrativity, temporality, memory and forgetting, with its emphasis on temporality. It focuses on how temporal ordering can be used and problematised by the archival researcher through different ways of reading time in archival materials such as diaries and letters. Chapters 3 and 4 are in a way concerned with two sides of the same archival research coin, one emphasising spatiality, the other temporality, while recognising that in practice these are conjoined. However, as Chapter 4 shows, whichever is foregrounded by the archival researcher will make a profound difference to research activities and practices, the selection of documents and other data, and the analysis of research materials.

4 Reading time backwards?

Archival research and temporal order

Andrea Salter

Introduction

Reading archival traces tells us things about the past, although much depends on what is meant by reading and also how time and the past are understood. Temporality is foundational to archives, their histories, contents and carrying out archival research. Should archival research always engage with the complexities of the temporal order, with how events, experiences and their representations are arranged in time? What is involved in using temporality in a methodological way to 'read the archive'? Are there transferable tools and practices here that other archival researchers can use in working with their own research?

My chapter explores these questions and shows how a methodological approach organised around temporality can be used in reading archival traces. It does so comparing two archival projects: one I was involved in as a doctoral researcher, working on the Mass Observation Archive's (MOA) collections, and the other as a post-doctoral Research Associate on the Olive Schreiner Letters Project, working on collections worldwide. It discusses how a focused attention to temporal order can provide an organising structure for archival research, shape the conduct of such research from its inception, and also frame the archival research process when looking back from the viewpoint of the 'products' – a dissertation, article and so on – that a project has produced.

Archival projects and temporality

Ideas about time and temporal order have strongly informed the two archival projects I worked on during my transition from a doctoral to post-doctoral researcher. These varied in size, scale, substantive focus, personnel involved and geographical and temporal reach. Both involved reading 'documents of life' (Plummer, 2001; Stanley, 2013), which are everyday texts of a wide variety that are marked with time and so lend themselves well to temporally framed investigations.

Thinking about this with hindsight, I realise my draw to the work of people who comment on their process of researching and writing and sometimes also invoke how their readers are positioned. Reflecting on methodology and its epistemological underpinnings is important in making available the procedures, practices and processes involved in knowledge production, as far as this is possible. My views have partly resulted from the frustrations of academic presentations and publications that tell remarkable research stories but give little indication of how the archival material drawn on was found and used and how arguments were formed on its basis. This obscures methodology and prevents learning from the practical experience of research and not just its sanitised results. Looking across the two projects, the chapter also explores some transferable skills that arise from focusing on the temporal aspects of these archival experiences.

The first example concerns my doctoral research, funded as a PhD studentship by the UK's Economic and Social Research Council (ESRC). This involved six months of solo archival research in 2004 and 2005 in the Mass Observation Archive (at that time part of Special Collections at the University of Sussex, today stored at The Keep, a purpose-built archive near Brighton, UK). In this, I constructed and analysed a sample of women's 'wartime' and 'day-diaries', written from the late 1930s to the 1960s, in the context of the social research organisation Mass Observation's various activities, with my PhD thesis resulting from this (Salter, 2008a). The second example is my post-doctoral research as a Research Associate on the Olive Schreiner Letters Project (www.oliveschreinerletters.ed.ac.uk) between 2008 and 2012, funded by the ESRC as a major research project. Among other things, this resulted in publication of a digital edition of transcribed letters, the *Olive Schreiner Letters Online* (www.oliveschreiner.org), a free access electronic scholarly edition which is also a dataset – a kind of meta-collection – of fully searchable and downloadable transcriptions of the 5,000+ extant letters written by South African feminist writer and social theorist Olive Schreiner (1855–1920), together with an extensive editorial apparatus and publications around this. Published through the Humanities Research Institute's HRI Online at the University of Sheffield, it has also been archived with the UK's Data Archive.

The Olive Schreiner Letters Project involved a Principal Investigator, two Co-Investigators, a full-time Research Associate (me) and two PhD Studentships, with three core research team members. There was also a three-member technical team based at the HRI at Sheffield. Schreiner's extant letters are located in more than forty archives on three continents and also in a number of private collections, so the project involved research in archives globally by one or more team members (and see Chapter 5 for a different process of assemblage). In addition to articles and book chapters on the research aspects of the project (Stanley, 2011a, 2011b, 2013; Stanley and Dampier, 2009, 2010, 2011, 2012; Stanley, Dampier and Salter, 2010, 2012; Stanley, Salter and Dampier, 2013a, 2013b; Stanley and Salter, 2009), an edited print volume of Schreiner's South African letters together with an extensive editorial apparatus has appeared (Stanley and Salter, 2014). Archival research for this particular project, then, has contributed to various different but related products, discussed later.

The structure of my chapter is informed by Paul Ricoeur's work on the hermeneutics of historical time and the intertwining of narrativity and temporality, memory and forgetting (Ricoeur, 1984, 2004). Ricoeur's comment, that when 'reading the ending in the beginning and the beginning in the ending, we also learn to read time itself backwards, as the recapitulation of ... a course of action' (Ricoeur, 1984: 67), provides a productive approach to use. There is of course a rich literature on reading and re-reading (and see Chapter 2 for its connections with writing), while this chapter is concerned with methodological matters using Ricoeur's broad frame to direct attention not only to reading forwards, to envisage an end-point and then plot the research moments or acts which enable this to be reached, but also to read research materials *against* chronological time. By this I mean strategically reading time backwards from the point of conclusion, so as to shed light on the actions and events that occurred in reaching that point.

Reading and interpreting chronologically forwards is how most archival researchers, indeed probably most researchers in general, work. Yet in practice, reading and interpreting backwards better characterises how archival researchers make sense of materials as well as the stance from which we write up our interpretations into arguments and publications. In research as in life, everything we do takes place through the lens of 'the present' and therefore involves us in an omnipresent way looking back. My doctoral research on Mass Observation's wartime diaries used this latter approach, acknowledging the effect that 'reading backwards' had on interpretation of the diaries I was researching, and also actively engaging with this in terms of the method I designed and deployed.

After introducing Mass Observation and its diaries, first, 'reading backwards' in archival research will be detailed and the implications of reading the 'beginning in the ending', to paraphrase Ricoeur, explored. The chapter, then, second, compares temporal strategies in reading Olive Schreiner's extant letters. It also, third, considers another temporal approach used in analysing the Mass Observation diaries, in looking at a number of diaries and entries written on and around specific days, instead of an individual diary over a length of time.

A fourth way of articulating the relationships between endings and beginnings in archival research is also discussed, drawing on Ricoeur in discussing the 'space of experience' and 'horizon of expectation', interrelated terms borrowed from cultural historian Reinhart Koselleck (1985 [1979]: 267–88; Ricoeur, 1988: 208–15; Koselleck, 2002). The 'space of experience' comprises past events that an individual remembers or is influenced by and is a site 'within which the acquisitions of the past are deposited' (Koselleck, 1985 [1979]: 210). And 'horizon of expectation' refers to unfolding future possibilities, to some degree guided by events occurring as part of the 'space of experience'. The present, then, is where both experience and expectations intersect. Differences and similarities between my doctoral and post-doctoral research experiences regarding 'spaces of experience' and 'horizons of expectation' will be discussed around some examples and how using these categories panned out in practice. Here ideas about a known, anticipated or imagined reader (colleagues, examiners, unknown future readers, and so on) were important and are also discussed.

Ricoeur's concepts of 'configuration' and 'emplotment' further illuminate how relationships between endings and beginnings can be understood. In any archival project, the complicated interweaving of the past and future at the present moment of 'doing research', and also in writing about it subsequently, informs both how expectations (regarding anticipated or promised products of a project) are articulated, and also how stories about research findings, archival experiences and so on are told. How such matters are managed gives clues about the co-ordinates from which we 'emplot' our archival research into stories or develop projects through building (whether prospectively or retrospectively) coherent narratives about them (Salter, 2010). The role of readers is important here, for readers too 'emplot' or configure to make sense of the stories told. Ricoeur's related three-tier conceptualisation of mimesis – as prefiguration, configuration and refiguration – can be defined in simple terms as representations of action or identity in narrative form. Mimesis forms part of the background to the theoretical structure developed in this chapter, as it has temporal aspects which are helpful in thinking about archival labour and the working practices involved in all archival research projects.

Mass Observation and its diaries

Home to the papers of the radical popular social research organisation Mass Observation, the Mass Observation Archive also holds its diaries and day-diaries (the latter sometimes referred to as day-surveys). There are also Monthly and Special Directive replies (which are responses written by its National Panel when asked specific questions around one or more themes), Topic Collections (including investigators' reports, correspondences, drafts and plans for particular topics investigated), File Reports (findings of studies Mass Observation's observers conducted from 1937 to 1951), and the Worktown Collection (MO's study of two towns in north-west Britain, Bolton [Worktown] and Blackpool [Holidaytown]). Some of these archival materials run from the late 1930s to the 1960s, and again from 1981 to today, with more detail on the MOA website (www.massobs.org.uk).

At the time of my PhD research, some MO diary materials were available on microfiche, while much was accessible only in manuscript form, the implications of which I discuss later. Today, all can be accessed via the subscription-based collection, Mass Observation Online, published in five parts since 2007 by Adam Matthew Digital (www.massobservation.amdigital.co.uk/Home/index). This includes the whole run of Mass Observation diaries (1939–1967) in an electronic but non-searchable form. It is important to emphasise that the varied character and specific location of what material was available to me at the time, and the form it was available in, shaped how I planned and conducted my research, as did the limited time-frame and finances I had, and the archive regulations, which specified no digital photography. Diversity and plenitude were also important with regards to the 5,000+ letters transcribed as part of the Olive Schreiner Letters Project. All the extant Schreiner manuscript letters were available in public and private sources to consult. There was also a grey area of different kinds of materials to be made sense of, importantly including typescript copies, extracts from letters and composite versions by Schreiner's estranged husband S.C. Cronwright-Schreiner (Stanley and Salter, 2009). How these different versions of Schreiner's letters came about was important in shaping the work that needed to be carried out. Similar kinds of issues arose in understanding how MO's diary materials came into existence initially, which strongly impacted on the hows and whys of their archiving, as well as how they developed over time.

In the beginning...

Around Geoffrey Pyke's idea of carrying out an 'anthropological study of our own situation' (Pyke, 1936: 974), the founders of Mass Observation, Charles Madge (then a *Daily Mirror* journalist and poet and from 1950 Professor of Sociology at the University of Birmingham; see Sheridan, 1984; Stanley, 1990; Calder, 1996; Hubble, 2001, 2006; Marcus, 2001; Hinton, 2013); Humphrey Jennings (a poet, artist and later well-known documentary film-maker); and Tom Harrisson (an anthropologist, ornithologist and writer; see Heimann, 2003), joined forces. They swiftly announced the official formation of Mass Observation in the *New Statesman and Nation* and called for 'not fifty, but 5,000 observers...' (Harrisson, Jennings and Madge, 1937). With the help of favourable press coverage, about 1,000 volunteers got in touch, half of whom responded to the observational tasks requested of them (Madge, 1976: 1395; Jeffrey, 1999). This National Panel of Voluntary Observers came from 'all walks of life' but were 'better educated and more intelligent than the average' (Ferraby, 1945: 1–2).

From the moment Mass Observation was formed, Madge's volunteers in Blackheath, London, began to send 'Directives' to its national observers, which 'directed the attention of the Mass Observers to the subject area which Mass Observation was studying at any one time', and included subjects such as their dreams, smoking habits, personal appearance and what was on their mantelpieces (Sheridan *et al.*, 2000: 75). The early Directives also included day-diaries, asking observers to write about their activities on the twelfth day of each month. The Coronation

Day of George VI, on 12 May 1937, however, presented MO with an opportunity to gather responses which were 'almost wholly concerned with one event, which affected the whole country' (Jennings and Madge, 1937: iii-iv); and from this and related data, the book *May The Twelfth* resulted. The day-diaries lapsed in February 1938, with more than 500 responses received by the end of 1937.

My doctoral research devised a sampling framework which selected a number of diaries written on particular days and, among other things, tested out a method for analysing their content as proposed in Jennings and Madge (1937). I shall return to this, but first want to discuss the origination of Mass Observation's wartime diaries, the 'backwards looking' methodological approach I adopted, and its interpretive consequences (see also Casey *et al.*, [2014] on Mass Observation as method).

Backwards looking

In August 1939, a 'Crisis Directive' asked MO's National Panel to write a 'Crisis Diary' (Sheridan *et al.*, 2000). While a Special Directive around the Munich Crisis had been issued in 1938, the 'Crisis Diary' was to be kept for a number of weeks from 22 August 1939 onwards (File Report 621, File Report 2181, Mass Observation Archive). On 28 August, Tom Harrisson suggested the National Panel might wish to transform their Crisis Diaries into 'Full Diaries'. These were later referred to as the 'Wartime Diaries' and formed an important strand of MO's research on the war (Willcock, 1943). Harrisson asked the National Panel to 'begin keeping day-to-day personal diaries of everything that happened to them' (Willcock, 1943: 450). Specifically, they were asked to 'concentrate on the details of every-day life, their own reactions, those of their family, and people they met' (FR 621, Introduction: 1).

Nearly 500 women and men wrote diaries for MO for varied spans of time between 1939 and 1967. In total, 227 women contributed diary entries, somewhat fewer than men, with a sample of women's diaries forming the empirical base for my doctoral research and the 'test ground' for the methodological activities I pursued. As well as wanting to add to the literature on interpreting 'documents of life', women's self-expression, and wartime experiences and activities, my focus on women's diaries specifically was also a practical one. The 'archival frame' (Hill, 1993) used to organise the MO diaries is both 'sexed' and 'chronologised' (Stanley, 1995b; see also Noakes, 1996; Sheridan, 2014) and almost constrains a focus on one or other of the sets, rather than both (for discussion of gendered aspects of MO as an organisation, see Sheridan 1990, 1993, 1994; Hinton, 2013). This is because the manuscript and also the microfiche versions of the men's and women's diaries are stored separately, making it difficult and time-consuming to work across both at the same time. The manuscript diaries are relatedly stored in folders by month and year, rather than containing a particular diarist's 'whole' diary (Hubble, 2014). The structuring of the MOA in this particular shape and order, then, clearly affects how it can be researched.

When I started this MO work, my concern was primarily methodological: how was I to research even a small sub-set of the whole and with what plan of action? This was very different in working later on the Olive Schreiner Letters Project, for the research strategy here was inbuilt: transcribe all of Olive Schreiner's letters. However, as a dataset, 'the Schreiner letters' was split across space and did not exist in just one collection or archive, and so was not framed by one single archival organising structure. There was then no reason to plan sampling Olive Schreiner's letters because this was not within the remit of the project, in fact was the antithesis of what it was trying to achieve.

Prior to visiting the MOA, I used search facilities regarding the collection on the University of Sussex library website to look up information, particularly around the periods for which women diarists wrote, to get a sense of time-spans and concentrated periods of diary-writing (www.sussex. ac.uk/library/speccoll/collection_descriptions/massobsdiaries.html). I began to construct charts recording information about this and took them to the MO archive with me during the two periods of pilot work I carried out, in March 2004 and December 2004. While there, I used the finding aids available, among other things to further check diarists and their periods of diary-writing. My purpose was to find an appropriate cross-section of diarists, by looking at age, location, date of writing and respondent number (a unique number given by MO). All the diarists cited here (and in Salter, 2008a) have pseudonyms because of the MOA's regulations (as of 2007) concerning anonymisation except if people's real names are publically known (most famously this includes Nella Last, but some others as well). The quotations later provide the unique identifying 'diary number' given each wartime diarist for identification purposes. I initially wanted to select a cross-section, but in the end my actual selection procedures deviated from this somewhat.

The first chart I produced was later used when in the archive. It records all 227 women diarists, with their names, years of birth, occupations, places of writing, household statuses, Diarist numbers, Directive numbers (if they also responded to Directives, which they mostly did) and day-diarist numbers, plus the months and years in which they wrote, as shown in Figure 4.1. I then produced a simplified version, including just diarist number and year and month of writing. The charts were immediately useful, as schematic overviews of periods of diary-writing by the diarists, and the information in them could be sorted to show the diarists with the longest and shortest periods of diary-writing, and also to look at temporal cross-sections.

This initial work concentrated my attention on time as a central organising feature of these materials. It was at that point, in firming up my interest in how temporal order structures these diaries, that I decided to operate two different sampling frames. The first strategy – which for shorthand I referred to as 'over time' – worked backwards across just one diarist's

HHS = Household Status   DR = Directive Respondent #
D = Domestic   DD = Day Diarist #
Hw = housewife

DIARIST#	DR #	DD #	Y.O.B	OCCUPATION	HHS	Residence	1939												1940											
							J	F	M	A	M	J	J	A	S	O	N	D	J	F	M	A	M	J	J	A	S	O	N	D
5332	1562		1905	Teacher	S	Cullercoats, Northumberland								x	x	x	x	x	x	x											
5333	2478		1909	D, domestic duties	S	Shepley, Huddersfield, Yorkshire								x	x	x	x	x	x	x	x	x	x	x	x	x	x	x	x	x	x
5334	2774		0	Forces, ATS	x	Leamington Spa, Warwickshire & Taunton, Somerset																									
5335	3003		1899	Teacher	S	Bedford, Bedfordshire																									
5336	104?		1904	D, hw	M	Cricklewood, London, NW2								x	x	x															
5337	3405		1882	D, hw	M	Fritwell, Bicester, Oxfordshire																									
5338	2675		1892	Civil servant	S	Morecambe, Lancashire																									
5339	2677		1870	D, hw	M	Leigh-on-Sea, Essex																									
5340	1070		1894	"Landed Gentry" independent means	S	Hatfield Peverel, Chelmsford, Essex								x	x		x	x	x	x							x	x	x		
5341	1040		1916	Shorthand typist, hospital library assistant	S	Liverpool, Lancashire								x	x	x	x	x	x	x	x	x	x	x	x	x	x	x	x	x	x
5342	1289		1902	D, hw	M	Blackheath, London SE3								x	x	x	x	x	x	x	x	x	x	x	x	x	x	x	x	x	x
5344	x		0	Nurse	S	Blackburn, Lancs																									
5345	1038		1915/6	Architect's assistant	S	Southampton, Hampshire								x	x	x															
5347	3110		1909	Telephonist	S	Hove, Sussex																									
5348	2182		1897	Teacher (music), hw	M	Rotherham, Yorks									x	x	x	x	x	x	x	x		x	x	x	x	x	x	x	
5349	1039		1905	Journalist	S	London, SE26								x	x	x	x	x		x			x		x		x	x		x	
5350	1286		1890	Teacher and reporter	D	London, N5								x	x																
5351	2043.1		1919	x	M	Westcliff-on-Sea, Essex												x													
5352	2043		1922	Student (art)	S	Northampton, Northants & London, N6								x	x		x	x	x	x		x		x							
5353	1061	824	1890	D, hw	M	Barrow-in-Furness, Lancs								x	x	x	x	x	x	x	x	x	x	x	x	x	x	x	x	x	x
5354	3645		0	x	x	Oxford, Oxfordshire																									

Figure 4.1 Women mass observation diarists – sample of entries by month, 1939–1944

diary-entries, that written by Nella Last. Last was a Mass Observation diarist who lived in Barrow-in-Furness in Lancashire, and wrote a diary for MO from August 1939 to February 1966, which was sent in weekly batches that were hand-sewn together on their left side with thread or wool. I shall return to the second strategy, which looked at eighty different diaries, later.

Nella Last's diary was chosen for several reasons. First, she was MO's second-longest writing diarist and so her diary lent itself to a longitudinal approach. She wrote a diary for MO on nearly every day of every week for almost twenty-seven years, with her last instalment sent in February 1966. The war years alone are estimated to comprise six million words and the sheer volume struck me profoundly, as did the considerable detail about her everyday life. Her diary's length, regularity and volume, plus the 'ordinariness' of her writing, intrigued me and were strong selection factors.

1941												1942												1943												1944											
J	F	M	A	M	J	J	A	S	O	N	D	J	F	M	A	M	J	J	A	S	O	N	D	J	F	M	A	M	J	J	A	S	O	N	D	J	F	M	A	M	J	J	A	S	O	N	D
x	x	x	x	x	x	x	x	x	x	x	x	x	x	x	x	x	x	x	x	x																												
							x	x				x	x	x					x																												
												x	x	x	x	x	x	x	x	x	x	x	x	x	x	x	x	x																		
																								x	x	x	x	x	x	x	x	x	x	x	x	x	x	x	x	x	x	x	x	x	x	x
								x	x	x	x	x	x	x	x	x	x	x	x	x	x	x	x	x	x	x	x	x	x	x	x	x	x	x	x	x	x	x	x	x	x	x	x	x	x	x	x
																																			x												
x		x			x			x		x	x																																				
x	x	x	x	x	x	x	x	x	x	x	x	x	x	x	x	x	x	x	x	x	x	x	x	x	x	x	x																				
																														x	x	x	x	x	x	x	x	x	x	x	x	x		x	x	x	x
																x			x			x		x																							
x	x	x																															x	x	x												
																														x																	
x	x	x	x	x	x	x	x	x	x	x	x	x	x	x	x	x	x	x	x	x	x	x	x	x	x	x	x	x	x		x	x	x	x	x												

Second, the fact that part of Last's diary – at that time just the war years, but subsequently the 1950s and later too – had been edited for publication was intriguing in a different way (Broad and Fleming, 1981, 2006; Malcolmson and Malcolmson, 2008, 2010, 2012). Interested in the 'architectural' activities of editors and biographers in shaping texts and lives, I was keen to explore questions regarding selection, omission, structure and construction, and I was also interested in MO's other edited published diaries and those used in edited collections as well. Retrospectively, I realise that this was important in my selection, for editorial activities shape how archival materials can be interpreted. In my PhD thesis I explored the editing aspect of diary collections in relation to how this shapes 'the diary/letter' and structures reading in consequential ways (Salter, 2008a); and later I was involved in examining how Olive Schreiner's estranged husband edited or bowdlerised her letters (Cronwright-Schreiner, 1924a, 1924b; Stanley and Salter, 2009).

5355	3377		1916	Teacher	S	Neath, Glamorgan, Wales	
5356	X		1889	Proprieter of X Bureau	W	London, W9	x x x x
5357	X	0		x	x	Kew, Surrey	
5358	3577		1915	Forces, Clerk in ATS	S	Grays, Essex	
5359	1650		1906	D, hw, librarian	M	Totland Bay, Isle of Wight	
5360	2888		1915	Health Visitor	S	Wellington, Surrey	
5361	3636	0		Clerk	S	Bridgend, Glamorgan, Wales	
5362	X		1913	Air Raid Warden (p/t)	M	East Sheen, London SW14	x
5363	X		1913	D, hw, mother	M	Shackleford, Surrey	x x x x x x x x x
5364	X	0		Secretary	S	Kingussie, Inverness, Scotland	
5365	X		1868	D, hw	W	Watford, Herts	
5366	2044		1894	D, hw	M	Croydon, Surrey & Cambridge, Cambs	x x x x x x x x x x x
5367	1059	0		Education officer	S	Warwick, Warwickshire	
5368	2485		1920	D, hw	M	Manchester, Lancs	x x x ... x
5369	3145		1918	Writer & voluntary worker	S	Mumbles, Swansea, Glamorgan, Wales	
5370	X		1923	Student	S	Romford, Essex	x
5371	X		1906	Manageress, Ofice	S	East Bridgford, Notts	
5372	2892		1892	D, hw	M	Minehead, Somerset & Sevenoaks, Kent	
5373	2486		1913	Teacher	S	Sheffield, Yorks	x
5374	X	0		Teacher	S	Campbeltown, Argyllshire, Scotland	
5375	3579		1914	D, hw	M	Sheffield, Yorks	
5376	1078		1900	Teacher	S	Burwash Weald, Sussex	x x x x x x x x x x x x x ... x
5377	2226		1871	D, home duties	W	Burwash Weald, Sussex	x x x x

Figure 4.1 (cont.)

And third, Last also wrote day-diaries and Directive responses, with these too retrievable in the MOA although having to be 'called up' from a different section of the collection, and I was interested in possible comparisons between her different kinds of writings for MO. Clearly, though, her involvement in writing for Mass Observation became a serious, long-term project for her.

Reading the beginning in the ending

For three months of archival fieldwork carried out in early 2005, I used the 'backwards' sampling method mentioned earlier. This involved me working back in Nella Last's diary and examining entries at pre-determined intervals, namely a month from each year in which she wrote. For each of these months, I fully transcribed a whole week of entries and made verbatim

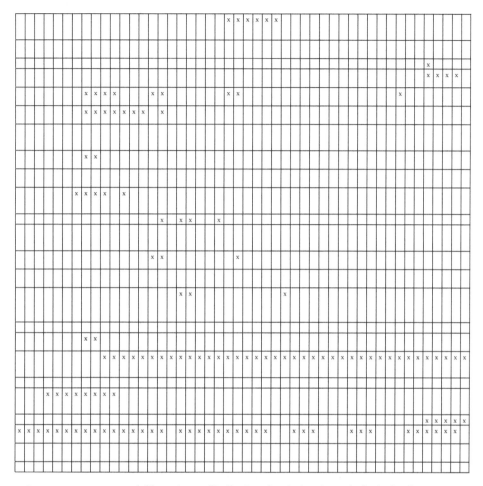

Source: www.sussex.ac.uk/library/speccoll/collection_descriptions/massobsdiaries.html

extracts from the remainder. This produced around fifteen word-processed A4 pages for each year and some 225,000 words in total. In literal terms, the sampling started with the last entry of Last's diary-entries, in February 1966, and moved sequentially backwards through the years, months and weeks of her writing. This involved sampling a roll of different weeks in each month, so that I would encounter as many different weeks of the month and year as possible in examining her diary over time.

There were some practical issues in using this sampling strategy. The 'Week 5' of some months was not accounted for in the strategy though dealt with by noting contents and transcribing relevant passages. Next, on two occasions my strategy 'closed in' on itself with, for example, January 1965 and December 1964 both identified in the sample. Here I decided to examine consecutive months. More difficult to manage, however, was the gap between January 1944 and April 1945 as these entries have been lost. Initially I wanted to 'fill' this with Last's response to an April 1944 Directive, but found its style of writing too different from her diary-entries for this to be sensible. Furthermore, leafing through her diary-entries, it became clear that the strict chronological frame was omitting important dates in event terms. For instance, while the frame specified transcribing 'Week 3' of September 1949, it was also important to look at 'Week 1', which was the tenth anniversary of the start of the Second World War and therefore also of Nella Last starting to write her diary, something she reflected on in it:

> Just about 10 years since I was asked to write an M. O diary, a long long time. I can never understand how the scribbles of such an ordinary person, leading a shut in, dull life, can possibly have value. No 'adventure' nothing spectacular, day after day, week after week, till the formidable total of 10 years – 3,650 entries – I cannot believe it!...
>
> (D 5353, diary for 2 September 1949, MOA)

In practice, then, I included material beyond the sampling strategy as initially designated – when faced with the vast realities of the MO diaries, I treated the frame as guidance rather than prescriptive. However, attempting to confine myself to it was important in terms of practically managing Last's voluminous diary and making sense of its length and breadth. The above example also highlights that deciding to include Week 1 in 1949 came from my contextual knowledge about when Last was likely to have been in reflective mode.

While focusing on MO's collection of women's diaries helped concentrate my investigation, looking across Nella Last's whole diary (1939–1966) brought me up against the archival frame in which the diaries had been curated, noted earlier. To sample her diary, I had to work out which storage boxes were required, with the women's diary-entries ordered alphabetically and stored accordingly in folders in boxes for each month of each year in which they wrote. Each box so identified then had to be requested, handing in 'Material Request Forms' by a particular time each day. It involved twenty-eight storage boxes, issued to me one by one because of regulations about only having one box to work on at a time. Within each box, I then had to search among many diary-entries to identify Last's, a process assisted by rectangles of card attached via brass paper clips to each diary-entry with the diarists' surnames on, and soon by recognising her handwriting and the chunky bundles her entries were grouped in.

Going 'against the archival frame' in this manner was not only hard work but also raised an odd thought: in doing this, was I trying to create a version of Last's diary as a whole and to what end? I had to recognise that Last would not have seen her diary-entries grouped together as a set in such a way, so this would have been a construction for myself as a reader rather than a recreation of anything that had once existed. There are similarities here with putting together the *Olive Schreiner Letters Online*, which is made up of transcriptions of Schreiner's 5,000 extant letters, sent to more than 100 different correspondents over the fifty years between 1871 and 1920, and which she would never have seen all together at any time.

Once my backwards chronological sampling brought me to the wartime years of Nella Last's diary, there was a further dilemma. The postwar years of the MO diaries at that time were available only in their original manuscript versions, while the wartime years were available also on microfiche and I was encouraged by the MO archivists to use the latter for reasons of preservation. I soon realised, however, that the text that the microfiche was taken from was in fact a transcribed, typed version produced by Broad and Fleming (1981) from their edited *Nella Last's War*, not the handwritten manuscript diary. Using the microfiche made for a dramatic change in how I handled the diary-entries, including the physical experience of 'sea-sickness' induced by whizzing across many entries to find those by Last. More importantly, there were important differences between the contents of the manuscript and the microfiche versions: these were different in kind, produced at different times for different purposes by different people; and there were also important differences in 'the words on the page', exemplified well by the 'false-start' to Last's diary given in Broad and Fleming's edited version.

Last actually began her wartime diary on 30 August 1939, not 3 September 1939, the day that war was declared, which was used as the start of Broad and Fleming's volume. By excluding the 30 August entry, they omit Last's comments about waiting for the declaration of war, gentle mockery of her neighbours' stockpiling of beer and whiskey at the expense of purchasing blackout materials, and concerning the bustling activity at her local Women's Voluntary Service meeting. They also exclude comments Last wrote before bedtime on 3 September 1939. In this she wrote, among other things, about her cat's techniques for securing a warm spot for the night, while mentioning her son Arthur having noticed 'a growing feeling against Jews – particularly foreign Jews', which perhaps explains their choice of starting place.

Approaching the diary 'backwards' was important for a number of reasons and provided useful insights. Reading it in this way meant I was gradually eased into what might have otherwise been hard to fathom cultural references. It also meant I had hindsight knowledge, which affected the interpretive lens through which I read all earlier (by date order) diary-entries. Also, Last did not acknowledge nor perhaps realise that her last entry was to be her final one, and she would not have known how her diary-entry written on one day would relate to that written a week or so later because sets of weeks of entries were dispatched at regular intervals once written. And my backwards reading meant that I could not know of connections between an entry I was reading and past entries until I came across them. By implication, then, I 'read the beginning in the ending', to paraphrase Ricoeur, learning to 'read time itself backwards, as the recapitulation of the initial conditions of a course of action in its terminal consequences' (Ricoeur, 1984: 67–68). This was not without its complexities, because Last frequently evoked 'pasts' and anticipated 'futures' in her diary, muddling the strict arrow-like order of chronological time by projecting other times from the perspective of her 'writing present'. Indeed, 'reading time backwards' like this encouraged me to explore the connections between the 'writing present' and the pasts and futures inscribed in it, while also alerting me to the structuring force that chronology has on representations of people and the order of action, events and experience.

Building on this, I drew on the diary material so retrieved in three particular ways to examine Nella Last's diary-writing over time. First, I looked at three diary-entries written at around ten-year intervals, doing so across the period she wrote her diary – 12 August 1960, 27 October 1950 and 13 December 1940 – in order to gain a sense of the 'narrative shape' of her diary-writing over time. Second, I traced one character – her Aunt Sarah (1957–1864) – backwards through the transcriptions I had made of Last's diary, following the twenty-six references to her that my sampling pinpointed. And, third, I compared the end and beginning of the diary.

There are four important points about this (Salter, 2008a provides more detail). First, overall my reverse chronological approach meant that, as well as acquiring an understanding of the narrative shape of Last's MO diary over time, I identified what I termed 'narrative threads' and 'micro-narratives' regarding connections between her representations of particular people and events over a number of diary-entries. Often reading one diary-entry enabled me to perceive implications regarding other entries: I inferred connections, linking together pieces of related information from different temporal points across the diary.

In her diary-entry for 27 October 1950, for example, Nella Last wrote about Mrs Atkinson, her neighbour, coming round to borrow 'a shilling for the meter' (D 5353, diary for 27 October 1950, MOA) and talking about her daughters Norah and Margaret and her home feeling 'dead' without them. Last quotes several remarks from this conversation in her entry, closing with a comment about her own children: 'I said 'you're lucky. I've not seen much of my two for years at either Xmas or New Year...'' (D 5353, diary for 27 October 1950, MOA). There are many passages across Last's diary implying her feelings about her sons living away from home, particularly Cliff who emigrated to Australia after the war, but also Arthur, who worked in Manchester then Belfast as a tax inspector. In 1942, for instance, Last wrote about an unnamed woman who 'Like myself she feels rather lost now her family have grown up & away & she has two lovely grandchildren she rarely sees & can only send presents to' (D 5353, diary for 1 March 1942, MOA), and there are many comments about her letters and later telephone calls bridging the distance between her and her sons.

Regarding the 27 October 1950 diary-entry, it is important to recognise that Last rarely mentions such sentiments and if I had read it in isolation I would not have appreciated that Mrs Atkinson's comment would have struck a tender chord. In other words, this is an implication I have perceived, not something immediately 'there in the text'. The basis for the interpretation comes from her other diary-entries, because reading Last's diary over time enabled me to infer a number of such implications. These inferences are, then, ones I have made by linking together comments inscribed over temporally different points, and are a result of my interpretive practices rather than being 'in' specific diary content. In addition, while my sampling strategy involved a strict reverse chronology, nonetheless the experience of working systematically through Nella Last's diaries meant that the intellectual work I was doing did not always readily obey the methodological procedures I had devised.

The second point is that through this work I became aware that Last's diary-entries were typically organised using 'temporal markers' such as eating and leisure times, which she developed over time, for they were not present in her earliest entries. Around these markers, Last sometimes chose not to record the day's events in strict chronological order, but to complete the arc of a story she was telling. For instance, on 12 August 1960, she wrote about making 'babies woollies' to give to Mr and Mrs Higham, the latter a colleague from the Women's Voluntary Service, whom she had hoped to meet that day (D 5353, diary for 12 August 1960, MOA). This rendezvous did not happen, so Last left the garments in the Highams' porch and mentions in the middle of this entry that Mrs Higham telephoned 'after tea' about them. Rather than writing the entry in a strict chronology, then, Last included the denouement of the 'woollies and Highams story' – the telephone call – in that particular micro-narrative, abandoning the chronology but maintaining the structure of the micro-narrative. The entry then reconnects with the main chronology, including her and her husband's choice of television or radio entertainment for the evening (D 5353, diary for 12 August 1960, MOA), which in the postwar years became the device Last regularly used to close an entry. This made me question the presumed 'presentness' of diary-writing and flagged up the importance of looking at the temporal complexities regarding not only how archival materials are archivally framed but also within such materials themselves (Salter, 2008b).

The third point is that in my backwards reading I effectively read 'the past' through the lens of 'the present', that is, reading the beginning in the ending, to paraphrase Ricoeur (and see Chapter 2's discussion of the now/past in relation to this). In other words, I knew the outcome of an incident before I knew the incident had even occurred. An example here concerns an accident befalling Nella Last's Aunt Sarah. Using the products of my sampling frame, the first mention of the accident was found in May 1957, when Last wrote that '…oddly enough, since the accident to her arm & shoulder, her face had plumped out, & grown pink & white, lost the sallow, wrinkled look' (D 5353, diary for 21 May 1957, MOA). At this point, I had no idea what had happened to Aunt Sarah, and even in the second entry I read about it, in April 1956, I still did not know the particulars of the accident: 'No sign of her "breaking up" after her accident, as the doctor had feared' (D 5353, diary for 20 April 1956, MOA). I had to wait until 1939 and the equivalent of seventeen years before Last specifically described the accident, when Aunt Sarah was 'knocked down by a car on Tuesday night, arm & left side very bruised' (D 5353, diary for 18 November 1939, MOA). Of course, I could have sampled Last's diary at different or shorter intervals, or in a forwards direction. However, it is likely that my interpretations would still have depended on particular dated entries and so would still have to be explored regarding how I made sense of the archival materials in hand.

Fourth, sampling backwards paradoxically increased my awareness of at least some of the consequences had I sampled Last's diary in a forwards chronological manner. I would have 'met' Aunt Sarah as an unnamed, then a named, relative; and I would have become aware that Last's written recollections of Aunt Sarah were more reflective and even sentimental after Sarah's death in 1957. Reading forwards would certainly have made me more aware of Last as a diary-writer engaged in building narrative threads and developing characters as her diary unfolded. Reading forwards would also have focused attention on her incremental inscription of information and the seeming continuities I read into this, while obscuring the fact that Last herself would not have written in this way because of posting off diary-entries at regular intervals and not retaining a copy. However, some MO diarists *did* keep copies: for example, Naomi Mitchison, one of the published diary-writers, kept a 'top copy' and she self-edited a version of this for the MO diary she sent in (Sheridan, 1985).

Reading backwards served to problematise the assumptions behind such perceived continuities. These include the assumed relationship of diaries to other forms of life writing, for instance to autobiographies or biographies, where continuities might be expected in order to construct the narrative whole, and also to letters, where continuities are as much a matter of reader perception as an actuality, for the form of letter-writing (as with a diary) is temporally fragmented by definition. Consequently reading backwards also highlighted the interpretive work done by myself as a reader in making sense across and within the diary-entries I sampled, something I return to later (see also Chapters 2 and 3 for different interpretational approaches). Another methodologically useful approach is to use a different sampling frame to provide a different vista on the Mass Observation women's diaries. However, before discussing this, I want to consider the experience of reading Olive Schreiner's extant letters.

In between? Temporal strategies in reading Schreiner's letters

A temporal or any other device for sampling was redundant when working on the Olive Schreiner Letters Project and producing the *Olive Schreiner Letters Online* because we were concerned with their totality, although temporality was still involved. At a simple level, much time was spent transcribing Schreiner's letters, sometimes just a few days on small collections and sometimes several weeks in archives holding large collections, such as at the University of Cape Town and the Ransom Center at the University of Texas at Austin. In order to transcribe, it is of course necessary to read, and also re-read to check for sense and accuracy, and both take place in time, although in a context where the letters concerned may be out of chronological sequence compared with a collection worked on before and after.

As a letter-writer Schreiner wrote to more than a hundred different people, sometimes just once or on a handful of occasions, but predominantly to a smaller number in long-term correspondences. The time-periods involved varied greatly. Also, in transcribing and following the order and contents of letters in each collection, this could involve transcribing letters Schreiner wrote to a number of different people at approximately the same time, rather than following a set of letters to a particular individual. 'The collection', then, had to be the frame worked with, given the particular kind of project this was, and also given the different sizes and temporal scope and varied locations of the collections concerned. However, this made gaining a clear sense of temporal order and rhythm something that had to be bracketed during the transcription phase (for a contrast see Chapter 3, where archival rhythms are bound up with spatio-temporalities rather than more material factors).

As fieldwork progressed, what was produced was an emerging set of letters, representing temporally and spatially differentiated parts of Schreiner's life, and the lives of her correspondents and the many people mentioned in her letters. At the same time, it was important to work *across* collections to understand the spans and sequences of her letter-writing across the board and its distinctive performative political character (Stanley and Dampier, 2012).

All 5,000 letters were read and re-read by the core research team at least twice in the process of transcribing and checking transcriptions, then preparing them for uploading into the Virtual Research Environment that eventually became the *Olive Schreiner Letters Online*, but in the temporally disjointed way just described. However, we all anticipated the value of re-reading the extant letters in a structured way then discussing such readings with each other (see also Chapter 2 for different reading processes). This was done in five tranches of letter-reading – which we called the 'Great Read' – in order to consolidate our impressions, provide a sound base for any joint analytical work, and also to think about how to structure and provide content for the editorial apparatus associated with the *Letters Online*. As a shared endeavour, the Great Read gave focus to analytical work, and later we held further meetings to discuss sets of particularly important letters and to carry out the groundwork for a series of journal articles. In addition, we read the letters in a more focused way, identifying letters which raised, for example, 'letterness', 'time and temporalities', 'transitions and turning points', and a set of 'must read' letters and letters which would populate the series of 'topic' collections appearing on the website (www.oliveschreiner. org/vre?page=257).

In working through all the letters, many beginnings and endings, lives, deaths, stops and restarts were experienced. The odd effect was of reading Schreiner as she grew older and more ill, her handwriting became larger and even harder to read, and she eventually died, but then came to life again; and with this happening repeatedly in re-readings, with her life almost on a play-back loop. The idea of the finitude of death producing the meaning of life struck me, although colleagues focused on the continued renewal aspects and repeated beginnings and restarts. There were corporal responses too, the anticipation as Schreiner neared joyful or mournful events we already knew from previous readings would shake her, including in 1890 meeting the much loved Mary Sauer, and the death of Schreiner's baby daughter in 1895.

The intellectual work done in the Great Read provided the bedrock for many publications (including Stanley, Dampier and Salter, 2012; Stanley, Salter and Dampier 2013a and Stanley, Salter and Dampier, 2013b). It also fed into the subsequent production of *The World's Great Question* (Stanley and Salter, 2014), another major project in reading and re-reading. This involved Liz Stanley and I in reading through all Schreiner's extant letters in order to identify the most important as well as evocative of Schreiner's relationship with South Africa, a focus shaped by an agreement to publish such a Schreiner volume with the Van Riebeeck Society, which specialises in publishing high-end primary sources in South African history. The first tranche of re-reading here identified a long list of contenders for inclusion. The second tranche was a more focused remit to select some 300+ letters (from 5,000) and doing so around a strong sense of Schreiner's position on race and ethnicity with regards to South Africa and its then-future. This resulted in something more manageable but still too long. Reluctantly, we agreed with our editor to omit letters from the earlier period of Schreiner's life and commence the selection when she returned from Europe to South Africa at the end of 1889. The last tranche finalised the key letters in which Schreiner commented on race as the 'world's great question', as she phrased it, and its connections with the women's and labour questions of the day. In these re-readings, temporality was both everywhere and nowhere. Nowhere because the emphasis needed to be on gaining some thematic or argumenta-tive unity; but everywhere because, having pinpointed this running thread of her thought, it was important to demonstrate its changing presence in Schreiner's letters over time.

'A day at a time' and going with the archival frame

While sampling Nella Last's diary, I was distracted by the many other diary-entries by women that her diary was located with. Often these were literally in my hands or on the screen of the microfiche reader, and

I sometimes looked at them. What would be the interpretive consequences of going with the archival frame, instead of against it? This led to my second methodological approach to the MO diaries, and took a further three months in the Mass Observation Archive.

As I worked on Last's diary, my gaze was sometimes engaged by the different ways in which the various diary-writers represented the same days, weeks, months. I began to note diarists 'of special interest'. The second sampling frame combined this with a list of events occurring on a day or group of days during or just after the war, arriving finally at seven events: the Declaration of War; Dunkirk and the Fall of France; D-Day; Hamburg, Dresden and Würzburg (Fire) Bombings; Victory in Europe (VE) Day; Hiroshima, Nagasaki and Victory in Japan (VJ) Day; and, Armistice Days. I transcribed diary-entries on these made by diverse women diarists, calling this approach for shorthand 'a day at a time', a phrase Last herself used quite often.

Because of the insights from my examination of the 'over time' aspects of Last's diary, I added an additional 'over time' dimension to the Armistice Days. Using this second sampling strategy, I transcribed diary-entries written by eighty different MO women diarists, more than a third of the total number of women who wrote for the organisation between 1939 and 1967. It resulted in over 270 pages of typed text containing nearly 175,000 words, which leant itself to different methodological experiments. One was my 'testing out' and developing Jennings and Madge's (1937) methodological ideas about the 12 May 1937 day-diaries, where they drew on surrealist montage techniques to represent the diary-writings of a range of people over that specific day.

This made it possible to explore differences between how different diarists used time in their diaries on the same days, or around the same events. Because my analytical work on these diaries followed what I had done on Last's diary, I was primed to notice shifts and changes in diary-writing over time, but my adaptation and application of Jennings and Madge's approach added a new aspect to this. That is, it highlighted that the 'moment of writing' in diary-writing (Stanley and Dampier, 2006) is not strictly bound to the particular time, day or date under which it might be located and there may be more going on, temporally; and also there are different relationships between experience and its representation inscribed across the diverse diary-entries I examined. These were constructed at the 'moment of writing' and tell the reader something about their 'time perspectives' (Roberts, 1999).

Having explored the ideas above in some depth, invoking theory, explaining my practice and drawing some inferences about these diaries, my doctoral thesis then stopped. It has only been through post-doctoral research, and then looking back in writing this chapter, that I have seen how to develop them. Part of this has involved my earlier thoughts about the temporal distance between experience and its representation. In a seminar group on 'documents of life', among other matters we discussed whether a time-lag necessarily existed, even if for instance someone wrote about what they were doing or feeling at the time of experiencing this, and whether diaries were better at representing this 'presentness' than other life documents (Salter, 2008b). There was a mixed verdict, but I was convinced there was a time-lag no matter how brief. Stanley and Dampier's (2006) analysis of Johanna Brandt-Van Warmelo's diary helped to firm up these ideas, demonstrating that the assumed-to-be direct relationship between 'the moment of writing' and 'the scene of what is written about' does not exist in her case, and I drew on this to develop thinking in my doctoral thesis. Only afterwards did I read about the role of the reader and archives in Ricoeur's (1984, 1988, 1998, 2004) writings on time, narrative, memory and forgetting and his use of Reinhart Koselleck's categories of 'space of experience' and 'horizon of expectation' (Koselleck, 1985 [1979]: 267–88; Ricoeur, 1988: 208–15; Koselleck, 2002).

Beginnings and endings

These categories of 'space of experience' and 'horizon of expectation' noted earlier are useful in thinking about the content of diary-entries written for Mass Observation (and other diaries, too). The idea of a 'space of experience' opens up the 'moment of writing' in a longer and broader sense. In this, past events, incidents and practices are gathered and coalesce to inform the individual's perspective, for instance the viewpoint presented by a particular MO diarist, or indeed by an archival researcher in building an argument, a thesis or such like. A 'horizon of expectation', on the other hand, is about opening up vistas from the perspective of the 'space of experience', and people's hopes and fears, dreams, curiosities and choices about the future. It involves 'every private or public manifestation aimed at the future' (Ricoeur 1988: 208). Two extracts from MO diaries provide examples of the space of experience populated by the past and projecting a future from that basis:

> I am writing this listening to the broadcast from the Cenotaph. I can't understand how it has carried on all those between years and yet so little was done to make a 'land fit for heroes'! I wonder if we'll make a better go of it this time? Or are we going on remembering on the '11th' after every war? I don't see much point in it, except that a great majority of people like a show … But why not let the dead bury the dead, and just make certain that they are dead to some purpose for a change? Will we ever learn?
>
> (D 5303, diary for 11 November 1945, MOA)

> I sat so still, barely conscious of Leo's drone about prospects & 'position' in life, the past nearer than the present, my mind such a queer jumble as I contrasted the light hopes & plans of those 1934–39 days

with the realities of today… I wondered what lay in store for Leo, & his generation – our little Peter & his.

(D 5353, diary for 19 August 1948, MOA)

The movements back and forth within and across time, encompassing past and future and present, are striking in both extracts, and Koselleck's categories could clearly be used to explore both Nella Last's and other MO diaries and also quite different archival materials.

However, rather than this I want to use them to discuss differences and similarities between the two archival projects I have been involved in, on Mass Observation's diaries and Olive Schreiner's letters. Ricoeur comments about 'reading the ending in the beginning' (Ricoeur 1984: 67). Focusing on the end, the goal of doing archival research, highlights that what we do as archival researchers at the 'moment of researching' is influenced by our experiences and expectations of other times, including future times.

'Space of experience' and 'horizons of expectation'

Archival research – whether conducted as multi-site funded research, a small fellowship project, a PhD thesis, or a family history tracing the stories of family members – is inflected by a 'horizon of expectation', or in more material terms, by an expected or anticipated future object or product (a book, an edition of letters, a thesis, an album, website) and the anticipated uses of this by different readers. The labour processes involved will therefore also have been oriented in one way or another towards this possible ending, because at least partly envisaged in the researcher's 'space of experience' when starting out. There were some very different initial spaces of experience associated with the doctoral Mass Observation and post-doctoral Schreiner letters projects.

The doctoral project involved me side-stepping from human geography to sociology as a discipline and reading between the lines regarding what this meant intellectually and what gaps I needed to fill. It involved working with a supervisor to develop a research proposal in the absence, at that point, of having spent any time in the Mass Observation Archive myself, instead drawing on secondary publications, the MOA website and my supervisor's experience, and revising this proposal after visiting the archive and examining the collections in person. With my doctoral research, I was able to govern the contours of intellectual scope and also the time spent on particular focuses. Although the intended readers of the resultant thesis were present in mind, this was on a distant time horizon (but came closer as I worked on the thesis, of course, and as it neared its end took on an embodied form as my examiners).

Regarding the Olive Schreiner Letters Project, I missed some of the preparation phase, although I read and commented on the draft-funding proposal, which most post-doctoral researchers will not have the opportunity to do.

I worked instead on specific tasks within a whole picture I could contribute to, but had less control over its overall shape. This was my first post-doctoral position and on a topic somewhat different from but with strong theoretical links to my doctoral studies. I was encouraged to read extensively in the period before the project officially started, guided towards particular literature which the Principal Investigator and main Co-Investigator, both experienced on South African topics, saw fitting with the emerging concerns of the project. I also participated in a pre-project month of archival research in Cape Town, working at the National Library of South Africa on a set of letter-extracts made by Schreiner's estranged husband Cronwright-Schreiner (www.oliveschreiner.org/vre?view=collections&archiveid=27&arrangeby=colorder). This was of relevance to the project and was also 'train me up' in the procedures of shared archival research (resulting in Stanley and Salter, 2009). However, my colleagues were responsible for devising the overall scope and timing of the research design, in contrast to my full responsibility for devising and designing my doctoral research.

Students or post-doctoral researchers working as part of larger funded projects are likely to have considerably less agency in constructing the shape and scope of their own work within the greater whole than I had. This is because project aims and objectives are usually already in place and their individual work will address these so as to fulfil promises to funders. Also working collaboratively requires different research skills from solo research, for example, working on shared concerns, arranging time in concert with others, negotiating divisions of labour and so on. Many post-doctoral scholars in the UK and elsewhere take on posts as contract researchers. Many will be building experience towards a permanent academic lectureship, which would enable them to apply for funding in their own capacity. Some may have the opportunity to craft an intellectual space for themselves. Few, however, will have the independence to pursue their own intellectual research agendas without some kind of external funding, whatever form this may take (interestingly, the notion of the struggling post-doc pursuing their own research agenda remains the idealised route).

Working collaboratively with colleagues means understanding your and their research rhythms, matching pace to maintain work flows, mapping a shared frame of reference grounded in the wide literature on a research topic, moving in and out of different kinds of project responsibilities, learning new skills according to what the broader project requires, and perhaps finding or being designated a part of the project to work on in greater detail. All these skills are valuable and are of course transferable to other research projects.

Regarding the Schreiner project, there were team meetings concerning how to organise, prepare for and conduct periods of archival research in the field, which necessitated wide reading on my part, and divisions of labour both within and outwith the archives worked in. As part of this, there were discussions concerning anticipated research outputs, mainly regarding

the design of the *Olive Schreiner Letters Online*, but also other publications, including articles and the print book mentioned earlier, *The World's
Great Question* (for ongoing publications, see www.oliveschreiner.org/
vre?page=318; Stanley and Salter, 2014). We talked about what the shared
'product' would look like, implicitly comparing aspects of various horizons
of expectation so as in a sense to align these. The horizons of expectation
projected were emergent, however, since each team member brought previous different levels of expertise and knowledge regarding the Schreiner
letters and wider academic interests. Some differences existed regarding
expectations for the project's overall outputs, and there were differences in
spaces of experience, but certainly the core research team shared a concern
for providing later readers with clear, readable and fully accurate transcriptions of Schreiner's letters. We thought it intellectually important to do this,
so that her letters could be read and used as a secondary dataset by other
researchers and by general readers from all manner of backgrounds; and
project activities were among other things directed towards this.

Team discussions were fed into by increasing 'on the job' experience
of what was and was not practicable to accomplish within the project's
thirty-nine months' time-frame. Also ideas from teaching on related topics,
including a postgraduate research training module on narrative, text and
discourse in my case, were involved too. These discussions were then con-
toured by reading around the substantive topic, including exploring other
digital letters and documents of life projects with respect to their working
practices and outputs, so as to inform ideas about what we did and did not
want to do with the online Schreiner letters.

Overall, while there were important differences in the spaces of experience, horizons of expectation and the methodological approaches between
the doctoral and post-doctoral projects, there were also considerable continuities. In my case, these were also aligned to my emergent career as a
researcher. Both projects enabled me to develop my research interests concerning documents of life, especially diaries and letters. They also enabled
me to focus specifically on women's lives, how they are represented, and
methodological approaches to these, a research priority starting with my
experience at the very beginning of my research career, discussed earlier. It
is clear, indeed, that I already had some sense of what I was most interested
in focusing on even at the very beginning stage – an early horizon of expectation – and therefore I have had a half-glimpsed ending or goal in mind
from the word go.

Readers

Early in the Schreiner project, we had developed a sense of the kind of reader
we wanted 'the letters' to engage with (Stanley, 2015c; Stanley, Salter and
Dampier, 2013a), a kind of embodiment of the horizon of expectation. Yet it
also became clear that 'the reader' was almost indeterminably broad, covering

unknown readers worldwide who would use the letters and the website in many ways over a potentially long time-period. Google Analytics data about usage of the *Olive Schreiner Letters Online* has provided subsequent detail about the range of uses of the site, but 'the reader' remains impossible to pin down in any precise way. However, the website was purposively designed around structuring the ways in which readers could use the website and how they would access letters. This always involves whole letters rather than selected passages and was crafted in principled ways (as detailed in Stanley, Salter and Dampier, 2013a).

How readers engage with the *Olive Schreiner Letters Online* as a product of archival research has been instantiated by the editorial architecture of the website and its editorial apparatus. This has been artful, with a deliberate play-off between the openness of making transcriptions of important letters by this perspicacious feminist commentator and theorist widely available for new audiences to read and use, and the project-designed structuring of how these letters are presented. The Schreiner Letters project has been a 'project' in the strong sense, then.

In the case of *The World's Great Question* (Stanley and Salter, 2014), as well as the different media of publication and scope, different reader expectations were present. These impacted on how readings of the letters translated into our work as researchers as well as editors. For example, while the approach to footnoted information for the *Letters Online* was light-touch, this had to be adapted for the edited book because its immediate readers – the Van Riebeeck Society editors and its target readers – expected 'on the page' contextual information about letter content and context to be provided, given over a hundred years of publishing and VRS conventions for such things. For the reader, reading the book would most likely be a stand-alone experience, without clickable links leading to diverse detailed information. For us as editors, this imposed a different kind of discipline and led to reading, selecting and representing Schreiner's letters in a different way so as to best-guess information that might be needed.

While 'the reader' for the *Olive Schreiner Letters Online* and *The World's Great Question* was hard to pin down, for my doctoral archival research there was a clear relationship between what was needed in my doctoral thesis and what its intended readers – that is, my external and internal examiners – were expecting to see and what they might do with this. That is, the thesis was produced for a very specific academic readership that would evaluate it according to particular degree regulations and guidelines to which I also had access. Therefore I needed to organise the scope and framing of my research topic, selection of archive materials, review of reading, interpretations, syntheses and theorisations to meet with the specified criteria. In this sense, the PhD research 'product' was tightly bound up with the concerns and responsibilities of its specific readers. This is also true on an ideas level too, for I read publications by the examiners when they were appointed to flesh out their intellectual framework in my mind and anticipate their expectations, and also cited these in the thesis.

Perceived readers always play an important role in shaping archival research and its outputs, whether situated in the present or future, whether real or imagined, fleshy or virtual. Ricoeur's (1988: 160) suggestion that the reader is the 'ultimate mediator between configuration and reconfiguration' is useful here, in seeing the reader as a mediator between the pulling or 'emplotment' of events to make a followable story and the casting of this story in relation to the living world. That is, according to the world of the reader. For much social science work, the reader can be conceived around how research might impact on the lives of the people who are researched, or those who read, implement or use research and its outcomes. Or perhaps such reader expectations will have a more diffuse aspect, such as hoping to add to or shake up bodies of scholarly work. Researchers of all kinds also position readers as the embodiment of some grounded horizons of expectation, such as in meeting the criteria we perceive examiners using for evaluating a PhD thesis, or those that editors and peer-reviewers bring to considering the possible publication of an article. And in archival research terms, readers are involved in how the stories that archival researchers tell about their research projects are shaped and filled (see Chapter 3 for more on this).

Envisaging 'the reader' in the early stages of a project – 'reading the ending in the beginning' (Ricoeur, 1984: 67) – encourages asking useful questions. What would we like to achieve and what questions do we want to address (acknowledging these might adjust as research proceeds)? What is the wider purpose and justification of our research agenda? How can the outcomes of the archival research best be represented to readers? What parts of a project will be of most importance for our arguments and to readers more generally? Intellectually 'checking in' with the reader and what we anticipate them to expect is a useful practice, then, and can be done both at the start of a project and at points throughout.

Doing this acknowledges that the 'reader function' is always present, shaping fieldwork activity and interpretation, providing a check for the credibility of arguments and whether sufficient relevant data is provided to make them stick. It is this view of the reader, one who will hopefully find the published outputs of both the Mass Observation and the Schreiner letters projects interesting, that is in my mind in thinking about the archival research I have been involved in. I have felt responsible to this reader for conveying as accurate, contextualised and meaningful representation of the archival trace as I possibly could, with this forming a core part of my broader archival sensibility.

In conclusion: archival research and time

This chapter has looked at time and temporality and how they can be used in designing and conducting archival research. It has discussed the different temporal sampling frames devised in researching Mass Observation diaries, and some of the temporal aspects of the Schreiner letters project. It has also explored looking back from the perspective of the products or outputs of an archival research project, and looking forward from the perspective of the present, or the space of experience, to a horizon of expectation, with the reader in a sense the embodiment of this.

Time and temporality are central to archival research, both conceptually and methodologically, and attending to them provides a creative strategy for other archival researchers to use too. Important in this is ensuring congruity between methodological approach and the archival materials under scrutiny, for these will have distinctive ways of framing time and temporality – such as the presumed 'presentness' of diaries or the sequential temporalities of letters – that will lend themselves to particular ways of working. A key question concerns which temporal strategies would be most suitable to the materials, collections and archives a project is intending to explore. What are the temporal features of this data? Would exploring these help to address project research questions, or perhaps generate some new questions? What does focusing on time add? And might it miss anything important?

To bring this chapter to a close, I return briefly to the questions raised at the start to draw out transferable aspects that other researchers might want to make use of. As a topic and as a resource, engaging with the complexities of time, temporal order and temporalities is certainly productive in planning and doing archival research. As a topic, time can be investigated in numerous ways, including looking at the content of documents for 'time perspectives' (Roberts, 1999), 'time orientations' (Schutz, 1945: 214–15) or temporal orders in the text, to examining wider constructions of social time, industrial time or other kinds of societal-level temporal structures or social change more broadly, concerns that can provide a conceptual frame for close reading of archival materials around a particular focus.

But which archival materials should be examined to begin this? Structuring archival research design around temporal categories enables data to be retrieved and examined according to a known framework. In addition, temporal strategies can be deployed as structuring tools for experimental sampling, whether this involves reading backwards, by reading across archival materials vertically, or horizontally, with linear time being subverted and different viewpoints and writings at the same time brought into view. Time and temporality also underpin and enable articulation of the narrative emplotments or configurations involved in representing and interpreting life events.

What, then, does it mean to deploy temporal methodological strategies to 'read the archive'? Clearly in methodological terms this further opens the black box regarding archival research, for as I have shown, reading is certainly not a self-explanatory practice, something we 'just do', but mindful and purposeful. Taking time seriously enables reading to be examined as a series of temporally located and consequential interpretive acts or engagements between reader/researcher/editor and text. It enables reading to be examined as a process of interpretation, meaning formation and re-representation or translation, and thus as core to archival research. This does not mean imposing a temporal structure when researching archival collections, but instead involves reading connections in archival materials across different times, connections which do not obey the order of chronological (or even reverse chronological) sampling frames, in order to work out how these interpretive threads came to be. To read the archive is also, then, to hear, feel, see, touch and sense connections between archival documents and the structures and stories of an archive and its collections.

Acknowledgements

I would like to thank Newcastle University, UK, and the ESRC for funding my doctoral research (PTA-030-2004-00614), and the ESRC for funding the Olive Schreiner Letters Project (RES-062-23-1286). Extracts from the Mass Observation diaries were reproduced with permission of Curtis Brown Group Ltd, London, on behalf of The Trustees of the Mass Observation Archive.

Archival sources

Harry Ransom Center, University of Texas, Austin; Olive Schreiner collections.
Mass Observation Archive, University of Sussex, UK; diaries, day-diaries, File Reports and Directive responses.
National Library of South Africa, Cape Town; Olive Schreiner and SC Cronwright-Schreiner collections.
Olive Schreiner Letters Online www.oliveschreiner.org.
Historical Papers, University of Cape Town, South Africa; Olive Schreiner collections.

Interlude

Chapter 4 has emphasised that how 'the data', the traces remaining, are understood is shaped by the strategies that archival researchers use and consequently should be engaged in mindfully. In foregrounding time and the temporal order, it shows the researcher as an active presence in constructing, not just reflecting on, such orderings through the methodological strategies deployed.

Chapter 5 continues the theme of researcher reflexivity and being aware of the differences produced by what we do and how we do it. Its focus is on how archives come into being, and shows that who archivists are, and how an archive, collection and trace are understood, is not immutable. It highlights the archive as process, as archive making, and in focusing on the making of community archives it helps expand the possibilities for archival research. In doing so, Chapter 5 explores a range of conceptual and methodological tools for understanding community archives by engaging with the process involved. While commenting on researching the contents of such archives, its emphasis is on process in the work of making archives and the archival researcher's role in this.

5 Weaving archival imaginaries
Researching community archives

Niamh Moore

Researching archival histories, beginning questions

How and why have different archives come into being and what can be learned from tracing archival histories? In what ways is our view of who is, or can be, an archivist transformed by exploring how an archive is created? And does what is an archive, and what is a collection in an archive, also change?

This chapter approaches such overarching questions through an account of the creation of a community archive, thereby raising some more detailed questions: What are community archives and are they different from other archives? What are the challenges of researching in community archives? What methodological tools can be developed in researching the making of community archives, and also the materials generated by them? In what ways and to what extent are the methodological tools for community archives research transferable to other kinds of archives and their collections? And, (how) does consideration of community archives reframe or reconfigure the archival imaginary in the social sciences?

Community archiving as research

In focusing on the creation of an archive, this chapter highlights the ways in which we can attend to the archive as process. In drawing attention to the making of community archives, it expands the possibilities of archival research, given that academics do not often use community archives. In doing so it draws on my involvement with Feminist Webs, a loose collective of feminist youth workers, young women, academics, artists and allies who have been collaborating with the aim of reinvigorating feminist youth work, and youth work with girls, in north-west England. Central to Feminist Webs has been the process of creating an archive of feminist youth work (oral histories, as well as materials from girls' work groups from over the last 40–50 years) and (re)using this archive in multiple ways. Through reflecting on the working practices of Feminist Webs, I develop some conceptual tools for thinking about community archiving projects, which I hope will also be useful regarding other projects. These are boundary objects, boundary infrastructures, archival webs and archival times. The chapter concludes by discussing how attention to archival histories, which include community archives, can help reconfigure the archival imaginary in the social sciences.

Community archives are burgeoning. In the UK, in 2006 the Community Archives website was set up by the Community Archives and Heritage Group and now runs annual conferences, provides cataloguing guidelines for groups, and offers annual awards to support best practice in archiving. It also has a directory of community archive groups and lists more than 300 community archives (www.communityarchives.org.uk). Also in the UK, the Heritage Lottery Fund has awarded £72.5 million specifically to oral history projects since its inception in 1994, funding more than 2,850 over that time, in addition to a diverse range of other community heritage projects. And there are countless numbers of other *ad hoc* community history projects, which represent both nascent grassroots archives and a vernacular social research about communities. So what are community archives? Andrew Flinn, in a significant effort to put community archiving on the broader archival agenda, proposes that 'Community histories or community archives are the grassroots activities of documenting, recording and exploring community heritage in which community participation, control and ownership of the project is essential. This activity might or might not happen in association with formal heritage organisations but the impetus and direction should come from within the community itself' (Flinn, 2007: 153).

This chapter takes up Flinn's invitation to pay more attention to the possibilities and practicalities of doing research with and in community archives, in particular through working through Susan Leigh Star's (2010) conceptualisation of 'boundary objects'. I draw on my involvement in a feminist and youth work project with a significant archival dimension – Feminist Webs – to explore the growth of community archives and their implications for rethinking the potentials of archival research, relationships with archives, and archival practices. As other chapters in *The Archive Project* have noted, rethinking the archive has been under way for some time – Stoler views it as moving from being seen as a taken-for-granted repository to being a site of critical inquiry, involving an engagement with the 'archive as subject' rather than as a mere 'source' (Stoler, 2002: 93). Here I remind researchers of the diversity of archives and the potential for extending this focus on archives 'as subject' to community archives. While the social sciences have a long history of documentary and archival research, recent discussions about archiving have largely focused on the re-use of qualitative data and the creation of archives holding quantitative and qualitative social research data. That these discussions have focused in this way is also suggestive of the lack of attention to and knowledge of the archival turn more broadly, which has constrained a wider-ranging discussion of archival imaginaries, a point I return to at the end of the chapter.

The transferable archival practices and methodologies of Feminist Webs

I approach community archiving around a particular archival project I have been involved in, Feminist Webs. Paying attention to the distinctive features of Feminist Webs usefully alerts us to the potentials of community archives. Feminist Webs is the inspired outcome of a meeting in York railway station in the UK between Alison Ronan and Jean Spence, both youth and community workers, academics and researchers and feminist activists (see Figure 5.1). They were returning from a youth work conference and shared their dilemma about what to do with all those feminist youth work materials under the bed/in attics/spare rooms – the tragedy would be for these to be lost, for all that work to disappear. This is a recognisable and familiar tale to many an archive or archival collection. Yet I want to tease out this story a bit more. While this may be familiar, not all such encounters produce a generative enterprise like Feminist Webs; many such conversations end instead with rueful grimaces and at best a trip to the recycle bin.

Alison Ronan returned to Manchester and began to engage in conversation with others about this dilemma, including Amelia Lee, Strategic Director of The Proud Trust and a feminist youth worker working with LGBT young people. In the conversations between Alison and Amelia, a plan for a meeting with feminist youth workers emerged. This was not just about the materials Alison had assembled over the years but about all the girls' work material in north-west England, an area with a long and dedicated history of girls' work.

From these initial threads, a thriving and ongoing project emerged. The sheer scale, energy and diversity of Feminist Webs is difficult to describe, but one way of introducing it is through an account of its herstory, and particularly funding phases. In 2006–2007 there was a project that led to a poster and online resource called 'Done Hair and Nails, Now What?'. And in the context of archival research, it is worth noting that this first project immediately used the materials gathered from youth workers and their attics. The creation and organisation of the archive in fact came later. The following year, when I became involved, there was a participatory oral history project and a short film, 'Feminist Webs, The Journey'. Then we took the archive on tour to girls' groups around Manchester and the North-West, and through workshops with young girls created a number of responses to the archival materials, including a 'zine, a banner, a short animation and a 'postfeminist booklet', which brought together responses to postcards which invited women and girls to write on 'what young women want'. This phase culminated in a launch at the Women's Library and excitement when the library took one of the 'zines for its own 'zine collection. The next funded phase was called 'Women and Girls are Strong' and it too involved working with a number of girls' groups to respond to archival materials and create artworks, which led to an exhibition at the People's History

Figure 5.1 A Feminist Webs' herstory
Source: Hebe Phillips, in *Feminist Webs*, 2012: 6–7

Museum in Manchester and the launch of the Feminist Webs' collaborative print-on-demand book, *The Exciting Life of Being a Woman: A Handbook for Women and Girls* (2012). Funding has mainly come from the Heritage Lottery and specific funds for girls and women, like the Rosa Fund (www.rosa.org), which supports activities that benefit girls and women in the UK. In between funded phases, various stages of the background work of managing the archive took place.

My involvement with Feminist Webs began with a muddy rather than a dusty encounter, more than a year after Alison and Amelia organised the initial meeting in Manchester. I was involved in a young women's allotment project, and was intrigued by my accidental encounters with feminist youth work there (Moore, 2013; Feminist Webs, 2012). Amelia Lee was the youth worker leading the allotment initially and mentioned a plan for an oral history project of feminist youth work and an application to the Heritage Lottery Fund, and hadn't I mentioned that I did oral history and could she ask me some questions when she was completing the application about what kind of support and training they would need. As I pondered the project that Amelia had sketched out, I was struck by its ambitions. So when she called, I suggested that a one-off day's training was not enough, that an oral history project was quite a complex process and that it would be good to have support all along the way. My interest in and curiosity about their plans grew. I found myself envious of the person who would get this job of work that I was describing, but this was before I fully appreciated just how resourceful Amelia is and how quickly she could spot someone who could be harnessed to the project.

My initial commitment to Feminist Webs was to offer support to the oral history project. This included providing training in oral history to young women during a residential weekend in a youth hostel, supporting the subsequent interviews and archiving, advising on consent and related matters in creating an archive, and depositing interviews with the North West Sound Archive in Manchester (sadly closed in 2015 – Feminist Webs' archival materials subsequently moved to Archives+ in Manchester Central Library; see www.archivesplus.org). This later included running workshops to make a 'zine, with Maggie Gee contributing to the creation of a Feminist Webs collaborative book (Feminist Webs, 2012), taking part in cataloguing workshops, being involved in conference papers and workshops on Feminist Webs and writing academic papers, and more. For me, Feminist Webs, with its participatory youth practices which morphed into transgenerational history-making practices, has stood as an intriguing success at a time of ongoing statements about the end of feminism and either its irrelevance for young women or that generational conflicts characterise its resurgence. It has not only informed my understandings of community archiving and feminist history-making but also provided a compelling instance of contemporary transgenerational feminist activism.

In thinking through the transferable methodological aspects of my involvement in Feminist Webs, I build on Flinn's (2007) conceptualisation of 'community archives' above and work through how Susan Leigh Star's (2010) ideas about 'boundary objects' might be used to think about participatory community archives. I link Star's work on boundary objects with the image and concept of 'the web', which is central to Feminist Webs. The key methodological tools derived from this are:

- boundary objects
- boundary infrastructures
- archival webs
- archival times
- archival imaginaries.

In what follows, I work through these concepts using my involvement with Feminist Webs to demonstrate them in process.

From black box to boundary object

In opening the black box of archival research (Hill, 1993; see also Chapter 2), Susan Leigh Star's (2010) work on 'boundary objects' offers generative resources for conceptualising and researching community archiving projects. For Star, a boundary object is 'a shared space, where exactly the sense of here and there are confounded' (Star, 2010: 602–603), and so a boundary here is perceived as not so much an edge or divide as a collectively generated space for working together. While the boundary object is a rather elegant way of manifesting what Star describes as the invisible processes of collaborative working, she also acknowledges the rather awkward nomenclature. Boundary seems to imply an edge, whereas the focus of the boundary object is on collective generation of a shared space. Indeed, the very awkwardness of the term can be seen as a manifestation of the messy nature of shared spaces, and the *ad hoc* processes which create them. The boundary object is consequently a useful term for exploring the entanglements that characterise community archives, where the need to be explicit about the qualifier, 'community' archive, highlights the unmarked assumption that archives are often understood as official repositories of knowledge, although in practice things are often more complicated, as all the chapters in this book emphasise.

Yet while the concept of boundary object has been taken up extensively in, for example, science and technology studies, and, significantly, information science disciplines, it has rarely been used to describe archives. This appears particularly curious given that one of Star and Griesemer's initial examples of what might constitute a boundary object was Berkeley's Museum of Vertebrate Zoology, and they developed their work in order to examine how various professionals, scientists, museum curators, administrators and amateurs worked together (Star and Griesemer, 1989). One of their examples of other possible sites where the boundary object might be used was in a repository, including libraries. Despite this absence, there are places in the archival turn literature where the boundary object has made appearances. If a record can be a boundary object, why not a collection of records too (Yeo, 2008, 2010)? Other examples of work on boundary objects outside of science include museum exhibitions (Burman, 2004) and producing a collaborative paper in a journal (Biglia *et al.*, 2005). Yet while the boundary object has not been applied extensively to the archive itself, it seems particularly well suited to understanding the complicated entanglements of a community archive. In addition, tracing the extent to which community archives are more or less successful in creating boundary objects might help to explain why some projects flourish more than others.

While community archiving has at times existed in an uneasy tension with the formal archival practices of professional archivists, Star's work on boundary objects offers an alternative way into thinking about archives and archiving. It does not foreground any contest between professional and amateur or official institutions and grassroots organisations, but rather reframes the key questions as to what is an archive and what is it for, and hence, what kind of infrastructure it requires. Here it is the nature of the archive itself that determines what kind of infrastructures it requires, and we can think of the archive, any archive, as a shared space, rather than a contest between different places and spaces or different archival practices.

Star was originally intrigued by the observation that many models 'of cooperation often began conceptually, with the idea that first consensus must be reached, and then the cooperation could begin', yet she also observed many groups 'where consensus was rarely reached and fragile when it was, but cooperation continued, often unproblematically' (Star, 2010: 604). Erica Burman's feminist account of a boundary object (describing group analysis) stressed its role as 'a means of producing sufficient coherence to enable interaction without this being predicated on the erasure of heterogeneity; nor on the imposition of uniformity or transparency. Thus boundary objects offer a site or medium for the negotiation of identity and difference' (Burman, 2004: 370). Feminist Webs can be understood as a shared space where a collective of youth workers, academics, young women, artists come together to work, in a way that unsettles any sharp separation of academia, activism, archiving and semi-professional domains such as youth work. Key to the concept of boundary object is the notion of 'interpretative flexibility', which can be seen in how Feminist Webs flourishes as an entity which is a youth work resource, a grassroots community archive, as well as a site of feminist activism, all at the same time – with the important consequence that Feminist Webs is meaningful as an exemplar with wider resonance.

While my focus is on community archives, which throw up these questions acutely, the argument also holds for other, more formal archives. In using the concept of boundary object to understand archives, I am extending work, particularly that initiated by Andrew Flinn and colleagues on community archives as well as those writing on feminist archival practices (Alexander and Bastian, 2009; Flinn, 2007; Flinn *et al.*, 2009; Eichhorn, 2010, 2013; Stevens *et al.*, 2010). Jeannette Bastian's work (2003) offers an evocative account of the importance of formal records for community memory. Collectively, these works have begun the project of tracing the many and complex relationships between activist archives, community archives and more formal archives. In introducing Star's work on boundary objects, I hope to develop understanding of and provide tools for conceptualising activist archiving and community archiving – and indeed for more formal archiving practices.

Boundary infrastructures

Star (2010: 602) also emphasises the importance of 'boundary infrastructures'. Her account of the work of 'tacking back and forth' between well-structured local and particular versions of boundary objects, and vaguer more general shared versions, is suggestive of the challenges both to professional archival standards and to academic research that are posed by community archiving projects. Feminist Webs too tacks back and forth across the domains of youth work, academia, community, activism, as well as across amateur and professional archival and research practices. Thus the boundary infrastructures idea is incredibly useful in understanding how Feminist Webs developed.

I became involved in Feminist Webs in my capacity as an academic experienced in oral history. I had training in oral history skills and had carried out oral history projects with feminist activists (Moore, 2001, 2007a, 2008, 2015). Together with Amelia and others, we created a plan for a residential weekend workshop involving oral history training as well as more general planning for the project. As best possible in two days and between meals and other activities, we led oral history training, covering a range of key issues, from what is an archive and what is feminist history to the practicalities of interviews, generating questions, as well as how to use recorders, why we needed consent forms, what ethical issues might arise, how to deal with difficult questions, as well as touching on the contingency of memory. In recognition of people's skills and the young women's availability, I prepared information sheets and consent forms for the project. But there were compromises, places in the process where decisions were made, or practicalities demanded departures from what I would have considered ideal. There was not much money in the budget for audio recorders. I would have liked better quality ones while we ended up with cheap MP3 audio recorders.

The assumptions about oral history interviews include that they are best carried out in people's homes. This was not really possible as many of the interviewers would be under 16, and in any case logistically it would have been difficult to arrange. Instead we planned 'memory days' in the youth centre where youth workers would come and be interviewed by young women in some of the many side rooms. This was the best that could be done. Actually we were interviewing women in part about their work histories, and so interviewing women in something like a workplace made sense, and even if the LGBT centre was not necessarily their own workplace, it would be reasonably similar. At the same time, I wasn't quite sure how it would work out, how we could co-ordinate interviews, arranging for interviewers and interviewees to align. And while I wanted to be there, relegated to data management, providing batteries, voice recorders, consent forms, information sheets, it would be a long day with lots of hanging around while the interviews went on. So we all turned up, handed out recorders and forms and sent pairs off to rooms, and I sat back to wait and wait. Until I was somewhat surprised and then confused and then horrified when the first young woman and youth worker came out of their room after about twenty-five minutes. At first I thought there was a problem, a need already for new batteries, something about consent or anonymisation that would require my expert intervention and explanation. But no, everything was fine, they had just finished the interview. Although we had covered all kinds of issues around consent, dealing with difficult answers, ethical questions, technology, and even broached the vagaries of memory, truth and contingency in interviews, and had created a huge bank of questions for young women to choose from, I had clearly neglected to give an indication of how long an interview should take, and that those with women with long histories of feminist and youth work activism could last for days and at least for an hour or two. Nonetheless, around the LGBT Centre, other pairs were emerging from their rooms, looking quite happy and content and interested and excited. All the while I was helping set up new interviews, new pairs, new batteries, new forms, collecting ones being handed back, and frantically thinking how I could retrieve the situation and rescue the project. But everyone, except me, seemed relaxed and happy and there was an air of shared conversations. It was a salutary lesson that oral history projects are not all the same; that this was not a PhD project, that oral history in a participatory youth work context might look somewhat different from what I was more familiar with, that fourteen year olds were unlikely to ever do an interview that would last hours, that twenty-five minutes was probably quite a good time. That success – or failure – does not look the same in all contexts.

Shortly afterwards I had a related experience, in a different community oral history project (with adults). This group had had one day's training from the British Library, and were taking the training very seriously, but had no one to provide ongoing advice as they worked their way through the project. They had used their small amount of funding to purchase two Marantz audio recorders, still the gold standard for archive quality recordings. However, their project involved interviews all around north-west England and they were having problems passing the recorders around as the interviews were in people's homes and were quite spread out. It was immediately obvious to me then that spending most of the budget on technology was not necessarily the best decision in this context – not least because there was no money left for getting together or for tea and sandwiches. Additionally, the Marantz recorders seemed complicated and people lacked confidence to use them. At a meeting, there was a long discussion about the need for silence when recording the interview, and one interviewer expressed concern that even after closing a nearby window there was still some noise from a school playground. There was a serious discussion then about possible access to a sound-proof room in the BBC building in Manchester to ensure the best quality recording. I did intervene here and insist that a little background noise should not detract hugely from the quality of the interview, that a sound-proof room at the BBC was likely to give rise to even further difficulties in arranging interviews, and was unlikely to encourage participants to feel very comfortable about speaking on the record. It is perhaps no accident that, although a fascinating project, I did not find the time to continue my involvement, and indeed the project has still carried out only a small number of interviews. At the same time, Feminist Webs had a number of memory days and has continued to generate new activities.

Yet, while the Feminist Webs interview recordings were mainly under thirty minutes and on low-quality MP3 recorders, it would be a mistake to think that it was not interested in professionalism or standards of any kind. Advice was initially sought from a range of relevant professionals and organisations, including the Ahmed Iqbal Ullah Education Trust in Manchester, which runs oral history projects on Black communities in Manchester, and this resulted in the purchase of a huge roll of acid-proof paper and brown cardboard archival boxes. A student from an archival studies MA was brought in to help organise the archive. While the original project concerned oral histories, as other community history projects have found, people began to bring 'stuff'. As well as the website, there was a physical archive. A room for the archive was initially found at Manchester Metropolitan University, which has a strong tradition of youth work, and several Feminist Webbers, youth work lecturers and former youth workers worked there. In fact, the archive first occupied, perhaps literally in the sense of unofficially squatted, the office of a retired colleague. But it wasn't long before the archive had to move, and it ended up in Room 101. This caused much amusement, recalling the torture chamber in the Ministry of Love in George Orwell's (1949) novel *1984*. While the archive spent a few years in Room 101, in the summer of 2014 it moved again, this time to a more explicitly archival space in a new university building – with Feminist Webber and youth work academic Janet Batsleer commenting on this shift, 'It's great isn't it! We have had the archive in an office for years, and now it is in the new building, in archive shelving, and feels like it's more integrated into the University and more accessible for the public' (www.feministwebs. com/2014/08/we-have-moved/).

That day, admiring the new archive shelving in the new building, it seemed a long way from the 'early days' when we hardly knew anything about archives. When Feminist Webs initially solicited donations to the archive, Amelia would get phone calls and emails and drive off to collect materials, bringing back boxes, plastic bags and armfuls of 'stuff', which we would unpack and wonder over. The archive includes books, magazines, postcards, photographs of youth work events, materials created in girls' work groups, including banners, posters, art projects, tee-shirts, badges, minutes of meetings of youth groups, plans of sessions for youth workers and accompanying resources, dissertations on youth work, and now also documentation of Feminist Webs itself. The existence of these materials and their emergence from attics, under beds and the backs of cupboards in youth centres also tells of a history of care, of saving materials even when there was not quite enough space for them. The sheer scale and diverse range of what ended up in the archive also seemed quite a contrast to Foucault's grey archival documents mentioned in Chapter 3 (see also Moore, 2015: 77–78). We did not really know where to start with this abundance (and for different responses to similar situations, see Chapters 2 and 4), but it became clear that we needed a way to organise all that had been gathered together. This was also pressing because the archive was given lots of materials related not directly to the history of feminist youth work specifically but to feminism more widely. For instance, and perhaps unsurprisingly, materials from feminist youth workers often contained many editions of *Spare Rib*, one of the most widely circulating feminist magazines in the women's liberation movement, published between 1973 and 1992. So it was not directly related to youth work, but on the other hand, it was clearly formative for the feminist youth workers we were engaging with. Our initial inclination was to gather these together to see if we had a full set but finding there were gaps and duplications and decisions to be made about duplicate copies. Eventually we learned about provenance, that archives are not necessarily organised by putting the same kinds of materials together, but by where a collection came from, who has donated or generated the collection. So instead of gathering together books, magazines, photos, minutes of meetings, we have the Manchester Collection, the Lancashire Collection, the Stockport Collection, the Wigan Collection as well as the National Youth Work (including the National Girls' Work Unit) Collection and the Regional Girls' Work Collection. But in the end, in our *ad hoc* approach to archiving, we did create a *Spare Rib* Collection, as it seemed an entity in its own right. Sitting around surreptitiously reading (or re-reading) *Spare Ribs* while we were supposed to be cataloguing was one of the not so guilty pleasures of producing the archive. We also had conversations about the possibility of digitising *Spare Rib*, bemoaning that this had not already been done and that we did not have the resources to do it. So there has been some excitement that since then the British Library has done just that (www.bl.uk/spare-rib). There is even a Feminist Webs Collection, because we are documenting and archiving our own process. It becomes quite difficult to know where the archive begins and ends, what is included and what might not be.

We were all drawn in by the copies of *Spare Rib*, but also recognised that they weren't really what we needed and that there were full sets in more accessible archives. So we drew up an 'Accessions Policy' and created an 'Ingest Form' so that we would have a policy on what materials the Feminist Webs archive would accept, and therefore, just as crucially, what we would not accept. The Ingest Form would mean that we would have at least some details of the materials in the archive, some account of provenance. The archive was in a closed, but unsupervised, room at Manchester Metropolitan and materials would appear unannounced, perhaps hurriedly dropped off by a Feminist Webber with no note of what they were or who they were from. Yet having an Accessions Policy and an Ingest Form didn't completely bring a halt to the experience of opening the door to another plastic bag, or little bundle of photos from a girls' work trip somewhere, some time.

The archive needed to be organised and catalogued. We sought advice from an archiving student about what was needed to organise the archive formally. We created a description of the archive to use in various ways, including for registering it with the Archives Hub (http://archiveshub.ac.uk/), an online gateway to archives throughout the UK, in the hope that unknown people searching for similar archives would find us. We registered also with the Community Archives and Heritage Group and added Feminist Webs to its online directory (www.communityarchives.org.uk/index.php). We used its guidelines on setting up a community archive and for cataloguing.

With these guidelines and with input from archives students, we planned cataloguing days, where women of all ages came together, and we began to organise all the material we had. These days are memorable for many of us. Even as we catalogued, as we tried to impose some order, provide definition of the materials, write summaries of the materials in our boxes, we could not help but create some chaos. Room 101 was a small office; there was not enough space for everyone to sit there to do cataloguing. The first time we had a mass cataloguing day, there was a huge group and we sprawled over the large staff common room on the weekend when there was no one about. We carried down all the archive boxes from Room 101 and Amelia divided them among us. There were photocopied sheets to fill in. We dipped into boxes, scanned what the item was, wrote a description in the boxes, trying to make it legible. And all the time we dallied, reading a bit more than we needed to for the sake of filling out description boxes. There was a hush in the room, and it lasted all of a long Saturday, a quiet, solitary yet collective reading of the contents of our magical boxes. There was more than cataloguing going on; or perhaps more accurately there was the realisation that cataloguing involves much more than what such an apparently bureaucratic, procedural word conjures up. There was a glimpse of how a catalogue can make up a world, how the old pages of some copies of *Spare Rib*, that somehow had not been thrown away, had been kept, almost disposable, but never quite, could make their way, re-valued, into the archive.

Another cataloguing day involved a smaller group and was midweek. We couldn't use the staff room and spilled out of Room 101 into the university corridor with our boxes and photocopied sheets and pens, and descended into a shared hush again as we read and scribbled and read and read. Meantime some were trying to go about their everyday work far away from our floor-reading, on their way to the photocopier, dashing to or from a lecture. Some were amused by our occupying of the corridor space, others were frankly irritated, huffed and puffed under their breath as they awkwardly threaded a path through the sprawling boxes and papers and bodies. Caught between being volunteer youth worker/amateur archivist/academic researcher, I shifted about uncomfortably, not only because I was unused to squatting for so long but because I was torn between feeling that, even if this was not 'my' university, as an academic I ought to be more amenable and tidier in the corridors, that we ought not to get in the way, that we could at least move to the side – but squatting on the floor did provide another perspective on academic corridors. Amelia was more accustomed to having groups of sometimes unruly young people under her wing and used to the stares, sideways glances and sometimes straightforward hostility to 'gangs' of young people being in the way and too noisy. She reminded me of cyclists announcing on t-shirts that 'we are not in the way of the traffic, we are the traffic', taking it for granted that young people should take up corridor space. But really we were barely aware of them climbing over us, so engrossed were we in our reading.

The often chaotic messiness of grassroots archives with amateur archival practices (or perhaps none at all), and a heavy reliance on volunteers, perhaps paradoxically begins to make explicit the labour that goes into the organisation and standardisation of more formal archives. Star uses the idea of 'invisible work' (Star, 2010: 606), in her case in relation to science, to focus on the gap between formal representations and the 'unreported back stage work', something highly pertinent in the context of archives. The flexible approach to professional standards in community archive projects reveals the extent to which more formal archives can be structured and 'cleaned'. At the same time, the urge in community archives to turn from collecting materials to finding ways to arrange them (often to make them more accessible and public) can lead to the creation of new boundary infrastructures, and to the *ad hoc* and variable take-up of professional standards. Focusing on this apparent flexibility of archival practices as taken up in informal sites draws attention to inconsistencies even in official archives, as in, for instance, Geiger's observations about the movements of documents into and out of George W. Bush's official archive depending on the political climate (Geiger, 2008).

Archival webs

While the boundary object concept was not explicitly in the shared lexicon of many involved in Feminist Webs, some of the metaphors and practices used, and in particular that of the web, are consistent with Star's work. And while it is hardly surprising that the term 'boundary object' was not common parlance, the existence of continuities between boundary object and the web metaphor should not come as a surprise. The movement of 'tacking back and forth' between professional and amateur practices, or perhaps between different professions – archivist, researcher, youth worker – noted above is also suggestive of the work of weaving a web.

The concept of the web has been both a founding narrative for Feminist Webs and a description of practice. Feminist Webs has been informed by women's involvement in Greenham Common and the use of web imagery and practices there (Cook and Kirk, 1983; Roseneil, 1995; Jolly, 2003). Alison Ronan, one of the initiators of the archive, has cited women's activism at Greenham Common as one inspiration for Feminist Webs. The Greenham Common Women's Peace Camp was an encampment at a nuclear weapons base in the UK beginning in the early 1980s with some spectacular instances of feminist activism, including the weaving of women's everyday belongings into fencing around the base as a reminder of the impact of nuclear weapons on everyday lives. The web also signified various activist practices of organising – a web of lists of contacts and phone numbers, enabling them to organise events with huge attendance or publicise what had been happening at the camp. Later, with the idea of an online archive, other versions of the web came to mind. The idea of a feminist web resonated, giving rise to Feminist Webs' name and a poem found from a group reflection from young women involved in it (cited in Batsleer, 2013; and Ronan, 2012: 40):

About forwardness
About interconnectedness
Full of spaces
And also lines which are the connections and the stories
They hold people together like a net
Points of understanding across generations
A way of representing what feminism is and making links with other social
    justice movements
Sticky: they hold people together
But people can also get stuck in them
Not unusual
Not innocent: ask the fly!

Feminist Webs

The following reflection on Feminist Webs too is suggestive of a boundary object:

> There are not specific roles in Feminist Webs, we support and energise each other … we did a lot of talking about the structure for Feminist Webs and identified that it's fluidity that's its great strength. We went down the road of discussing a committee structure – but no-one wants to impose a structure so we are trying to think about it in a creative way about how it should operate. Women can identify with it in the way they want to – a different way – organising is needed but we don't know what it is yet. It needs to be loose and fluid.
>
> (Cited in Batsleer, 2013: 204)

Star's account of a boundary object sees it as 'something people act toward and with. Its materiality derives from action, not from a sense of prefabricated stuff or 'thing'-ness' (Star, 2010: 603), and this echoes chants at Greenham that 'we are the weavers, we are the web'. The concept of the web begins to blur the boundaries of the inside and outside of the archive, and also those of academic/activist/archivist.

The web metaphor shifts focus to the movements of the archive – the movements of materials into the archive, the arrangements and rearrangements of these materials, and the people who move and are moved by them. Community archives often come late to standard archival practices of documenting provenance, of developing accessions policies, and of organising materials in collections. Nonetheless, it is worth recognising that more formal archives often lack full (or any) accounts of provenance because of the haphazard ways in which materials often end up in archives. In addition, formal and informal archives are not exclusive entities. There is considerable interest in some larger archives in addressing the ephemerality of organisations, groups and materials that may not last, for instance. Thus Feminist Webs, while involving a physical and a virtual archive, also has its online presence preserved as part of the British Library's efforts to create an archive of UK websites (www.webarchive.org.uk/ukwa/target/60293326/source/subject).

While there remains a likelihood that the web, and Greenham Common, will for some conjure up an essentialised naturalised straw woman (Sturgeon, 1997), I want to draw on Donna Haraway's work on the game with string called cat's cradle (Haraway, 1994) to develop the idea of web as boundary infrastructure. It is probably no accident that Haraway, with her penchant for cyborgs rather than goddesses, coyote tricksters rather than spiderwoman, turns to the cat's cradle rather than the web, which may seem an overdetermined metaphor for her. Nonetheless the cat's cradle is another web, and Haraway's account of cat's cradle is useful for thinking through the world-making of community archiving (as well as Greenham) and what is at stake in these stories. For Haraway, cat's cradle is about the holding and passing on of patterns, through the process of making new knots or new webs (Haraway, 2011: 18). This description seems well suited to the passing on of feminist histories and the boundary object of community archiving – movements back and forth, creating new patterns and new knots. For Haraway, echoing Star's account of collaboration without consensus, 'it's a figure for building relationships that isn't agonistic' (Haraway, 2000: 156). This is serious play, however, as she forthrightly insists on the need to learn how to play well – and that making a 'tangled mess' is not the same as learning about the process through which 'some worlds get made and unmade, and for whom' (Haraway, 1994: 70). While Haraway is discussing technoscience, we might see the official archive with its knowledge practices, gatekeepers of truth and (the illusion of) modernist bureaucratic processes as a good exemplar of the kind of technoscience she has in mind, and of the need to make worlds differently.

Playing cat's cradle is not about handing on the same pattern, it is about making different patterns altogether. Haraway introduces the concept of 'diffraction', which also captures the multiplying and diversifying patterns of the cat's cradle, as against what she sees as the limits of representational modes. Diffraction creates interference that might 'make a difference in how meanings are made and lived' (Haraway, 2011). So with the Feminist Webs archive, materials are gathered not just to preserve them, but rather materials are generated in order to make a difference. The archive, the 'zine, book, or other activities, were not intended to mirror existing possibilities for being a girl.

Feminist Webs' first project was to immediately re-use and repurpose materials gathered from feminist youth workers to create a large booklet that also folded out as a poster called 'Done Hair and Nails, Now What?'. This contains a detailed breakdown of topics for discussions in girls' youth groups, ranging from body image to sex and sexuality, faith, women and asylum to work and leisure, with links to the website for further resources to follow up (www.feministwebs.com/resources/). These resources include a 'Beauty Image Timeline', which musters historical research to demonstrate the shifting standards of beauty ideals. Materials on sex and sexuality include a link to the 'Sex and Relationships Booklet' produced by the Young Women's Health Project for young lesbian and bisexual women, which crucially focuses on sexual pleasure as well as safety. One section of the booklet uses photos of Barbie dolls to explain and illustrate in detail some of the possible answers to 'what do two girls do in bed together?.' In this way, the booklet takes the culture jamming techniques of the Barbie Liberation Organization, which famously switched the voice boxes of Barbie and Ken, to have Ken wistfully suggest, 'let's plan our dream wedding' and Barbie announcing 'vengeance is mine' (https://sniggle.net/barbie.php), to a queer conclusion.

It was some time before I appreciated the full significance of the work that went into creating the 'Done Hair and Nails, Now What?' poster and the resources it made available to youth workers and youth groups. As my only encounter with youth work was through the Young Women's Health Project at the allotment and The Proud Trust, I didn't really appreciate that not all youth groups operated with similar values and practices and commitments to participation, informal learning and anti-oppressive practice. I didn't really grasp the extent of some of the difference until I visited a nearby youth group with Amelia Lee in a later phase of Feminist Webs, when we were bringing them details of an opportunity for girls to participate in. We arrived at a busy youth centre during school holiday activities. Two girls bounced up, stuck out their hands displaying their newly painted fingernails and announced that they had just won the baking competition with their cupcakes, while the boys were playing sports. It was a struggle to assemble some girls in a room upstairs where Amelia and I tried to engage them in conversations about why a free residential weekend with the Feminist Webs project might be fun. And once it emerged that one of the other youth groups on the residential would be the Young Women's Health Project with young lesbian and bisexual women, even lukewarm inclination to come ran cold as the young women mumbled about not sharing a room with anyone from that group. There were no youth workers at that youth centre with the knowledge, skills and training to work through these issues with the young women. Only one young woman from that club ended up coming on the residential.

It was some time, too, before I fully appreciated the lack of resources for youth work, the ongoing cuts in budgets and services, just how strapped these youth groups were and how much work they carried out on the proverbial shoestring. 'Done Hair and Nails, Now What?' was Feminist Webs' work to expand the range of possibilities available to girls' groups and offer an alternative to what Batsleer has described as the '"target-driven" focuses on teenage pregnancy, personal safety and anti-obesity eating practices, or the "pampering" offered as part of outreach to girls via hair and beauty sessions' (Batsleer, 2013: 52). 'Done Hair and Nails, Now What?' is one response to what Haraway describes as 'how to have simultaneously an account of radical historical contingency for all knowledge claims and knowing subjects, a critical practice for recognizing our own "semiotic technologies" for making meanings, and a no-nonsense commitment to faithful accounts of a "real" world, one that can be partially shared and friendly to earth-wide projects of finite freedom, adequate material abundance, modest meaning in suffering, and limited happiness' (cited in Haran, 2013). Also, how the passing on of patterns might make a critical difference in the world.

Archival times

Archives might appear as collections of records of the past, but archives themselves have histories and biographies, as Nicholas Dirks (1993) has pointed out. Approaching community archives as boundary objects opens up the possibilities for examining communities – as well as history – in the making, or more precisely, for examining the making of communities through the making of history. Thus the scope of archival research expands to include not only the materials in the archive but also a focus on the relationships that create the archive and how these have influenced its nature. As an archive of feminist youth work, Feminist Webs provides a particularly resonant exemplar for discussing archival times.

Feminist Webs emerged in the mid-2000s when stories of the end of feminism persisted alongside accounts of third- and fourth-wave feminisms, of revivals of feminism by young women, and of rejections of feminism by young women. Feminist Webs also emerged at a time of a proliferation of feminist history projects – including those by Bolton Women's Liberation Group (www.feministarchivenorth.org.uk/catalogue/index.htm), Nottingham Women's History Group (www.nottinghamwomenshistory.org.uk/about.html), the Women's Liberation Music Archive (http://womensliberation-musicarchive.co.uk/) and the national archive of the Women's Liberation Movement, Sisterhood and After (www.sussex.ac.uk/clhlwr/research/sisterhoodafter). There is a risk that, in the context of endless reports of the ongoing death of feminism, it might seem that history is all that feminism has left. Yet we might want to remember that a founding moment for the Women's Liberation Movement in the UK was the first Women's Liberation Movement conference at Ruskin College in Oxford in 1970, which in part emerged out of challenges in the History Workshop movement over the need to develop a specifically women's history. Thus history was an important site for the emergence of feminism, as the initial conference focus broadened out from women's history to women's issues more generally. Making history, in the doubled sense of both changing history and the generative work of materialising a specifically women's history which otherwise would not come into being, has long been crucial for feminism.

What might have looked like a legacy or memorial project transformed in conversation. Ideas of weaving women and materials, Greenham style, to create an archival web morphed in the encounter with feminist youth work. This web would not only be of older women gathering their materials to pass on to younger youth workers and young women; the archival project would itself be a practice of feminist youth work. Feminist youth work, especially as practised in north-west England, is strongly participatory and young women would be centrally involved in gathering and, crucially, (re) using the materials. While this might still look like a legacy model, there are distinctive features that make it different. Young women were hearing and gathering histories of women who had been committed to girls' work for many years, who had passionately campaigned to make girls' work possible. This was not a legacy of straightforward narratives of progress or decline, but rather stories of young women, and their value by older feminists who continued to value that work and wanted to create an archive of it. This was also obvious in older feminists' ways of engaging with young women and their interest in being involved, not only so that their histories could be documented but also so that they could learn about feminism in the lives of young women. Other points were the interviews, where youth workers 'successfully' turned the interviews around and asked young women for their own stories. Thus, against a legacy model of feminist history, Feminist Webs' transgenerational, collaborative, participatory herstory-making practices offer a more timely version of feminist herstory, one which certainly refuses any end or death of feminism, or linear progress or decline narratives, or any straightforward account of conflict between generations. Rather, Feminist Webs echoes Puig de la Bellacasa and Bracke's reflection that 'when translating feminist struggles and their achievements into theories, we would rather be *better with/because of* – than *better than* those who came before us' (2004: 314, emphasis in original). Histories of feminist youth work offer a provocative site for thinking through conflictual histories of feminism. Feminist Webs offers histories of a feminist practice – feminist youth work – which has always been transgenerational.

Considering the practices involved in establishing the Feminist Webs archive, and also in researching its contents, disrupts linear histories and dominant narratives which rely on generational conflict as a key defining crisis for feminism. This provides a salutary reminder that feminist generations do not always experience conflictual relationships. Michelle Bastian suggests that one way of tackling the limits of linear histories 'is to develop an account of time which will enable contradictory histories and contradictory ways of acting to share the same time, to be coeval with each other, rather than be divided from each other as they are within linear accounts of time' (Bastian, 2011: 14). The idea of contradictory simultaneity can provide a helpful reading of the possibilities of feminist and other histories, countering narratives of the death or end of feminism through conflict. This attention to contradictory simultaneities offers another instance of the complex temporalities of the archive, explored in particular in Chapter 4.

These contradictory simultaneities do not necessarily erase conflicts (generational or otherwise), but also any conflict is not constitutive of the end of feminism. However, legacy is reworked as an active process of relationship, where older youth workers also ask and listen about young women's experiences, where legacy can be bequeathed at least both ways, to young women and from young women to older feminists. This transgenerational ethos is also evident in some creative outputs from Feminist Webs. *Femzine*, a Feminist Webs online and printed 'zine (www.feministwebs.com/about/femzine/), operates as a contemporary 'mashed up' version of the *Spare Ribs* that made it into the archive. *Femzine* juxtaposes images from *Spare Rib*, Jacky Fleming cartoons and other materials from the archive with responses from young women involved. This juxtaposition of apparent past and present creates a montage where engagement with archival materials does not just relegate the materials to history but through writing and rewriting reworks meanings for now. In addition, the Feminist Webs book, *The Exciting Life of Being a Woman,* contains side-by-side chapters written by young women and older feminists, all reflecting on the experience of being involved, drawing on archival materials or writing anew. Thus both *Femzine* and *The Exciting Life of Being a Woman* offer popular examples of the re-reading of and rewriting of the archive signalled by the archigraphics of Chapter 2.

Feminist Webs, as an archive of youth work, demonstrates the contradictory simultaneities of feminism particularly well, and especially in the fraught context of feminist histories and generations. Thus the complex temporal logics of a participatory history of feminist youth work, I would suggest, offer powerful possibilities for reconceiving community archiving more broadly, through shifting from a notion of preserving community to an attention to the temporal dynamics of the making and passing on of community (see also Chapters 3 and 4 on archival rhythms and temporal dynamics).

From Feminist Webs to archival genealogies

While, for some, Feminist Webs might seem a curious anomaly, I want to locate Feminist Webs in histories of community and activist archiving, as well as in a complex relationship with mainstream archiving and histories.

Andrew Flinn's (2007) account of the community archive movement points to its long history in the UK and internationally, involving the History Workshop movement and the public history movement, as well as traditions of Black, working class, feminist and LGBT archives (Flinn *et al.*, 2009). Commonly these archives, and Feminist Webs in particular, straddle academia, activism and a range of publics, with the shared space of the community archive as a boundary object supporting the weaving of other webs and the construction of alternative genealogies.

Here I take up our interest in genealogy (see also Chapter 3), to situate the Feminist Webs archive in the context of other queer archival histories, including, for instance, the Hall-Carpenter Archives, now housed at the London School of Economics. One of the impetuses for the setting up of the Hall-Carpenter Archives came from within the British Sociology Association's Sex and Gender Study Group and Gay Research Study Group in the late 1970s and early 1980s. The idea was for the archive to be driven by the gay community, while ultimately it moved to the LSE (Donnelly, 2008). Similar stories of links across academia and political communities and considerable debate about appropriate sites for community archives could be told regarding other archives, including where different decisions were made, such as the insistently independent New York Lesbian Herstory Archives (Nestle, 1979; Nestle, 1990). This version of genealogy is certainly informed by Foucault, but also by feminist thinking (Moore, 2015: 23–4). For instance, Adrienne Rich's essay 'When we dead awaken: writing as re-vision' was first published in 1979, the same year that Foucault's 'Nietzsche, genealogy, history' appeared. Clearly aware of the constitutive power of histories and the (re)writing of these histories, Rich (1979: 35) wrote about re-vision as 'the act of looking back, of seeing with fresh eyes, of entering an old text from a new critical direction' and as an act of survival, for 'until we can understand the assumptions in which we are drenched we cannot know ourselves... We need to know the writing of the past, and know it differently than we have ever known it; not to pass on a tradition but to break its hold over us'.

Rich's call for re-visioning history points not only to juxtapositions of then and now but also to the importance of being able to imagine and re-imagine history – and archiving – as crucial knowledge-making practices which support the possibilities of alternative presents and futures. For Feminist Webs, this includes the possibility of different relationships between generations and different histories and futures for feminism. A genealogical approach to the archive, then, foregrounds the labour of creating an archive and acts to contextualise not only the 'truths' of archival documents but also the archive itself. This way of approaching archival genealogies goes further than Dirks' call for 'a biography of the archive' (Dirks, 1993) and later for 'an ethnography of the archive' (Dirks, 2002), to think more extensively about the connections which archives generate. Relatedly, applying Foucault's account of the imaginary to archives seems productive, because for him the imaginary 'is not formed in opposition to reality as its denial or compensation; it grows among signs, from book to book, in the interstice of repetitions and commentaries; it is born and takes shape in the interval between books. It is the phenomena of the library' (Foucault, 1977: 91).

What this points up is that Feminist Webs exists not only in relation to feminist and youth work histories but also in relation to mainstream histories, or what the oral history concerns of the Occupy Movement (http://occupyoralhistory.wordpress.com/about/) refer to as conversation with the '1%'. This calls not for reading along or against the archival grain (Stoler, 2009) but for tracing webs of connections, that is, archival genealogies. This point has been made powerfully by Jeannette Bastian in *Owning Memory: How a Caribbean Community Lost Its Archives and Found Its History* (2003). This details the challenges faced by Virgin Islanders whose archival records have been split between Denmark and the USA, as it was once a Danish colony and is now a US territory. Through an account of the creation of oral and local histories and their complicated relationship with the distant official records, she details the construction of the collective memories of the island community, and this in turn highlights the important role of formal archives in the creation of community and collective memory.

Refiguring social science archival imaginaries: some methodological conclusions

Rich's re-visioning of history, re-imagining the past so that we might imagine ourselves otherwise, is suggestive for thinking about the purpose of community archives – and for reflecting on what I suggest is the social sciences' ambivalent relationship with the archive. This is perhaps most obviously manifest through the social science struggle to imagine its own archive. While there are notable exceptions – including in the UK the Mass Observation Archive, the Foundations of British Sociology: The Sociological Review Archive, ESDS Qualidata, now part of the UK Data Archive, and Timescapes – the social sciences are not overburdened with archives. Relatedly, the at times fraught debate over archiving and (re)using research data has compounded this ambivalent overall relationship with archives. The failure of imagination regarding archival research is also evident in research methods textbooks, a strong impetus for writing this book. New textbooks detailing how to do archival research are rarely published, compared with qualitative methodology in general and interviewing in particular. Archival research does not usually figure in generic social science research textbooks, even as a solo chapter. Despite the current focus on 'innovations' in methods – including sensory methods, mobile methods, more-than-human methods, big data and the digital – archival research does not appear as one of the sites of innovation in the social sciences. At best there may be marginal references to re-use or secondary analysis in methodology textbooks, with little attention to the archives and archival practices that enable research data to be re-used.

In exploring how archival research figures, or more often fails to figure, in the social sciences, I turn to the work of historian and philosopher of science Helen Verran, who links the concept of 'imaginaries' with knowledge production. The idea of archival imaginaries underlines the relationship between archives and the possibilities of knowledge-making. While there have been many iterations of the concept of the imaginary, I draw particularly on its take-up in feminist science and technology studies (with Jasanoff and Kim, 2015 and McNeil *et al.*, 2016 providing useful overviews). Verran has extended Michèle Le Doeuff's (1989) work on the philosophical imaginary to practices of knowledge-making more broadly, working through a detailed case study of a court case on land ownership in Australia, where she identified different imaginaries at play in claims to the land. Le Doeuff reworks Kant's account of reason as requiring the exclusion of the imaginary, pointing out that he could present this exclusion only through images and metaphors, pictures and storytelling. This, then, is not a psychoanalytic or Lacanian 'imaginary' (though see Lennon, 2004, 2015 for versions including Lacanian and non-Lacanian psychoanalytic accounts). Verran takes up the imaginary to stress how it is implicated in how we know the world. In particular, for her the imaginary is necessarily involved in 'knowing and knowledge-making', and is 'constitutive of, and constituted by ontic and epistemic commitments: a politics over what there is and who/what can know it' (Verran, 1998: 238). Here the imaginary is not invoked in its common-sense understanding as that which is not real, or existing only in imagination, but as crucially bound up with the possibilities of knowledge, with knowledge politics – and knowledge practices. So, for Verran, imaginaries are not only about possible futures but also about knowledge production itself.

The concept of an archival imaginary suggests that it is not merely that archives are sites where social science knowledge can be produced (or social science methods can be applied), but also that the archival imaginary is constitutive of the possibilities for knowledge-making. Verran insists that imaginaries are not located in minds but in practices, and while this distinction may not be as clear-cut as she implies, nonetheless her assertion that 'it is in the everyday messing around with murky, obdurate stuff, and in the conversations and other texts – official and unofficial – that imaginaries are enacted and enact' (Verran, 1998: 252) is instructive. A corollary of this is that an impoverished archival imaginary constrains the possibilities of social science research and knowledge – of what constitutes the archive and who can know it. The project of transforming archival imaginaries is not as straightforward as simply claiming a new imaginary, however. A transformed archival imaginary requires transformed archival practices and methods, and also the work of cultivating an archival sensibility.

Elsewhere, with colleagues I have noted how some sociological commentaries on the archive are revealing of an impoverished archival imaginary (Geiger *et al.*, 2010). Relatedly, it has been proposed that sociologists should have a role in re-imaging the archive:

> [O]ne might imagine, indeed, a sociological history of such places of storage, deposition, testimony and administration; a history that would also be a history of the relevant agents of the archive. It would be a history of at least two kinds of people – archivists and historians – who tend to inhabit such dry, dark, forbidding places.
>
> (Osborne, 1999: 52)

The sociologist here is positioned on the outside of the archive, looking in to a place where the proper occupants are seen as archivists and historians. Featherstone (2000: 167) has asked, 'who will archive cultures in the future – the state, or the corporations or the public?', but with no suggestion that social science might play any role. However, the reference to corporations has been taken up in one, perhaps dystopian, version of social science futures. Mike Savage and Roger Burrows' (2007) account of the 'coming crisis of empirical sociology' has proven an influential vision of the academic near future concerned with the multiple transactions of a global corporate digital age. Pointing to the wealth of data generated through mundane everyday transactions, and that this exists behind a paywall and is largely inaccessible to academic researchers (and the people whose actions, often purchases, constitute the data), sociology is seen as unable to compete. If we are to avoid these limited visions for social science futures, however, a much richer archival imaginary is needed.

In making this point, I also want to point to another site of archival research, which does occupy some space in the methodological literature. This is the growth in genealogical research, particularly the practice of family history commonly examined as a site of kin-making, identity and belonging. However, only rarely is this approached as a popular *research* practice (Gilchrist *et al.*, 2015) and specifically of *archival* research, and as such it surely ought to interest those exploring everyday practices and cultures of participation. Yet the present impoverished social science archival imaginary means that all this activity is primarily seen as about family and kinship, and not as a site of everyday archival research. To repeat Verran's (1998: 238) point, imaginaries are centrally about 'a politics of what there is, and who/what can know it'. Paying attention to genealogy and community history as sites of everyday archival research has the potential to change understanding of what social science is, who does it and where it happens.

In this chapter I have pointed to different possibilities for the social sciences, through pointing to a long history – and flourishing present – of community history and genealogical research, and in particular community archives and research practices. Against the exponential accumulation of digital data, I point to other sites of data production and research practice. While big data triumphs with the sheer quantity of data generated through financial and other transactions, community archives and family history research are rich sites of archiving and archival research and they offer a fertile site for refiguring the archival imaginary.

I have drawn on Feminist Webs in this chapter as both a particular kind of archive and one located in a wider genealogy of popular archival practices, including community archives and family history projects. Through tracing the constitution of Feminist Webs as a boundary object and its connections with other archival projects which straddle the boundaries of activism and academia (Verran, 1998; Cvetkovich, 2003; Benson and Nagar, 2006; Eichhorn, 2010, 2013; Jolly *et al.*, 2012), this chapter has proposed a reconfiguring of the social science archival imaginary, in which community archives come into view, not as oppositional to other more formal archives but rather as bound together in a genealogical web.

The chapter has emphasised the possibilities of research in community archives – and crucially has also stressed how this focus on the creation of the archive highlights the ways in which we can attend to the archive as process. The chapter has relatedly offered a range of conceptual and methodological tools for understanding the work of community archives and how they relate to the communities they gather around them, as well as to more formal archives and archival practices – boundary objects, boundary infrastructures, archival webs, archival times and genealogies. I have also suggested that paying attention to community archiving and its complicated histories and relationships, both with the archival profession and with academic research, can help refigure and reweave the limits of existing social science archival imaginaries.

Acknowledgements: Many thanks to Ali Hanbury and Joan Haran for comments on an earlier draft and to Feminist Webbers from whom I have learned so much, including Janet Batsleer, Sally Carr MBE, Maggie Cole, Heather Davidson, H. Gibson, Lily Grey, Ali Hanbury, Claire Holmes, Sophie Lau, Amelia Lee, Damien Massey, Neelum Mehmood, Omena Osivwemu, Hebe Phillips, Rachel Roantree, Alison Ronan – and many others.

Interlude

The discussion in Chapter 5 has opened up the process and activities that go into the making of archives and collections and provided a range of methodological tools for engaging with this. In doing so, two constants across our individually written chapters have been highlighted. The first is the agentic presence of the archival researcher (indeed, all researchers) in thinking, deciding, collecting, selecting and making, and to which can be added writing and reading, designing, analysing and interpreting. All the chapters engage with this active presence and show not only the hows and whys but also the ways this plays out in the processes and also concerning the products of archival research. The second is that archives are made, not found. And regarding the collections discussed across Chapters 2–5, it should be noted that these all had their origins as 'community' archives of different kinds.

These and other key points across our book are now picked up in Chapter 6 and the epilogue. Together, they square the circle by returning discussion to common ground and synergies – and also to differences and departures.

6 The beginning in the ending
Reassembling archival practices

The trace and the craft

'What is the use of history?' Marc Bloch (1991 [1954]: 3) asked in the first line of *The Historian's Craft*, his famous book left unfinished when he was executed in 1944 by the Nazis. In raising questions around historical facts, evidence and interpretation, Bloch brought forward the notion of the trace, that which has been left over from earlier periods and enables the craft of writing about the past. Readers of the English translation of Bloch's book will find that his notion of '*la trace*' has been rendered there as 'track', in the sense of a track of footprints. The same term, '*la trace*', in Derrida's work has been translated by Gayatri Chakravorty Spivak as 'trace' because of its similarity with the English word, although as she also notes in her translator's preface to Derrida's (1974: xvii) *Of Grammatology*, 'the French word carries strong implications of track'. Therefore, following Spivak, we have opted for 'trace' in relation to Bloch's work as this better carries the conceptualisation of *la trace* as he uses it and also as the term has been deployed in the archival turn subsequently.

Taking the trace as a central concept in Bloch's reflections concerning the how of historical method, he drew parallels between the writing of history and sociological analytics and commented that 'the sociological school... has taught us to analyse more profoundly, to grasp our problems more firmly, and even, I dare say, to think less shoddily' (Bloch, 1991 [1954]: 15). His book is in itself a trace, the trace of an intellectual's struggle to go on thinking and creating in the midst of a world disaster, when imprisoned and without access to a library or archive, and it is 'the memorandum of a craftsman... the notebook of a journeyman' (19). That is, it is a methodology text.

It goes without saying that methodology should not be collapsed into method. It is rather a set of ideas and practices, adding up to a framework, which emerges from situated theoretical perspectives and maps the exploration of specific research questions and problems. It is our shared way of seeing methodology as embedded in overall epistemological concerns and theoretical orientations that has provided the impetus for this book and the methodological strategies deployed in each chapter. Questions around how to map and write the archive were raised in Chapter 2; rhythms were discussed as a means of analysing the experience of archival research in Chapter 3; problematising what it means to read the archive was the focus of Chapter 4; while the idea of re-imagining the archive was the frame for Chapter 5.

Complex and situated as they are, methodologies still include methods, and the key argument that runs like a red thread throughout the book is that methods should be appropriate to methodologies, rather than treated as a pick and mix add-on. 'Archigraphics' was thus presented as a methodological framework regarding methods for writing the archive in Chapter 2; narrative methods were deployed in Chapter 3; reverse temporalities as a method for reading the archive were discussed in Chapter 4; and configuring the archive as a boundary object was an approach considered in Chapter 5. If we were to present our approaches to archival research as verbs, then, our methods might be presented as writing, feeling, reading and remaking the archive, with all of these applying to all four chapters.

In this light, is there 'an' archival methodology after all, something that stands over and harnesses the differences of our different approaches? Our reflections on how we have worked in diverse archives in different parts of the world suggest that there is, or at least there should be, an archival methodology, so long as this is taken not as a closed framework but rather as an open process, a toolbox for the craft of finding, recognising and reassembling traces, something which brings us full circle to Bloch. Although the trace is the only way 'for returning through time [via] the materials provided by past generations', nonetheless not all traces 'lend themselves equally well to this evocation of the past' (Bloch, 1991 [1954]: 57). This is where the skills of the craft of archival research become important: we need to know and practise how to discern, assemble, read and rewrite and make interpretive meaning of the traces, while being aware of their epistemological possibilities and also their limitations. As Bloch put it, it is upon traces that 'the methods of observation remain almost uniformly dependent' (78).

Commenting on Bloch's approach to history as a reassemblage of traces, Paul Ricoeur (1998: 23) noted appreciatively that Bloch had shown that 'the historian's apparent bondage of never being in the presence of his past object but only its trace by no means disqualifies history as science'. The notion of the trace as the fundament of all inquiries about the past has become part of the air that archival researchers breathe. Even when working with tangible sources such as transcripts of oral interviews or written documents, we are dealing with mere traces of the complex and visceral ways that such things were lived, told or written, and subsequently recorded in the researcher's notes or databases, transcriptions or digital photographs. And yet this acknowledgement of the impossibility of reaching 'the real', the aporias of representation and communication, and the fleeting meanings of language-in-use, does not reduce the validity of human and social sciences research generally, or archival research specifically. No researcher can be 'in the presence of his past object', as Ricoeur puts it; it is always their traces we grapple with, however seemingly close the proximity between the object, its representations and our engagements with these. In this last chapter of *The Archive Project*, a book about the craft of archival research, we take up Bloch's notion of the trace, which appears, although fleetingly, in all the earlier chapters to explore the question of 'what is the use of the archive', doing so from different angles and perspectives and with the focus on the part that the trace plays in this.

There are nothing but traces in archive documents and collections: things that hint at what has been left behind, and which more profoundly raise what has been forgotten, never recorded, or lost, or destroyed either intentionally or unintentionally. We are quite clear on this. The archive has consequently been conceptualised herein as an assemblage of faded presences and shadowy absences, a spatio-temporal matrix wherein the past is penetrated by and is also part of the present. This is a clear reminder that the traces that are still to be excavated are wider than the trace already encountered: there is an outside and a beyond, as well as undiscovered regions within, archival spaces. It is in this light that the trialectics of the archive become visible, by being configured as an institution, as a project, and as a process. What follows reflects upon this tripartite configuration, taking up threads that connect and also noting tensions between the different approaches.

More specifically, thinking about the archive as an institution returns to attention our different approaches to genealogies, genealogical analytics, and also to heterotopias and heterotopics, and archival imaginary and archival sensibility, initially raised in Chapter 1. All the chapters in this book have followed different genealogical histories in tracing the origins and connections of their archival collections. They have also showed that, even as a power/knowledge institution, the archive is mapped on shifting grounds, its structures are unstable, and the relations that are deployed within it are labile and changing.

Taken as a project, the archive opens up space/time inquiries that follow different trajectories regarding configuration and rhythmanalysis. Focusing on the project of grappling with the world of archival documents, time becomes its central organisational axis. The surrounding spaces of the archive and the idea of listening to their rhythms, however, can be equally important in shaping the archival project.

In addition, the openness of the process engaged in has created a plane of consistency for different conceptualisations of the archival imaginary and the archival sensibility to come together. All four chapters have opened up different but mutually supporting processes in re-imagining the archival collections they have either worked with or created, including by bringing together an assemblage. In doing so, they have all addressed questions and issues concerning our shared archival sensibility in distinct and yet largely harmonious ways.

The archive as an institution

Throughout *The Archive Project*, we have mapped archives as institutions of power/knowledge relations, among other things drawing on Foucault's (1986) and Derrida's (1995) influential theorisations as well as the rich body of literature that has used their work. We have further considered community archives, as well as family archives and shoeboxes, photograph albums and so on. But what are the effects of such a multi-faceted approach, given that the archive is an ambiguous institution and has become even more complicated with the advent of digitisation, as commented on across our chapters? What we are dealing with, when entering 'archival discourse', is a playing field inhabited by two often antagonistic forces: 'the conflation of libraries, museums and archives', on the one hand, and on the other, 'the inflation of the term "archive", which has become a kind of loose signifier for a disparate set of concepts' (Manoff, 2004: 10). It is by reference to recognising this field of contending forces that we have approached the archive as an institution, doing so from different angles and contributing to archival discourse by adding our own archival formations.

In this light, Chapter 2 made a strategic decision from its outset to focus on 'the archive' in an institutional sense, to explore how archival research on race and racism in such places can be operationalised while also recognising the wider discourse and debates marking this field of competing forces. It associates the black box aspects of such research with the vast inflations of the term 'archive' as the source of the mystification and panic experienced by many beginning researchers. As a counter, it has instead explored the grounded practices involved in making new knowledges as a challenge to the power/knowledge configuration of the archive-as-law.

While situating archival research in a well-known knowledge institution, the New York Public Library, Chapter 3 has shown that the archives of memory of women garment workers went beyond the institution's walls, boxes and microfilm reels. The archive was thus extended not only into the NYPL's wider spaces and activities, such as the 'Lunch Hour in NYC' exhibition', but also in the streets of the New York fashion district, as well as the buildings that still carry the scars and stains of the garment industry's bloody past.

In discussing the Mass Observation Archive and the *Olive Schreiner Letters Online*, Chapter 4 has explored radical archive projects that have deliberately gathered everyday documents of life around particular political and social concerns, disrupting conventional ideas of what should be collected and archived. It adds to this by providing a methodology attuned to temporality, and like other chapters shows how productive it can be using concepts to work out from a body of traces rather than looking in at archival research through the lens of its mythologies.

Chapter 5 has also shown that, whereas once the archive was viewed as a site of institutional power, now community groups like Feminist Webs are claiming their place in history by 'occupying the archive'. This has involved not only entering archival spaces but also creating archives; not only working against the archive but working with archivists and archiving standards to secure a new archive.

It is worth remembering at this point the observation made in the interlude at the end of Chapter 5, that the collections we have discussed in detail, although now mainly located in institutional archives, all had their origins as 'community' archives of one kind or another. We would also make the further observation that the majority of archival collections, certainly in the Anglophone context, have similarly diverse origins. However, many researchers work in the archives of the state and other large governmental or powerful corporate entities, or combine this with other archival environments, and there are three helpful comments to make around this. The first is that it has been the focus on, and indeed preoccupation with, state and juridical archives to the exclusion of others that has led the 'power of the archive' view discussed in Chapter 1. Indeed, in some cases the impression is given of not realising that other kinds of archives exist, with generalisations made that do not hold true in other kinds of archives. The second is that we can say with some certainty from our collective experiences that the skills and practices and methodologies we have provided are transferable ones that work just as well across the range of different archives, for it has been by working across the range that we have honed them. The third is that while distinctions between different kinds of archives and collections can be useful, mapping this onto state and governmental archives versus others helps perpetuate the mythologising around the former that has been a factor in inhibiting the development of more realistic archival research methodologies.

In thinking about the archive as an institution, related questions arise about the origin and purpose of its foundation, the mode of its organisation and accessibility, the ways it is funded, preserved and maintained, and last but not least the role of its subjects and figures. It is the latter that we now consider by exploring the question, 'what is an archivist?'

'The archivist' is principally considered here as a professional whose role is to collect, organise, preserve and provide access to archival documents. Some archivists are working researchers in various fields in history and the social sciences. In addition, archivists can be amateurs, family members, enthusiasts and people who want to preserve the history of organisations, causes, families or publicly significant figures. Such collectors, assemblers and archivists will create their own 'other archive', and they have been encountered in a number of chapters: Joan Findlay organised the Findlay family papers, Kate and Dave Forbes junior put together the Forbes Family collection, Fannia Mary Cohn and Rose Pesotta reassembled their own personal papers, Mass Observation was formed by three young political radicals, while a group of feminist activists brought Feminist Webs into being. In thinking about the intricacies involved, Chapter 4 points out that the

Olive Schreiner Letters Project team researched Schreiner's letters in three continents to produce transcriptions assembled in an online, searchable meta-repository and to provide an editorial apparatus around these, thereby combining the activities of researchers, editors and archivists.

Considered as professionals and within institutional settings such as museums, state archives or libraries, archivists have often been portrayed either as neutral and objective figures who receive records then pass them to researchers or other interested parties, or as grey controlling figures who constrain or prevent research and enshrine selectivity and elitism. Alongside this, Chapter 2 notes that, bucking the stereotype, archivists can also brave institutional restrictions and support dissident academics. In the light of such split views of 'what is an archivist', we are interested in the institutional limitations and constraints that create the conditions of possibility for the archivist's work, as well as the effects of these upon the theory and praxis of archival research. In doing so, we shall explore 'the archivist function' along the lines of 'the author function' that Foucault (1972) has famously theorised.

In borrowing and extending this Foucauldian notion, the archivist function needs to be considered in the light of the social, material and cultural conditions that underpin the institutional foundation and organisation of archives. Here questions are raised about how collections are inherited, created and maintained, as well as wider questions regarding the position of a specific archive or library within the wider power/knowledge relations of the nations and states and countries they are embedded in. The archivist function is complex and many-sided, with a paradox at its heart, that its management and placing of records and collections both makes these findable and available and also governs and shapes access (from the archivists' perspective see, for example, contributors to Craven, 2008; McKemmish et al., 2005).

As Joan Schwartz and Terry Cook (2002: 1) have pithily summarised it, 'Through archives, the past is controlled. Certain stories are privileged and others marginalized. And archivists are an integral part of this story-telling'. Through the various positions that archivists inhabit in cultural institutions such as libraries, museums and archives, they inevitably become the gatekeepers of how knowledge is produced . . . 'in the pursuit of their professional responsibilities, archivists – as keepers of archives – wield power over those very records central to memory and identity formation through active management of records before they come to archives, their appraisal and selection as archives, and afterwards their constantly evolving description, preservation, and use' (Schwartz and Cook, 2002: 2).

Archives and archivists are significant components in an incessant cycle of power/knowledge relations. There is no doubt about it. And this should not be denied or hidden behind a screen of professional integrity: 'Power recognised becomes power that can be questioned, made accountable, and opened to transparent dialogue and enriched understanding' (Schwartz and Cook, 2002: 2). But – and it is an important but – what is lacking in Schwartz and Cook's analysis is the recognition that it is not only archivists who are entangled in this field of power/knowledge relations but archival researchers too, as players and major gatekeepers in the knowledge production process, and that ratios of power are complicated and can change. Relatedly, what needs to be recalled here from discussions in Chapters 2 and 3 particularly is that archives are not monolithic but rather heterotopic sites, wherein different spaces, opportunities and subjectivities emerge and interact. Archivists and archival researchers are both entangled in this matrix of power/knowledge relations, inhabiting different but interrelated positions in the distribution and circulation of power/knowledge within the archive and beyond.

At the same time, while we recognise that, in collecting, organising, assessing and preserving archival documents, the researcher inevitably takes on some aspects of the archivist function, there are important differences between the archivist as a professional and the archivist as a researcher. While the professional archivist mostly works within the limitations of the institution, the researcher with their 'archive of the other archive', discussed in Chapter 2, works in the interface between the traces and the archive. This is not to say that the researcher is unconstrained by discursive limitations and institutional structures – we all are, in different ways and configurations. The point here, however, is that the figures of the researcher as archivist, and the archivist as researcher, emerge from different fields of action involving different dynamics that need to be understood and mapped in their specificity. Such dynamics are difficult to manage, and on both sides, not least because many professional archivists have well-founded stories to tell of researcher behaviour, in/competence and so on, including misreadings and misuses of source materials. 'Access' brings troubles on both sides of the relationship, then.

Archivists – be they researchers, professionals, activists, enthusiasts or family historians – can be constrained within the bureaucratic, material and political conditions shaping their position and role, but as noted earlier they can also transgress institutional boundaries and limitations. Throughout the book, we have problematised rigid distinctions, troubling boundaries in terms of the creation of meta-archives or the 'other archive'. At the same time, we have shown that researchers and archivists can have conflicting interests and facilitate or frustrate each other's work. Such tensions depend in part upon geopolitical conditions, diverse cultures and colonial and metropolitan histories, which are here to stay. It is also crucial to recognise the power of classification and the role of cataloguing practices that impact not only on what enters but also on what can be found or is lost in an archive. In reflecting upon archival practices, Arnold Hunt, a curator at the British Library, has written: 'As a curator myself, I'm intrigued by the ways that the physical organisation of archives can affect – and sometimes obstruct – their use by historians. As the old saying goes: where do you hide a leaf? In a forest. Where do

you hide a document? In an archive' (www.cam.ac.uk/research/discussion/
qa-how-archives-make-history). It is in this context that across all our
chapters we have raised the question of, 'what is a collection?'

What brought together collections in the past was a theme, an organisation or a person around which sources and data were gathered, either before
they were deposited in a library or an archive, or after. Chapter 2 explores,
among other things, the archive of a large dispersed family involved in many
economic activities that was assembled by family members and which sits
on the boundaries of being a family collection and an organisational one.
As Chapter 3 notes, Tamboukou went to one archive to read Rose Pesotta's
papers, and to another to work with Jeanne Bouvier's *fonds*. It is important here to note that the French notion of the 'fonds' is much more than a
mere collection of papers, usually around a figure; it rather reflects a much
more conceptual arrangement of documents, their contexts, as well as their
authorial and discursive relations (Eastwood, 1992). The concept originated
in France, when in 1841 archivists were asked to create *fonds*, that is 'to
unite all the deeds which come from a body, an establishment, a family, or
an individual' (Thibodeau, 1993: 256). Although initiated in France and
used primarily in Francophone and Soviet-influenced contexts, the concept
of the *fonds* has more widely influenced the idea of creating collections of
documents that are 'naturally' and/or 'originally' accumulated around a
theme, a country, an organisation or a person more widely. But it goes without saying that concepts such as 'origins' or 'natural accumulation' have
been highly interrogated in archival discourse well before the advent of the
digital turn, and particularly so in its wake. Within current problematics,
the creation of *fonds* fleshes out the way documents connect within a collection, promoting their indexical qualities and inevitably bringing forward
hierarchical orderings in the catalogues and beyond, although digital environments with their multiple orders, relationships and contexts challenge a
hierarchical *fonds*-like approach. The initiator of the *fonds* is also of interest
here, with the archivist function already discussed above, while *fonds* as an
analytical mode of ordering documents has opened up questions around
boundaries and linkages that keep recurring.

But in addition to structural, analytical and conceptual decisions and
activities, collections have been brought together through commercial
routes, the buying and selling of objects and writings of the famous. It was
this, for instance, that led some of Olive Schreiner's letters to be located in
particular collections, although many more were collected and donated by
family, friends and feminist colleagues. As Chapter 4 observes, some collections are headed 'Olive Schreiner', but more often her letters are small
components within other sometimes very large collections, such as the
Alfred Milner papers in Oxford, the Jan Smuts collection in Pretoria, the
Aletta Jacobs archive in Amsterdam and so on. The assemblage and publication of an e-edition of her complete letters was intended both to support Schreiner scholarship by making available transcripts of the complete

corpora traversing such boundaries and to shape readership and usage in specific ways. Foremost here was organising the meta-archive and its searching and finding aids in such a way that users are always returned to whole letters rather than to particular passages in them, and also organising the meta-data and editorial apparatus surrounding the complete letters so as always to return a researcher to the letters as components within collections and collections in particular archives.

Chapter 5 has recounted the unannounced arrival of materials without apparent provenance in the Feminist Webs archive, as well as finding the archive had been moved from its original squatted office to a different location. This was a rather chaotic move, with things literally thrown about on the floor and mixed up with another collection of books and papers. In reassembling the archive, Moore and her colleagues had to sift through everything and make rather random decisions about what they thought belonged in Feminist Webs and what should go to other (youth work) collections.

But no matter how it has been brought together, a constitutive component of a collection is the physical proximity of its sources and documents, as well as its particular organisation in files and boxes. With the advent of digitisation, however, the aspect of proximity is troubled and in some circumstances seemingly dissolved. Digital collections can bring together versions of documents from diverse archives around the world, and as flagged up across our chapters, there are consequences of these new technologies, both ontological and epistemological. As Julia Flanders (2014: 166), among other digital humanities scholars, has commented, 'we now understand a collection as a predominantly informational construct', an approach that radically changes what a collection is in an ontological sense and what it can do. However, while a digital collection seems to offer multiple possibilities for exploration and research, its tools necessitate layers of technological interventions that are tacit yet powerful, imposing their own systems governing how a collection is conceived and used, something that has been analysed within the framework of 'cultural assemblage' regarding the Schreiner letters (Stanley *et al.*, 2013a).

Perhaps surprisingly, few digital collections are open about the technologies of interpretation they have created and imposed, although new discussions have started emerging in the field (Manoff, 2015). A counter-example explored in Chapter 4 is Schreiner's letters, where how texts are transcribed and marked up for e-publication through to the analysis and interpretation of particular texts is provided and readers are explicitly invited to reflect upon the collection. Such interpretational analytics inform good practice in other archiving projects too, shown in Chapter 5 with the Feminist Webs archive containing materials about the process of making this archive and related projects, including texts, photographs and film, among others. Also, the wider Whites Writing Whiteness project, of which Chapter 2 explores a small part, is assembling a digital set of data that includes within its remit letters, maps, memoirs, wills, diaries, inventories, photographs, tallies, receipts and so forth.

While the space of physical collections was previously demarcated and limited, in the digital context there are no longer clear boundaries between what 'belongs' to a collection or not, when a researcher 'enters' an archival space and 'exits' from it. There are interesting questions arising from this virtual experience of transgressing boundaries: 'how do the boundedness and internal cohesion of a collection help to define its intellectual purpose?... who experiences it?... for whom is the collection modelled?' (Flanders, 2014: 168–9). In addition, we need to ask what the effects of boundlessness might be in terms of archival ethics and responsibility towards the living and the dead. There are important questions here to be addressed and new aporias and problems are opened up as digitisation expands and transposes what used to be viewed as the archival researcher's craft. We shall return to the idea and reality of going digital in the epilogue and provide some final reflections.

All chapters in this book have discussed exemplars of working with different kinds of documents and different types of collections, including the process of creating some new ones, both physical and digital. We now move on to reassemble these diverse practices, through focusing on the second configuration, that of the archive as a project.

The archive as a project

In reflecting upon the function of classification and cataloguing as tacit practices that impact on what we can find out and how, Foucault's (2000: xv) famous opening to *The Order of Things*, where he reads a passage from Borges and laughs at 'the ordered surfaces and all the planes with which we are accustomed to tame the wild profusion of existing things', inevitably comes to mind. Archival documents can definitely be wild things that archivists need to tame, to order, label, file and box, in the process creating a system of taxonomy and classification that all future researchers are required to decipher, understand and work with. The politics of classification and the politics of knowledge are thus inextricably interwoven, decisively shaping every archival research project.

Thinking with Foucault about the power/knowledge relations of the archival project, the genealogical questions and archaeological practices presented and discussed particularly in Chapters 3 and 5 come into play. In this light, how important is provenance (how a document or a collection was assembled, when and by whom, and how it ended up in the particular archival location it has) and in what ways does it shape understandings of contents and collections? Archival ordering does not emerge out of the blue: it is usually underpinned by pre-classification practices, which have often conditioned the very existence or formation of a collection, for it has been standard practice among professional archivists for many decades now that the original order of a collection on arrival is preserved and embedded in collection inventorising (Wisser, 2011).

But it is also not unusual that the details of provenance are less than fully known, particularly perhaps when archival materials are purchased from collectors or auction-houses, but sometimes concerning donations, too. Generally, archives will systematically record dates of purchase/donation, from whom and where, and such other information as is available. For example, as Chapter 2 comments, the Cory Library in Grahamstown, like some other archives worldwide, has kept detailed records of every incoming item from when it was founded. Also most other archives, even if they do not have a 'book of lore' in this way, will have a file of information per collection that researchers can access on request. However, some archives have longer and more unsettled histories, with such information only patchily available, as is clear from Feminist Webs in Chapter 5. Exceptionally, the codified information about provenance may have been entirely lost. This may not sound particularly important, but in fact provenance can often provide important information vital to analysis and interpretation. In Chapter 3, for instance, Tamboukou has discussed how knowing that both Cohn and Pesotta organised the papers that they bequeathed to the NYPL had an effect on how she read the selections, deselections, presences and absences of these particular collections. Similarly, everything that Chapter 2 writes about has to take into account the prior assemblage of the Forbes family/business papers by the Forbes themselves. Indeed, the whole point of the wider Whites Writing Whiteness project is that it is precisely the representational practices engaged in by white people that point to complexities in how the racial order was seen and these are therefore an important analytic focus.

Another important question that Foucault urges us to consider is, why is it necessary to understand how catalogues work and what are the effects of such understandings in analysis, interpretation and the multiple rewritings of research results? As noted in Chapter 2, a catalogue is a system of representation and it theorises/interprets the structure and reach of what is catalogued. It enables finding things – so long as one works and thinks in the framework or mind-set used by the catalogue compiler (as also with filing systems and indexes). A catalogue is consequently necessary, helpful, an imposition, to be interrogated and – metaphorically – to be burned. Regarding such matters, Chapter 3 considers the restrictions and limitations in narrative understanding while working with files entitled as 'letters sent' or 'letters received' and shows how microfilm enables an immediate reordering of the archive in 'letters to and from significant others' or the synchronisation of letters within some significant years or months. Chapter 4, alternatively, discusses the making of a kind of self-built, purposive 'catalogue of diarists' which distilled relevant information from the pre-existing online database of Mass Observation diarists into something specifically useful for a particular archival project in conjunction with other finding aids. In Chapter 5, cataloguing Feminist Webs was shown as a process of reading and re-reading. Here perhaps the absence of a strict adherence to archival practices meant more time for reading. This is a reminder that, as Dorothy Sheridan (2000), formerly head archivist of the Mass Observation Archive, has commented, the archivist is the first user of archival documents. This raises the question, when the archivist is also a leading researcher, as with Sheridan: what does the archivist know from doing this? The question reminds us that knowledge is embodied not only in the archive but in the archivist function, too.

Related to the interpretive analytics of the catalogue is the question of the role that inventories and finding aids discussed in a number of chapters play in this. Chapter 2 details different styles of inventories and the ways their content and structure impact on the 'how and what' of the research carried out, so they should be seen as working documents which need to be revised in the light of a researcher's work on the collection or collections in question. In Chapter 3, Tamboukou discusses how the NYPL's inventory aids have facilitated archival research with women trades unionists in the garment industry, juxtaposing this with her early experiences of 'losing and finding' Clara Collet's diary in the Modern Records Centre at the University of Warwick.

A related question concerns why national registers are important. A national register of archives is a kind of meta-catalogue of all the collections held in the main archives of a country, although as Chapter 2 comments regarding the UK's National Register of Archives and the wider Access to Archives (A2A) mega-list from across the UK, this provides information about connected collections in other countries, too. There are issues here regarding which people, organisations and collections are included and which are not, with the emphasis on state, government, local government, large public libraries, universities and colleges. There are alternative collections of archives, such as the archive directory maintained by the Community Heritage and Archive Group, or AIM 25, an online gateway to archives in London and the M25 area (www.aim25.ac.uk). However, helpful though such registers can be, and just as with catalogues, they fix boundaries of inclusion and exclusion and classify around a particular mind-set, and this needs to be kept in mind when using them. These search engines/hubs certainly provide previously unparalleled tools for the researcher, but issues arise concerning both what should be done about the material that isn't there and how the researcher can find out about this. Relatedly, such resources are not always clear about what they include and what they do not. More worryingly, are we perhaps now in a situation where, if an archive is not on A2A or similar facilities, it does not really exist for most researchers because the skills of other ways of finding relevant sources are being lost?

As shown throughout *The Archive Project*, exploring and excavating the multi-levelled features of archival practice and archival research has important epistemological, methodological and ethical effects regarding how we understand how knowledge is produced and circulated, with this in turn raising further questions around relationality, context and boundaries. All of these are important in mapping any archival project. In addressing them as we have done, by drawing on our experiences of doing archival research in diverse archives and collections, we have pointed to the blurred boundaries between institutions and projects, archivists and researchers, rules and practices. But acknowledging the porous character of boundaries, as well as the possibility of productively crossing and re-crossing them, does not mean that the archival structuring side of this can be neglected or erased. Archival documents are the objects of inquiry, after all: they need finding, access, attention, smart methodologies and nuanced theoretical and epistemological frameworks to be managed, decoded, read, understood and rewritten. Throughout, we have argued that as archival researchers we need to throw light on our practices, instead of clouding, mystifying or vanishing them, including through the claimed magic of serendipity and chance. Without denying the profound pleasure of finding something precious or unexpected, we have also insisted that archival encounters involve a studious and many-layered process of hard graft, which brings us to the last configuration of the tripartite schema introduced at the start of the chapter.

The archive as a process

What is the difference between a project and a process? Conceived as a project, archival research has concrete plans, aims and objectives that need to be designed, practised, managed and finally delivered on and circulated. As a process, however, archival research is labile and open, inviting the researcher not only to deliver but also, and perhaps more importantly, to throw herself or himself into the adventure of ideas, the excitement of uncovering, learning, knowing and understanding. Conceptualising this as a never-ending process does not mean downplaying the importance of findings or outcomes produced at any one point in time, but rather indicates that there is little that is definitive about researching the past (or indeed the present). There are rather new processes for experimentation and knowledge-making that are repeatedly put in motion as times and understandings change.

In this sense, opening up processes and knowledges is the foundational aim and product of archival research, as shown in all chapters in *The Archive Project*. Chapter 2, for instance, explores a range of archival research practices, and a research process in which these fit together, and this includes analysis and interpretation as part of process and refuses any easy product/process distinction. Chapter 3 emphasises that analysis always starts in the archive and it is in the process of doing archival research that new projects emerge. Chapter 4 plays with process, subverting the usual chronological order of archival research to see what can be understood by working through data backwards. It unpacks the interpretive implications of this, showing the analytical connections between project, process and product.

In Chapter 5, the commitments of participatory feminist youth work meant that involving young women in youth groups and youth workers, artists and feminist activists of all ages, was central. Thus process was always in the foreground when creating the Feminist Webs archive as well as in the production of collaborative outputs such as *Femzine* and *The Exciting Life of Being a Woman* (Feminist Webs, 2012).

It is around understanding archival research as an open process that we provide our concluding thoughts and suggestions, as a tentative manifesto for doing archival research under the banner of archival sensibility. Here we are aware of writing this from the situated position of feminist politics, noted in Chapter 1. In this context, how do we understand archival sensibility and how has it unfolded in our individual research practices?

Archival sensibility, relational ethics

Throughout this book we have highlighted the fact that we do not consider archival documents as a backcloth to the researcher's discourse, but rather as a formative component of this. It is for this reason that versions of many such documents have been included across its chapters. We need to point to the source and let it guide our analysis and understanding. Lines from archival sources, the traces of traces, are not captions of our conceptual images nor illustrations of what we have already decided to say or write, but are rather taken from the records of past lives and events and are variously refractory, dull, difficult, tantalising, boring, disturbing, puzzling, fragmentary, incomplete – and to be respected.

Archival documents are thus taken as crystallisations of processes – the processes of 'then', meeting the processes of 'now', and forming the 'now/past', as discussed in Chapter 2. In this sense they have an ontological specificity, a life that started before they were deposited in an archive and one that will continue in their future circulation through rewritings and transpositions of them. The fact that only traces, fragments, can be found in an archive does not mean that archival researchers should perpetuate their fragmentation, by scattering and dispersing them even more in the investigations we make, the interpretations we provide and the ways we write. On the contrary, once we are confronted with the fragments and fissures of lives and events, we take on epistemological and ethical responsibility for offering a design, a pattern that has a meaning, at the same time facilitating possibilities for the creation of different meanings: the other archive, the other understanding and interpretation.

Moreover, once our research design has begun to take shape, its structures and limits can be explored. What are the indexical knowledges (Garfinkel, 1967) drawn on to devise the design? What ramifications does this have for sense-making and its boundaries? Are there themes and patterns that are better understood by deploying this design and within what limitations? What does the design prevent us from seeing, doing? There are examples across all the chapters in *The Archive Project*. Chapter 2, for instance, has built in suggestions for stopping, sitting, thinking and scribbling notes in a process of reflection, and indicates that the research it details takes somewhat different forms in other aspects of the wider Whites Writing Whiteness project. Chapter 3 discusses how the well-rehearsed private/public schema did not work very well with Pesotta's supposedly 'private self' of the diaries or 'social self' of the letters; it was rather in her creative writings that understandings about the constitution of the self could dimly be discerned.

Developing out of an interpretation of work where time and temporality appear as key analytical threads, Chapter 4 has discussed benefits and drawbacks of using these as structuring devices in reading Mass Observation's wartime diaries, and how they impinge too on reading and making sense of Olive Schreiner's letters. It has shown that in deploying the backwards sampling frame the chapter discusses, researchers' interpretive acts are not so neatly organised, with complicated interconnections made across times in the process of interpretation. In addition, Chapter 5 demonstrates how pauses between funding applications, as well as the need to tailor applications to funding streams, have impacted the rhythms of Feminist Webs, as well as how these pauses have provided important down-time between funded activities to carry on the actual work of archiving, which has tended to fall outside the remit of much youth work funding.

In all this, we place relationality at the heart of archival sensibility, in exploring multifarious connections between archival documents, events and persons, discourses and practices, histories and geographies, other spaces and different temporalities. Most significantly, it is on a relational plane that the ethics of archival research unfold. As noted in earlier chapters, the people, events and situations of our archival projects, while belonging to that vast realm of the past, are nonetheless full of life and continuing significance for us. As we have the privilege of exploring the matters discussed across *The Archive Project*, so we are fully aware of our ethical responsibility to honour the trace and to represent past lives and circumstances as imbricated with meaning, no matter that this meaning is always already disputed and negotiated, and also open to further layers of understanding and interpretation.

Epilogue

Niamh Moore, Andrea Salter, Liz Stanley and Maria Tamboukou

This epilogue is where we bid adieu to readers. We do so with open-ended thoughts on some matters touched on elsewhere in the book but which are hinted at or taken for granted, as background to the foreground concern of its composing chapters. We commence, as is right and proper, with readers, the archive and the data, to provide some collective last thoughts about the things that have driven our concern to configure *The Archive Project* in the ways we have. We then move to some individually authored observations and clarifications, concluding with departures and what each of us is doing 'after the book'.

Readers, the archive and the data

Readers

'Dear Readers' is the best way to open these comments, for *The Archive Project* was conceived, designed and written with the needs of potential readers in mind. Archival research, together with re/reading and re/writing and documentary analysis, is among the few aspects of method and methodology that remain mysterious because there are still few detailed accounts of a 'how to' kind which are joined up with relevant theory and a clear sense of the core conceptual issues in this area of social inquiry. Opening the black box and relating what happens inside to important theoretical ideas and a deep appreciation of foundational conceptual issues has been our driving concern.

We hope, dear Readers, that as a result the practical skills, activities and tools involved can be seen more clearly, the importance of taken-for-granted skills in organising, writing and reading at their heart better appreciated, the feelings and entanglements that infuse the analysis and interpretation of research materials realised, the insights that arise from different ways of ordering archival inquiries grasped, the importance of who and where the archival researcher is situated better understood, the centrality of process accepted. We also hope that recognition of the actually blurry line between collector, archivist, researcher, author and reader – both now, in the midst of the archival turn, and back then when collections originated – becomes widespread and over-simple distinctions are rejected.

The archive

In a very real sense, the whole of this book has been an exposition of our collective and individual ideas about the archive and the archival turn, and there is no need to repeat in summary what has already been explained in detail in its unfolding contents. Instead, we want to recognise another important blurry line in addition to that involving the collector/archivist/researcher/writer/reader. This second one is often lost sight of in archival turn literature, while our chapters place it firmly on the agenda for consideration, as we commented in Chapter 6.

It is that *all* of the collections that our individual chapters are concerned with started out as 'community archives', the archives of smaller or larger, more or less formal, communities of interest, including of a family (Forbes), a trades union (women garment workers), a radical social research organisation (Mass Observation) and a close-knit epistolary network (Schreiner), as well as of Feminist Webs. All except the latter are now part of the formal archives system, including with Mass Observation having a purpose-designed archival presence. Ironically given its origins, because of funding issues, the barriers to research use in terms of permissions and possible costs are higher for Mass Observation and similar bodies, and lower for collections in some but not all state and public archives. (For a discussion of some more general aspects of this, see www.theguardian.com/higher-education-network/blog/2013/may/23/history-research-costs-archive-fees#comment-23790432.) This raises the issue of commercialisation and its effects. It also raises the question of whether there might be ways to future-proof community and alternative archives so that, while they may become – and want to become – part of formal systems, the more radical participatory urges that helped initiate them can be built-in and non-eradicable. We see this as an important task for further consideration, for it is clearly crucial to opening up archives and repositioning and empowering readers and users of archival materials, important concerns for all of us.

The data

Big/numbers, small/words? Let's think beyond tired old binaries! It is sometimes assumed that documents are just about words, are always small-scale, and must be analysed qualitatively, although this is not necessarily so. In fact, in archival research, the more usual conjunction is 'words/big'. However, as the preceding discussion has shown, the traces that remain can be of all kinds, including the numerical, the visual and the material, and also the large-scale. Consequently, the ideas and arguments we have discussed are highly relevant to archived statistical data and the secondary analysis of both quantitative and qualitative social science research, too (Moore,

2007b; Stanley and Dampier, 2009). Relatedly, the 'big data' trend in social research raises some key issues concerning archiving and re-use of such data and how these should be conceptualised (for example, Halford *et al.*, 2013), and this can be usefully drawn on. In addition, we are clear that some big data research would benefit from greater awareness of the methodological issues involved and discussions about these in the archival turn literature.

Underpinning our discussion about the trace and archival data is the fact that many aspects of archival research have 'gone digital' and digitisation continues to make important differences. Of course, personal photocopies made of a part and sometimes all of a collection were possible in the past and became components of many 'archives of the other archive'. However, it was difficult to share or manipulate these records in the way this is possible now with digitised images of objects and collections. Given our collective experience and the methods described, the digital is one of the themes that runs right through the book, with every chapter referencing the changes and new possibilities afforded. In Chapter 1, we raised a number of important points about digitisation and return to the topic here for final reflection, now that readers can see how we have responded to them in the details of our chapters.

The seduction effect and the tendency to treat digital forms as though real, in the sense of being the thing itself that they are actually representations of (in fact, representations of representations), indicates a worrying failure to think seriously about the ontological complexities that come with digitisation. Such worries are reinforced by sweeping references to the 'born digital', when such things are actually rooted in profound materialities. However, as noted earlier, collectively our main concern is focused on the loss of historical and archival relational contexts and their replacement by faux versions referencing other digital forms.

Nonetheless, these are concerns and not impediments, and as noted previously we are enthusiastic originators and proponents of digitisation in all its aspects. But. One 'but' here is that we reject seduction in favour of some hard thinking about the ontological complexities involved and ensure that these matters are discussed in our own working practices. The other 'but' is that things are still very much under change, and archives and sourcing research in them have in some respects been in the eye of the storm, and so in five or ten years' time we may well have different responses.

At this point, we now want to disaggregate and also complicate authorship by giving voice to our different approaches on a number of matters, including some differences of thinking, emphasis and focus between us.

Observations and clarifications

Scribbles

Andrea: Scribbles are everywhere in archival research. They include scribblings that have been curiously or mysteriously written by others and found on the archival materials we work with, as well as our own notes-to-self in research notebooks, typed up in project diaries, jotted on Post-it Notes. They may be bullet-point lists or spider diagrams, testing out intellectual connections between aspects of the research and its data. Often they ask questions or volunteer ideas and structures in transit without committing these to final thought status. Scribbles consequently make room for new ideas to come to mind and provide a snapshot of those already in progress.

Niamh: Scribbling can seem random, messy, written over, rewritten, crossed out, disposable, not neat, not tidy, not intended for ever. But throughout this book the importance of process has been highlighted, with scribbles too a crucial part of archival processes. They may appear to go round in circles, seeming not to go anywhere in particular, until a thought or a line breaks free and wanders off, gathering a sense of direction en route. Scribbling offers an evocative image of the entanglements and archigraphics of archival research. Finding someone else's scribbles is a powerful reminder that the supposedly fragile and ephemeral can sometimes persist, and scribbles may turn into something more enduring than perhaps anticipated.

Liz: Scribbles bring to mind *scritti politti*, political scribblings inscribed in graffiti and other transitory forms. Scribbles are the backcloth not only of archival research, as small asides to self that are memory aids and an essential part of research practices, but also of archigraphics. Scribbling fixes in the mind, so what is scribbled might never need to be returned to, its work done. Scribbling is what Barthes (1986: 11–12) calls an intransitive verb: there is a linguistic time specific to scribbling and its moment of writing; 'I' and 'you' become conjoined, for scribbles are in fact notes to self; and also scribbling is never fixed, always up for revision.

Maria: Scribbles leave traces of moments of thought, ideas that come up in the archive or when thinking about it, while our mind is still preoccupied with the documents we have read during the day. They can as well become redundant or obsolete, material for the writer's desk bin. Scribbles can also be the beginnings of more articulate fieldnotes, or the abstract of a paper to be written, or even the idea for a book.

Spectrums

Andrea: Working with colleagues on archival research projects means learning how to balance and operationalise sometimes different and sometimes similar conceptual stances, including handling the relationship that exists between the here and now and there and then aspects of archival research, between the depths and surfaces it entails, and also managing the speeds at which work can and should take place. It also requires accommodating the working curves of others, to preserve the individual within the team. In team-based research projects, the rhythms of archival research are by necessity collaborative, and ideally work towards synchronising and harmonising our research and writing practices as the team works towards its common goal.

Maria: Feeling the rhythms of an archive and its collections is both a physical and intellectual process and cannot be separated as such. The researcher is entangled in the physical world of the archive in terms of its geographical location, but also enmeshed in the grey world of its documents, moving within and along different temporalities. An awareness of the researcher's entanglements in the archive does not mean that the focus is turned on the researcher him- or herself: it is the traces and what can be understood from them that archival research should be about if it is to have value as a methodological approach.

Liz: Organisation, strategies and the orderly scoping and mapping of collections do not preclude having depth to the detailed analysis of particular documents or other archival traces, nor prevent interpreting the deep connections between linked examples. Indeed, they do not just 'support' this in an ancillary way – they actively enable it because it is these orderly activities that provide the contextual knowledge essential to good interpretation. There is, then, no binary aspect to the iterative back and forth of surface and depth, for in research practice they are inseparable, two sides of a coin and so both surfaces at once.

Niamh: Funding and 'project time' can hugely impact the rhythm of archival work. Feminist Webs has had its own waves or cycles of activity, with dense work in the archive when there is a grant. Often with Feminist Webs this means taking the archive on tour to youth groups. Access, perhaps especially with volunteer-run archives, is difficult. Opening hours, or the lack of them, also impacts the rhythms of archives. Perhaps paradoxically, it is in the quieter times between funding that some of the work of maintaining the archive can happen.

Diffractions

Liz: Since late 2014 when writing actually started, 'it', aka 'the book', has stood plum centre to my working life, with other things eddying around it or bumping into it, then skeetering off in other directions. A Blog for Whites Writing Whiteness? Well, if it's on archival research. Do a book on epistolarity? No, there's 'it' to finish first. Conference to attend? Of course, if I just pop in the Bodleian. Supervision meetings with graduate students? Yes, around how to analyse documents. Pile of new books to read? Just Martha Cooley's *The Archivist*, thanks. Time off? Only little bits until 'it' is completed and dispatched.

Maria: I have always felt a little uneasy with the compulsion to be reflective, thinking that it was actually destroying the very purpose of reflexivity. This is how I ended up liking the idea of diffractions: both reflections and diffractions are optical metaphors, but if I look back at my research in archives, it has always been diffractions that I have worked with – Foucauldian insights interfering with feminist analytics, narrative approaches stumbling on the death of the subject, material rhythms running in parallel with intellectual intensities, striated academic spaces co-existing with imaginative freedom.

Andrea: On reflection, my chapter is about emplotting lines of diffraction, making sense of the eruptions or events that shift or propel research activity, which trails or also forges paths. The diffractions that mark the course of emergence from doctoral to post-doctoral studies and beyond involve both continuity and change simultaneously. They have been embedded in the structure of my working practices, and so have by definition a 'moving with the times' character. These contingent bends, twists and turns are ones that all beginning archival researchers face.

Niamh: The interference patterns of diffractive readings complicate archival temporalities. My passion for making feminist history came long before Feminist Webs, but involvement with Feminist Webs has reworked prior thinking. I am revisiting oral history interviews from the 1990s (for example, Moore, 2015) and working to create an online archive of these, inspired by what I have learned with Feminist Webs. This involves open source archival software, Omeka (www.omeka.org), which may subsequently be used to rework the Feminist Webs archive. The interferences/diffractions continue.

Palimpsests

Niamh: Archives, projects, books, 'zines, Post-its, scribbles, all layered over and between each other, making new connections through queer juxtapositions. With Feminist Webs, new conjunctions of feminist histories emerge through the weaving together of previous and current feminisms.

Liz: I see my chapter as through a glass, darkly, because overlaying traces of earlier projects, including other Whites Writing Whiteness collections, Olive Schreiner's letters and a lineage tracing back to my 1980s' work on the diaries of Hannah Cullwick, Emily Wilding Davison and her comrades in the UK's suffragette movement, gay and lesbian networks in 1880s' England, Mass Observation. But, the other side of palimpsest, there are new projects faintly prefigured too, possibilities that can't yet be pointed to with any certainty: a book on South Africa, 'race' and change, another on letters and epistolary theory, another on Schreiner's unpublished manuscripts... and better live for ever!

Andrea: Looking back over the archival projects I have worked on, there are overlaying aspects of earlier projects, seeds sown but not seen as such at the time, and later revisionings, rewritings, which gather together at the 'moment of research' to confirm or change the ending or 'horizon of expectation' they point to. The emergence of an archival palimpsest is halted when outputs are produced because these are a fly-in-amber moment when this apparently stays still. Where does palimpsest stop, and as researcher can I define its boundaries?

Maria: Archival research is a process of doing, learning and understanding, an ongoing becoming emerging after layers of actual experience mingle to create moments of concrescence and awareness. It was only at the end of my various archival expeditions over the years that I was able to look back and see a pattern of my already taken steps and movements. These patterns initially guided my next journey, until a new problem or impasse emerged and new trails had to be taken or old ones changed. In the end, a book about archival methods is always, already a palimpsest.

Differences and departures

Along with opening the black box of archival research so as to better explore methodology matters, we have sought to open up the processes constituting our individual and collective authorship of *The Archive Project*. There are large areas of agreement between us, in particular concerning the importance of methodology conceived in broad ways and of looking for synergies and overlaps rather than emphasising disagreements that in practice may turn out to be not so significant. Some points of disagreement were outlined in theoretical terms in Chapter 1; there are also differences of methodological choices, and in emphasis and focus, as represented in our individual chapters. But as what follows indicates, when we sat down to write about them, the differences did not seem to be major or insurmountable, and largely concerned the difficulties of working jointly, regarding different responsibilities and working practices, all important in any collaborative project. Delving a little deeper into differences that were stimulating and/or challenging, by and large when we wrote about differences these things were largely bracketed. They concern the process/product continuum and the somewhat different positions we take up along this, and the different ways of unpacking the concerns of the past and those of the present that inform the different kinds of archival research we do. For more on these we must point readers back in the direction of our chapter discussions, and forward to the more practical matters raised below, and also emphasise again that in practice differences have been less significant than agreements.

Differences

Maria: Finding the rhythm of writing with other authors who all have different timescales has been a challenge and a learning curve for me in *The Archive Project*. The fact that my immediate readers were much more in the flesh and some of them would immediately respond to my ideas changed my overall way of writing compared with having an abstract audience in mind. My writing technologies changed overall in the process of writing with others.

Niamh: I see this book itself as a boundary object, with us all tacking back and forth between the shared space of our collective archive project and our own trajectories, jobs, commitments and other projects. Key for me is the insight that building consensus does not mean the elision of differences, as it is sometimes taken to mean. Rather, it is an active process of valuing differences and of working to stitch something new together. From Feminist Webs, from participatory feminist youth work, from feminism more generally, and also from this book, I learn that learning is different done together and is not always easy (as if it ever is on one's own), and I also want to say that differences can be stimulating, compelling, challenging, inspiring. *Andrea*: Theoretical and analytical differences have been surprisingly few, but our methodological approaches to archival research (and to writing about it) are of course inflected by the rest of our lives and the constraints and responsibilities we inhabit. Methodological imagination, and also travelling to conduct periods of archival research, are bounded by available funding and other responsibilities. And our different career paths mean that more experienced colleagues have more points of reference to draw on. *Liz*: Theoretical, conceptual and methodological differences have been balanced by our larger areas of agreement, and held in check by the structure of the book and how authorship was organised, with its combination of the individual and the collective helping shape all the chapters. Practical differences have included different ways of working that at times have been out of synch, varied ways of handling the product/process relationship, and in my own case, feeling at times quite constrained by producing a practical 'try this' sort of chapter. But overall, it flies!

Departures

Niamh: Hopefully I will get to depart 'back' to the archive. Being so involved in creating archives means a certain frustration with not being able to spend time actually reading the materials there. I have been fascinated to learn about feminist youth work and want to write more about this compelling history of women and girls working together, and how this might refigure histories of feminism that revolve around stories of generational conflict. *Maria*: There are three areas I am most interested in: a) writing archival genealogies, that is, mapping discourses and practices that have created and shaped particular archival collections, as well as their subsequent readings, re-readings and rewritings; b) following up questions around archival troubles and failures; and c) creating digital meta-archives. *Andrea*: During the life of producing this book, starting with getting the contract for it in 2013, I left working as a two-job contract researcher to focus both on research facilitation and on writing about documents of life and the methodologies used to explore these, including narrative, archival and digital ones. *Liz*: Pastures new? No and yes. The Whites Writing Whiteness project is still in process, with publications from this proceeding along lines already set, so watch this space at www.whiteswritingwhiteness.ed.ac.uk. However, it will be completed by a book on social change and South Africa, which will provide the opportunity to write in a more holistic way about work over the last decade. And in palimpsest fashion, traces of other books-to-be are in mind, too. But who knows, when the wind changes...

The end

References

Adams, Tony, Jones, Stacey Holman and Ellis, Carolyn. 2015. *Autoethnography: Understanding Qualitative Research*. New York: Oxford University Press.

Alexander, Ben and Bastian, Jeannette A. (eds.) 2009. *Community Archives: The Shaping of Memory*. London: Facet Publishing.

Altman, Janet Gurkin. 1982. *Epistolarity: Approaches to a Form*. Columbus, OH: Ohio State University Press.

Andrews, Molly. 2013. Never the last word: revisiting data, in *Doing Narrative Research*, edited by Molly Andrews, Corinne Squire and Maria Tamboukou. London: Sage, 2nd edition, 205–22.

Arendt, Hannah. 1990. *On Revolution*. Harmondsworth: Penguin.

———— 1998 [1958]. *The Human Condition*. Chicago, IL: University of Chicago Press.

Archives Hub. www.archiveshub.ac.uk/ [accessed 15 June 2015].

Barbie Liberation Organization. https://sniggle.net/barbie.php [accessed 15 June 2015].

Barta, Peter, Miller, Paul, Platter, Charles and Shepherd, David. 2001. *Carnivalizing Difference: Bahktin and the Other*. London: Routledge.

Barthes, Roland. 1986. To write: an intransitive verb? in his *The Rustle of Language* (trans. Richard Howard). Berkeley, CA: University of California Press, 11–21.

Bastian, Jeannette, A. 2003. *Owning Memory. How a Caribbean Community Lost Its Archives and Found Its History*. Westport, CT: Libraries Unlimited.

Bastian, Michelle. 2011. The contradictory simultaneity of being with others: exploring concepts of time and community in the work of Gloria Anzaldua. *Feminist Review*, 97(1), 151–67.

Batsleer, Janet. 2010. Feminist Webs: a case study of the personal political and professional in youth work, in *Critical Practice with Children and Young People*, edited by Martin Robb and Rachel Thomson. Bristol: Policy Press, 217–33.

———— 2013. *Youth Working with Girls and Women in Community Settings: A Feminist Perspective*. Farnham: Ashgate, 2nd edition.

Beinart, William. 2001. *Twentieth-Century South Africa*. Oxford: Oxford University Press.

Benjamin, Walter. 2002. *The Arcades Project*. New Haven, CT: Harvard University Press.

———— 2007. *Walter Benjamin's Archive*. London: Verso.

Benson, Koni and Nagar, Richa. 2006. Collaboration as resistance? Reconsidering the processes, products, and possibilities of feminist oral history and ethnography. *Gender, Place & Culture*, 13(5), 581–92.

Berry, David, M. (ed.) 2012. *Understanding Digital Humanities*. Basingstoke: Palgrave Macmillan.

Best, Stephen and Marcus, Sharon. 2009. Surface reading. *Representations*, 108, 1–21.

Biglia, Barbara, Clark, Jude, Motzkau, Johanna and Zavos, Alexandra. 2005. Feminisms and activisms: reflections on the politics of writing and the editorial process. *Annual Review of Critical Psychology*, 4, 9–24.

Blanchot, Maurice. 1982 [1955]. *The Space of Literature*. Lincoln, NE: University of Nebraska Press.

Bloch, Marc. 1991 [1954]. *The Historian's Craft* (trans. Peter Putnam). Manchester: Manchester University Press.

Borges, Jorge Luis. 1998. *Fictions*. Harmondsworth: Penguin.

Boulter, Jonathan. 2011. *Melancholy and the Archive: Trauma, History and Memory in the Contemporary Novel*. London: Bloomsbury.

Broad, Richard and Fleming, Suzie with Mulford, Jeremy (eds.) 1981. *Nella Last's War: A Mother's Diary 1939–45*. Bristol: Falling Wall Press.

—— (eds.) 2006. *Nella Last's War: The Second World War Diaries of 'Housewife, 49'*. London: Profile Books.

Brockmeier, Jens. 2015. *Beyond the Archive: Memory, Narrative and the Autobiographical Process*. New York: Oxford University Press.

Brundage, Anthony. 2013. *Going to the Sources: Historical Research and Writing*. Molden, MA: John Wiley & Sons, 5th edition.

Burman, Erica. 2004. Boundary objects and group analysis: between psychoanalysis and social theory. *Group Analysis*, 37(3), 361–79.

Burton, Antoinette. 1992. 'History' is now: feminist theory and the production of historical feminisms. *Women's History Review*, 1(1), 25–39.

—— (ed.) 2006. *Archive Stories: Facts, Fictions and the Writing of History*. Durham, NC: Duke University Press.

Calder, Angus. 1996. Obituary: Charles Madge. *The Independent*, 20 January 1996. www.independent.co.uk/news/people/obituarycharles-madge-1324861.html [accessed 21 January 2015].

Casey, Emma, Courage, Fiona and Hubble, Nick. 2014. Special section introduction: Mass Observation as method. *Sociological Research Online*, 19(3), 22, www.socresonline.org.uk/19/3/22.html [accessed 3 July 2015].

Certeau, Michel de. 1998. *The Writing of History*. New York: Columbia University Press.

—— 2000 [1990]. *The Possession at Loudon*. Chicago, IL: University of Chicago Press.

Chakrabarty, Dipesh. 2000. *Provincializing Europe: Postcolonial Thought and Historical Difference*. Princeton, NJ: Princeton University Press.

Cohen-Meyers, Ricki, C. 1976. *Fannia Cohn and the International Ladies' Garment Workers' Union*. Unpublished PhD thesis, University of Southern California.

Cohn, Bernard. 1987. *An Anthropologist Among the Historians*. New York: Oxford University Press.

—— 1996. *Colonialism and Its Forms of Knowledge*. Princeton, NJ: Princeton University Press.

Community Archives and Heritage Group. www.communityarchives.org.uk [accessed 15 June 2015].

Comparative Critical Studies. 2011. 8:2 and 8:3. Special issue on 'Archive Time'.

Cook, Alice and Kirk, Gwyn. 1983. *Greenham Women Everywhere: Dreams, Ideas and Actions from the Women's Peace Movement.* London: Pluto.

Craven, Louise. (ed.) 2008. *What Are Archives? Cultural and Theoretical Perspectives.* Farnham: Ashgate.

Cronwright-Schreiner, Samuel Cron. 1924a. *The Life of Olive Schreiner.* London: Fisher Unwin.

——— (ed.) 1924b. *The Letters of Olive Schreiner.* London: Fisher Unwin.

Cunningham, Adrian. 2008. Digital curation/digital archiving: a view from the National Archives of Australia. *American Archivist*, 71, 530–43.

Cvetkovich, Ann. 2003. *An Archive of Feelings: Trauma, Sexuality, and Lesbian Public Cultures.* Durham, NC: Duke University Press.

Dampier, Helen. 2008. Re-reading as methodology. *Qualitative Research*, 8, 367–77.

Danto, Elizabeth. 2008. *Historical Research.* New York: Oxford University Press.

Deleuze, Gilles and Guattari, Felix. 1994. *What is Philosophy?* (trans. Hugh Tomlinson and Graham Burchell). London, New York: Verso.

Derrida, Jacques. 1972. Freud and the scene of writing. *Yale French Studies*, 48, 74–117.

——— 1974. *Of Grammatology* (trans. Gayatri Chakravorty Spivak). Baltimore, MD: The Johns Hopkins University Press.

——— 1989 [1982]. *Memoires for Paul de Man.* New York: Columbia University Press.

——— 1997 [1995]. *Archive Fever: A Freudian Impression.* Chicago, IL: University of Chicago Press.

——— 2008 [2003]. *Geneses, Genealogies, Genres and Genius: The Secrets of the Archive.* New York: Columbia University Press.

Dinshaw, Carolyn. 2007. Temporalities, in *Twenty-First Century Approaches: Medieval*, edited by Paul Strohm. Oxford: Oxford University Press, 107–23.

Dirks, Nicholas. 1993. Colonial history and native informants: biography of an archive, in *Orientalism and the Postcolonial Predicament: Perspectives on South Asia*, edited by Carol Breckenbridge and Peter van der Veer. Philadelphia, PA: University of Pennsylvania Press, 279–313.

——— 2002. Annals of the archive: ethnographic notes on the sources of history, in *From the Margins: Historical Anthropology and its Futures*, edited by Brian Keith Axel. Durham, NC: Duke University Press, 47–65.

——— 2015. *Autobiography of an Archive: A Scholar's Passage to India.* New York: Columbia University Press.

Dobson, Miriam and Ziemann, Benjamin (eds.) 2008. *Reading Primary Sources.* London: Routledge.

Donnelly, Sue. 2008. Coming out in the archives: The Hall-Carpenter Archives at the London School of Economics. *History Workshop Journal*, 66(1), 180–4.

Eastwood, Terence. 1992. *The Archival Fonds: From Theory to Practice.* Ottawa: Bureau of Canadian Archivists.

Eichhorn, Kate. 2010. D.I.Y. collectors, archiving scholars, and activist librarians: legitimizing feminist knowledge and cultural production since 1990. *Women's Studies: An Interdisciplinary Journal*, 39(6), 622–46.

——— 2013. *The Archival Turn in Feminism: Outrage in Order.* Philadelphia, PA: Temple University Press.

Elias, Norbert. 2008. *Essays II: On Civilizing Processes, Collected Works, Volume 15.* Dublin: University College Dublin Press.

—— 2012. *On the Process of Civilisation, Collected Works, Volume 3.* Dublin: University College Dublin Press.

——2013. *Studies on the Germans, Collected Works, Volume 12.* Dublin: University College Dublin Press.

Farge, Arlette. 2013 [1989]. *The Allure of the Archives.* New Haven, CT: Yale University Press. [*Le goût de l'archive.* Paris: Gallimard.]

Farge, Arlette and Foucault, Michel. 1982. *Le désordre des familles: lettres de cachet: Des Archives de la Bastille.* Paris: Gallimard.

Featherstone, Mike. 2000. Archiving cultures. *British Journal of Sociology,* 51(1), 161–84.

—— 2006. Archive. *Theory, Culture and Society,* 23(2–3), 591–6.

Feminist Webs. www.feministwebs.com/the-archive/ [accessed 15 June 2015].

Feminist Webs (eds.) 2012. *The Exciting Life of Being a Woman: A Handbook for Women and Girls.* Bristol: Hammeron Press.

Ferraby, John, G. 1945. Planning a Mass-Observation investigation. *American Journal of Sociology,* 51, 1–6.

First, Ruth and Scott, Ann. 1980. *Olive Schreiner.* London: The Women's Press.

Flanders, Julia. 2014. Rethinking collections, in *Advancing Digital Humanities: Research, Methods, Theories,* edited by Paul L. Arthur and Katherine Bode. Basingstoke: Palgrave, 163–74.

Flinn, Andrew. 2007. Community histories, community archives: some opportunities and challenges. *Journal of the Society of Archivists,* 28(2), 151–76.

Flinn, Andrew, Stevens, Mary and Shepherd, Elizabeth. 2009. Whose memories, whose archives? Independent community archives, autonomy and the mainstream. *Archival Science,* 9(1), 71–86.

Foucault, Michel. 1967. Of other spaces/heterotopias. www.foucault.info/documents/ heteroTopia/foucault.heteroTopia.en.html [accessed 15 June 2015].

—— 1972. *The Archaeology of Knowledge* (trans. Alan Sheridan). London: Tavistock.

—— 1975. *I, Pierre Rivière, Having Slaughtered....* New York: Pantheon Books.

—— 1977. The fantasia of the library, in *Michel Foucault: Language, Counter-Memory, Practice,* edited by Donald F. Bouchard. Ithaca, NY: Cornell University Press, 87–111.

—— 1980a. *Herculine Barbin.* Brighton: The Harvester Press.

—— 1980b. 'The history of sexuality', an interview (trans. Colin Gordon), in *Power/Knowledge: Selected Interviews and Other Writings 1972–1977,* edited by Colin Gordon. London: Harvester Wheatsheaf, 83–193.

—— 1986. Nietzsche, genealogy, history (trans. Donald F. Bouchard and Sherry Simon), in *The Foucault Reader,* edited by Paul Rabinow. Harmondsworth: Peregrine, 76–100.

—— 1988. The concern for truth, in *Michel Foucault, Politics Philosophy, Culture,* edited by Lawrence D. Kritzman. London: Routledge, 255–70.

—— 1994. Lives of infamous men (trans. Robery Hurley and others), in *Michel Foucault: Power, The Essential Works 3,* edited by James D. Faubion. New York: The New Press, 157–75.

—— 1998. Different spaces (trans. Robery Hurley and others), in *Michel Foucault, Aesthetics, Method and Epistemology, The Essential Works 2,* edited by James D. Faubion. Harmondsworth: Penguin, 175–85.

—— 2000 [1966]. *The Order of Things* (trans. Tavistock Publications). London: Routledge.

Garfinkel, Harold. 1967. *Studies in Ethnomethodology*. Englewood Cliffs, NJ: Prentice-Hall.

Geiger, Till. 2008. George W. Bush and the war on the archive. 'The Ontology of the Archive' Conference. University of Manchester, 25 April. www.cresc.ac.uk/events/archived/archiveseries/documents/Geiger25April.pdf [accessed 3 July 2015].

Geiger, Till, Moore, Niamh and Savage, Mike. 2010. The archive in question. No 16. NCRM, Southampton. http://reprints.ncrm.ac.uk [accessed 15 June 2015].

Gidley, Ben. 2011. Doing historical and archival research, in *Researching Society and Culture,* edited by Clive Seale. London: Sage, 249–64.

Gilchrist, Paul, Holmes, Claire, Lee, Amelia, Moore, Niamh and Ravenscroft, Neil. 2015. Co-designing non-hierarchical community arts research: the collaborative stories spiral. *Qualitative Research*, 15, 459–471. Open access at: www.emeraldinsight.com/toc/qrj/15/4

Guglielmo, Jennifer. 2010. *Living the Revolution: Italian Women's Resistance and Radicalism in New York City, 1880–1945.* Chapel Hill, NC: University of North Carolina Press.

Halford, Susan, Pope, Catherine and Weal, Mark, J. 2013. Digital futures? Sociological challenges and opportunities in the emergent semantic web. *Sociology*, 47(1), 173–89.

Hamilton, Carolyn. (ed.) 2013a. Special issue on 'South African archives'. *South African Historical Journal*, 65, 1.

—— 2013b. Forged and continually refashioned in the crucible of ongoing social and political life: archives and custodial practices as subjects of enquiry. *South African Historical Journal*, 65, 1–22.

Hamilton, Carolyn, Harris, Verne, Pickover, Michele, Reid, Graeme and Salem, Razia. (eds.) 2002. *Refiguring the Archive*. Dordrecht, The Netherlands: Kluwer Academic.

Haran, Joan. 2013. Screening naturecultures: Haraway, Starhawk and a magical experiment. Paper given at the UFAL Conference, Maceio, Brazil. 4 October.

Haraway, Donna. 1988. Situated knowledges: the science question in feminism and the privilege of partial perspective. *Feminist Studies*, 14, 575–99.

—— 1994. A game of cat's cradle: science studies, feminist theory, cultural studies. *Configurations*, 2(1), 59–71.

Haraway, Donna and Goodeve, Thyrza Nichols. 2000. *How Like a Leaf: Donna J. Haraway: An Interview with Thyrza Nichols Goodeve*. London: Routledge.

Haraway, Donna. 2011. SF: science fiction, speculative fabulation, string figures, so far. Pilgrim Award Acceptance Talk. Lublin: Poland. 7 July.

Harrisson, Tom, Jennings, Humphrey and Madge, Charles. 1937. Anthropology at home. *New Statesman and Nation*, 30 January, XIII (310) (New Series), 155.

Heimann, Judith. 2003. *The Most Offending Soul Alive: Tom Harrisson and His Remarkable Life*. London: Aurum Press.

Hetherington, Kevin. 1997. *The Badlands of Modernity: Heterotopia and Social Ordering*. London: Routledge.

Hill, Michael, J. 1993. *Archival Strategies and Techniques*. Moreno Valley, CA: Sage.

Hinton, James. 2013. *The Mass Observers: A History, 1937–1949*. Oxford: Oxford University Press.

History of the Human Sciences. 1998, 1999. Special issues on 'The Archive', 11:4 and 12:2.

Hubble, Nick. 2001. Charles Madge and Mass-Observation are at home: from anthropology to war, and after. *New Formations*, 44, 76–89.

—— 2006. *Mass-Observation and Everyday Life: Culture, History, Theory.* Basingstoke: Palgrave Macmillan.

—— 2014. Review of James Hinton's 'The Mass Observers: A History, 1937–1949'. *Reviews in History*, www.history.ac.uk/reviews/review/1603 [accessed 5 August 2015].

Hughes, Jason and Goodwin, John (eds.) 2013. *Documentary and Archival Research.* London: Sage.

Hunt, Arnold. 2014. How archives make history. www.cam.ac.uk/research/discussion/qa-how-archives-make-history [accessed 3 July 2015].

Jasanoff, Sheila and Kim, Sang-Hyun. 2015. *Dreamscapes of Modernity: Sociotechnical Imaginaries and the Fabrication of Power.* Chicago, IL: University of Chicago Press.

Jeffrey, Tom. 1999 [1978]. *Mass-Observation: A Short History*, Mass-Observation Archive Occasional Paper No. 10, University of Sussex Library.

Jennings, Humphrey and Madge, Charles. 1937 [1987]. *May The Twelfth: Mass-Observation Day-Surveys 1937.* London: Faber & Faber.

Jolly, Margaretta. 2003. After the seventies: Greenham Common women and dreams of a common language, in *The Feminist Seventies,* edited by Helen Graham, Ann Kaloski, Ali Neilson and Emma Robertson. York: Raw Nerve Books, 173–86.

Jolly, Margaretta, Russell, Polly and Cohen, Rachel. 2012. Sisterhood and after: individualism, ethics and an oral history of the Women's Liberation Movement. *Social Movement Studies*, 11(2), 211–26.

Jobs, Sebastian and Lüdtke, Alf. (eds.) 2010. *Unsettling History: Archiving and Narrating in Historiography.* Frankfurt: Campus Verlag.

Jordanova, Ludmilla. 2000. *History in Practice.* London: Arnold.

—— 2012. *The Look of the Past: Visual and Material Evidence in Historical Practice.* Cambridge: Cambridge University Press.

King, Michelle. 2011. Working with/in archives, in *Research Methods for History,* edited by Simon Gunn and Lucy Faire. Edinburgh: Edinburgh University Press, 13–29.

Kirsch, Gesa and Rohan, Liz. (eds.) 2008a. *Beyond the Archives: Research as a Lived Process.* Carbondale, IL: Southern Illinois University Press.

—— 2008b. Introduction: the role of serendipity, family connections and cultural memory in historical research, in *Beyond the Archives: Research as a Lived Process,* edited by Gesa Kirsch and Liz Rohan. Carbondale, IL: Southern Illinois University Press, 1–12.

Klein, Lauren. 2013. The image of absence: archival silence, data visualisation, and James Hemings. *American Literature*, 85, 661–88.

Koselleck, Reinhart. 1985 [1979]. Space of experience and horizon of expectation: two historical categories, in his *Futures Past: On the Semantics of Historical Time* (trans. Keith Tribe). Cambridge, MA: The MIT Press, 267–88.

—— 2002. *The Practice of Conceptual History: Timing History, Spacing Concepts* (trans. Todd Samuel Presner). Stanford, CA: Stanford University Press.

Ladurie, Emmanuel Leroy. 1980 [1978]. *Montaillou.* Harmondsworth: Penguin.

Lalu, Premesh. 2009. *The Deaths of Hintsa: Postapartheid South Africa and the Shape of Recurring Pasts.* Cape Town: HSRC Press.

Leeder, Elaine. 1993. *The Gentle General, Rose Pesotta, Anarchist and Labor Organizer.* New York: State University of New York Press.

Le Doeuff, Michèle. 1989. *The Philosophical Imaginary.* London: Continuum.

Lefebvre, Henri. 1991 [1974]. *The Production of Space* (trans. Donald Nicholson-Smith). Oxford: Blackwell.

———— 2004. *Rhythmanalysis: Space, Time and Everyday Life* (trans. Stuart Elden and Gerald Moore). London: Continuum.

Lennon, Kathleen. 2004. Imaginary bodies and worlds. *Inquiry,* 47(2), 107–22.

———— 2015. *Imagination and the Imaginary.* London: Routledge.

Levy, David. 2011. *Scrolling Forward: Making Sense of Documents in the Digital Age.* New York: Arcade Publishing.

McKemmish, Sue, Piggot, Michael, Reed, Barbara and Upward, Frank (eds.) 2005. *Archives: Recordkeeping in Society.* Wagga Wagga, New South Wales: CIS.

McNeil, Maureen, Arribas-Ayllon, Michael, Haran, Joan, McKenzie, Adrian and Tutton, Richard. 2016 (forthcoming). The concept of imaginaries in Science and Technology Studies, in *Handbook of Science and Technology Studies,* edited by Clark Miller, Laurel Smith-Doerr, Ulrike Felt and Rayvon Fouché. Cambridge, MA: MIT Press.

Madge, Charles. 1976. The birth of Mass-Observation. *Times Literary Supplement,* 5 November, 1395.

Malcolmson, Robert W. and Malcolmson, Patricia (eds.) 2008. *Nella Last's Peace: The Postwar Diaries of Housewife, 49.* London: Profile Books.

———— (eds.) 2010. *Nella Last in the 1950s: Further Details of Housewife, 49.* London: Profile Books.

———— (eds.) 2012. *The Diaries of Nella Last: Writing in War and Peace.* London: Profile Books.

Manoff, Marlene. 2004. Theories of the archive from across the disciplines. *Libraries and the Academy,* 4, 9–25.

———— 2015. Human and machine entanglement in the digital archive: academic libraries and socio-technical change. *Libraries and the Academy,* 15(3), 513–30.

Mass Observation Archive. www.massobs.org.uk/index.htm [accessed 15 June 2015].

Mass Observation Online, Adam Matthews Digital. www.massobservation.amdigital.co.uk/Home/index [accessed 25 June 2015].

Marcus, Laura. 2001. Introduction: the project of Mass-Observation. *New Formations,* 44, 5–20.

Matienzo, Mark, A. 2008. Canonization, archivalization, and the 'archival imaginary'. Paper presented at Archive Fervour/Archive Further: Literature, Archives, and Literary Archives, Aberystwyth, Wales, 9–11 July.

Merewether, Charles. (ed.) 2006. *The Archive.* London: MIT Press/Whitechapel Gallery.

Miller, Jane. 1990. *Seductions: Studies in Reading and Culture.* London: Virago.

Moore, Niamh. 2001. Paths to ecofeminist activism: life stories from the North East of England, in *The Roots of Environmental Consciousness: Popular Tradition and Personal Experience,* edited by Stephen Hussey and Paul Thompson. London: Routledge, 160–73.

———— 2007a. Imagining feminist futures: the third wave, postfeminism and ecofeminism, in *Third Wave Feminism: A Critical Exploration,* edited by Stacy Gillis, Gillian Howie and Becky Munford. London: Palgrave Macmillan, 2nd edition, 125–41.

———— 2007b. (Re)using qualitative data? *Sociological Research Online,* 12(3), www.socresonline.org.uk/12/3/1.html [accessed 3 July 2015].

———— 2008. Ecofeminism, non-violence and the future of feminism. *International Feminist Journal of Politics,* 10(3), 282–98.

———— 2013. Growing collaborative research, in The CRESC Encounters Collaborative. '(Un)doing Collaboration: Reflections on the Practices of Collaborative Research', *CRESC Working Paper 127.* Manchester: University of Manchester. www.cresc.ac.uk/publications/working-papers/year/2013/, 7–8 [accessed 15 June 2015].

———— 2015. *The Changing Nature of Eco/feminism: Telling Stories from Clayoquot Sound.* Vancouver: University of British Columbia Press.

Nestle, Joan. 1979. Notes on radical archiving from a lesbian feminist standpoint. *Gay Insurgent,* 4–5, 11.

———— 1990. The will to remember: the Lesbian Herstory Archives of New York. *Feminist Review,* 34, 86–94.

Nicholson, Bob. 2013. The digital turn. *Media History,* 19(1), 59–73.

Noakes, Lucy. 1996. Sexing the archive: gender in contemporary history, in *The Contemporary History Handbook,* edited by Anthony Seldon, Brian Brivati and Julia Buxton. Manchester: Manchester University Press, 74–83.

The Occupy Movement. http://occupyoralhistory.wordpress.com/about/ [accessed 15 June 2015].

Olive Schreiner Letters Online. www.oliveschreiner.org [accessed 15 June 2015].

Orwell, George. 1949. *Nineteen Eighty-Four.* London: Secker & Warburg.

Osborne, Thomas. 1999. The ordinariness of the archive. *History of the Human Sciences,* 12(2), 51–64.

Petersen, Bhezizwe. 2002. The archive and the political imaginary, in *Refiguring the Archive,* edited by Carolyn Hamilton, Verne Harris, Michele Pickover, Graeme Reid and Razia Salem. Dordrecht, The Netherlands: Kluwer Academic, 29–37.

Plummer, Ken. 2001. *Documents of Life 2.* London: Sage.

Puig de la Bellacasa, Maria and Bracke, Sarah. 2004. Building standpoints, in *The Standpoint Theory Reader,* edited by Sandra Harding. London: Routledge, 309–16.

Pyke, Geoffrey. 1936. King and country. *New Statesman and Nation,* 12 December, XII(303) (New Series), 974.

Rich, Adrienne. 1979. When we dead awaken: writing as re-vision, in her *On Lies, Secrets and Silence: Selected Prose, 1966–1978.* New York: W.W. Norton, 33–49.

Richards, Thomas. 1993. *The Imperial Archive: The Knowledge and Fantasy of Empire.* London: Verso.

Ricoeur, Paul. 1984. *Time and Narrative, Volume 1* (trans. Kathleen McLaughlin and David Pellauer). Chicago, IL: University of Chicago Press.

———— 1988. *Time and Narrative, Volume 3* (trans. Kathleen McLaughlin and David Pellauer). Chicago, IL: Chicago University Press.

———— [1955]. *History and Truth* (trans. Charles A. Kelbley). Evanston, IL: Northwestern University Press.

—— 2004. *Memory, History, Forgetting* (trans. Kathleen Blamey and David Pellauer). Chicago, IL: University of Chicago Press.

Roberts, Brian. 1999. Some thoughts on time perspectives and auto/biography. *Auto/Biography*, 7, 21–5.

Rogers, Helen. 2008. Searching questions: digital research and Victorian culture. *Journal of Victorian Culture*, 13(1), 56–7.

Ronan, Alison. 2012. Herstory: why we gathered things from under people's beds, in *The Exciting Life of Being a Woman: A Handbook for Women and Girls*, edited by Feminist Webs. Bristol: Hammeron Press, 39–41.

Roseneil, Sasha. 1995. *Disarming Patriarchy: Feminism and Political Action at Greenham*. Buckingham: Open University Press.

Said, Edward. 1983. *The World, the Text and the Critic*. New Haven, CT: Harvard University Press.

Salter, Andrea. 2008a. Women's Mass-Observation diaries: writing, time and 'subjective cameras'. Unpublished PhD Thesis. Edinburgh: University of Edinburgh.

—— 2008b. Engaging with 'the present'? Nella Last's Mass-Observation diary. Edinburgh Working Papers in Sociology, No. 26, University of Edinburgh. www.sociology.ed.ac.uk/__data/assets/pdf_file/0006/13011/WP26_Salter2008.pdf [accessed 12 July 2015].

—— 2010. Filling the silences? Mass-Observation's wartime diaries, interpretive work and indexicality. *Life Writing*, 7(1), 53–65.

Savage, Mike and Burrows, Roger. 2007. The coming crisis of empirical sociology. *Sociology*, 41(5), 885–99.

Schutz, Alfred. 1945 [1973]. On multiple realities, in his *Collected Papers, Vol. 1: The Problem of Social Reality*. The Hague: Martinus Nijhoff, 207–59.

Schwartz, Joan and Cook, Terry. 2002. Archives, records and power. *Archival Science*, 2, 1–19.

Sheridan, Dorothy. 1984. Mass-Observing the British, *History Today*, 34, 42–6.

—— (ed.) 1985 [2000]. *Among You Taking Notes: The Wartime Diary of Naomi Mitchison*. London: Gollancz.

Sheridan, Dorothy (ed.) 1990. *Wartime Women: A Mass-Observation Anthology*. London: Heinemann.

Sheridan, Dorothy. 1993. Ordinary hardworking folk?: volunteer writers for Mass-Observation 1937–50 and 1981–91. *Feminist Praxis*, 37/38, 1–34.

—— 1994. Using the Mass-Observation Archive as a source for Women's Studies. *Women's History Review*, 3(1), 101–13.

—— 2014. Response from Dorothy Sheridan to Nick Hubble's review of James Hinton's 'The Mass Observers: A History, 1937–1949'. *Reviews in History*, www.history.ac.uk/reviews/review/1603 [accessed 5 August 2015].

Sheridan, Dorothy, Street, Brian and Bloome, David. 2000. *Writing Ourselves: Mass-Observation and Literacy Practices*. Creskill, NJ: Hampton Press.

Sheringham, Michael. 2010. Michel Foucault, Pierre Riviere and the archival imaginary. *Comparative Critical Studies*, 8, 235–57.

Smith, Sidonie and Watson, Julia. (eds.) 1998. *Women, Autobiography, Theory: A Reader*. Madison, WI: University of Wisconsin Press.

Stanley, Liz. 1983. New women, free women, all women: Olive Schreiner, in *Feminist Theorists*, edited by Dale Spender. The Women's Press, London, 229–43.

——— 1984. *The Diaries of Hannah Cullwick*. London: Virago and New Brunswick, NJ: Rutgers University Press.

——— 1988. *The Life and Death of Emily Wilding Davison*. London: The Women's Press.

——— 1990. An archaeology of a 1930s Mass-Observation project. *Sociology Occasional Paper No. 27*. Manchester: University of Manchester.

——— 1992. *The Auto/Biographical I: Theory and Practice of Feminist Auto/ Biography*. Manchester: Manchester University Press.

——— 1995a. *Sex Surveyed, 1949 to 1994: From Mass-Observation's 'Little Kinsey' to the National Survey and The Hite Reports*. London: Taylor & Francis.

——— 1995b. Women have servants and men never eat: issues in reading gender using the case study of Mass-Observation's Day Diaries. *Women's History Review*, 4, 85–102.

——— 2002. *Imperialism, Labour and the New Woman: Olive Schreiner's Social Theory*. Durham: Sociology Press.

——— 2008 [2006]. *Mourning Becomes: Post/Memory and the Concentration Camps of the South African War*. Johannesburg: University of Witwatersrand University Press and Manchester: Manchester University Press.

——— 2004. The epistolarium: on theorizing letters and correspondences. *Auto/ Biography*, 12(3), 201–35.

——— 2011a. The epistolary gift: the editorial third party, counter-epistolaria: rethinking the epistolarium. *Life Writing*, 8(3), 137–54.

——— (ed.) 2011b. Olive Schreiner & company: Schreiner's letters and 'drinking in the external world'. *Olive Schreiner Letters Project Working Paper on Letters, Letterness & Epistolary Networks* no.3, University of Edinburgh. www.oliveschreinerletters. ed.ac.uk/OSandCompany2011PDF.pdf [accessed 17 July 2015].

——— (ed.) 2013. *Documents of Life Revisited: Narrative and Biographical Methods for a 21st Century Critical Humanism*. Farnham: Ashgate.

——— 2015a. The scriptural economy, the Forbes figuration and the racial order. *Sociology*, 49, 5.

——— 2015b, in press. What is a migrant letter and do settler colonial letters make a difference? *Journal of Family History*.

——— 2015c. The reader, the text and the editor. On the making of Olive Schreiner's letters and *The World's Great Question*. *English in Africa*, 42, 59–76.

Stanley, Liz and Dampier, Helen. 2006. Simulacrum diaries: time, the 'moment of writing' and the diaries of Johanna Brandt-Van Warmelo. *Life Writing*, 3, 25–52.

——— 2009. The number of the South African War (1899–1902) concentration camp dead: standard stories, superior stories and a forgotten proto-nationalist research investigation. *Sociological Research Online*, 14(5), www.socresonline. org.uk/14/5/13 [accessed 17 July 2015].

——— 2010. 'Men selling their souls & the future – & fate watching them' – Olive Schreiner on Union. *Quarterly Bulletin of the National Library of South Africa*, 64(3), 121–36.

——— 2011. Towards the epistolarium: issues in researching and publishing the Olive Schreiner epistolarium. *African Research and Documentation: Journal of the SCOLMA*, 113, 27–32.

——— 2012. 'I just express my views & leave them to work': Olive Schreiner as a feminist protagonist in a masculine political landscape with figures. *Gender and History*, 24, 677–700.

Stanley, Liz, Dampier, Helen and Salter, Andrea. 2010. Olive Schreiner globalising social inquiry: a feminist analytics of globalization. *Sociological Review*, 58(4), 656–79.

——— 2012. The epistolary pact, letterness and the Schreiner epistolarium. *a/b: Auto/Biographical Studies*, 27, 262–93.

Stanley, Liz, Salter, Andrea and Dampier, Helen. 2013a. The work of making and the work it does: cultural sociology and 'bringing-into-being' the cultural assemblage of the Olive Schreiner letters. *Cultural Sociology*, 7, 287–302.

——— 2013b. Olive Schreiner, epistolary practices and microhistories: a cultural entrepreneur in an historical landscape. *Journal of Cultural and Social History*, 10, 577–97.

Stanley, Liz and Salter, Andrea. 2009. Her letters cut are generally nothing of interest: the heterotopic persona of Olive Schreiner and the alterity persona of Cronwright-Schreiner. *English in Africa*, 36(2), 7–30.

——— 2014. *The World's Great Question: Olive Schreiner's South African Letters*. Cape Town: Van Riebeeck Society.

Stanley, Liz and Wise, Sue. 1983. *Breaking Out: Feminist Consciousness and Feminist Research*. London: Routledge.

——— 1993. *Breaking Out Again: Feminist Ontology and Epistemology*. London: Routledge.

Star, Susan Leigh and Griesemer, James. 1989. Institutional ecology, 'translations' and boundary objects: amateurs and professionals in Berkeley's Museum of Vertebrate Zoology, 1907–39. *Social Studies of Science*, 19(3), 387–420.

Star, Susan Leigh. 2010. This is not a boundary object: reflections on the origin of a concept. *Science, Technology & Human Values*, 35(5), 601–17.

Steedman, Carolyn. 2001. *Dust*. Manchester: Manchester University Press.

——— 2008. Romance in the archive. Keynote address, 'Archive Fervour, Archive Further' Conference, University of Wales, Aberystwyth, 9–11 July.

——— 2011. After the archive. *Comparative Critical Studies*, 8(2–3), 321–40.

——— 2015. On a bridge. *Changing English*, 22(3), 245–59.

Stein, Leon. 1962. *The Triangle Fire*. Ithaca, NY: Cornell University Press.

Stengers, Isabelle. 2011. *Thinking with Whitehead* (trans. M. Chase). Cambridge, MA: Harvard University Press.

Stevens, Mary, Flinn, Andrew and Shepherd, Elizabeth. 2010. New frameworks for community engagement in the archive sector: from handing over to handing on. *International Journal of Heritage Studies*, 16(1–2), 59–76.

Stoler, Ann Laura. 2002. Colonial archives and the arts of governance: on the content in the form, in *Refiguring the Archive*, edited by Carolyn Hamilton, Verne Harris, Michele Pickover, Graeme Reid and Razia Salem. Dordrecht, The Netherlands: Kluwer Academic, 83–102.

——— 2009. *Along the Archival Grain: Epistemic Anxieties and Colonial Common Sense*. Princeton, NJ: Princeton University Press.

Stryker, Susan. 2010. ed. Introduction. Bodies of knowledge: embodiment and the archival imaginary. *Australian Feminist Studies*, 23(64), 105–8. Thematic issue on 'Embodiment and the archival imaginary'.

Sturgeon, Noël. 1997. *Ecofeminist Natures: Race, Gender, Feminist Theory and Political Action*. London: Routledge.

Tamboukou, Maria. 2000. Of other spaces: women's colleges at the turn of the century. *Gender, Place and Culture*, 7(3), 247–63.

——— 2003. *Women, Education, the Self: A Foucauldian Perspective.* Basingstoke: Palgrave Macmillan.

——— 2010a. *In the Fold Between Power and Desire: Women Artists' Narratives.* Newcastle-upon-Tyne: Cambridge Scholars Publishers.

——— 2010b. *Nomadic Narratives, Visual Forces: Gwen John's Letters and Paintings.* New York: Peter Lang.

——— 2010c. Working with stories as multiplicities, opening up the black box of the archive. *Life Writing,* 7, 19–33.

——— 2011. Archive pleasures or whose time is it? *Forum: Qualitative Research,* special issue on 'Qualitative archives and biographical research', 12(3), Art. 2, http://nbn-resolving.de/urn:nbn:de:0114-fqs110327 [accessed 5 June 2015].

——— 2012. Heterotopic and holey spaces as tents for the nomad: rereading Gwen John's letters. *Gender, Place and Culture,* 19(3), 275–90.

——— 2013a. Educating the seamstress: studying and writing the memory of work. *History of Education,* 42(4), 509–27.

——— 2013b. Good night and good-bye: temporal and spatial rhythms in piecing together Emma Goldman's auto/biographical fragments. *BSA Auto/biography Yearbook.* Vol. VI, 17–31.

——— 2013c. Love, narratives, politics: encounters between Hannah Arendt and Rosa Luxemburg. *Theory, Culture and Society,* 30(1), 35–56.

——— 2014a. The female self as punctum: Fannia Cohn's archival technologies of the self. BSA *Auto/Biography Yearbook.* Vol. VII, 99–113.

——— 2014b. Archival research: unravelling space/time/matter entanglements and fragments. *Qualitative Research,* 14(5), 617–33.

——— 2014c. The autobiographical you: letters in the gendered politics of the labour movement. *Journal of Gender Studies* (online first).

——— 2014d. Imagining and living the revolution: an Arendtian reading of Rosa Luxemburg's letters and writings. *Feminist Review,* 106, 27–42.

——— 2014e. Narrative personae and visual signs: reading Leonard's intimate photo-memoir. *a/b: Auto/Biography Studies,* 29(1), 27–49.

——— 2015a. 'Not everything that the bourgeois world created is bad': aesthetics and politics in women workers' education. *Discourse: Studies in the Cultural Politics of Education,* 36(3), 424–36.

——— 2015b. Feeling narrative in the archive: the question of serendipity. *Qualitative Research* (online first).

——— 2015c. The work of memory: embodiment, materiality and home in Jeanne Bouvier's autobiographical writing. *Women's History Review* (online first).

——— 2015d. *Sewing, Fighting and Writing: Radical Practices in Work, Politics and Culture.* London: Rowman & Littlefield.

Thibodeau, Sharon. 1993. Review of Eastwood (ed.), The Archival Fonds: from theory to practice. *Archivaria,* 36, 256–8.

Trouillot, Michel-Rolph. 1995. *Silencing the Past: Power and the Production of History.* Boston, MA: Beacon Press.

Valles Martínez, Miguel, S. 2011. Archival and biographical research sensitivity: a European perspective from Spain. *Forum Qualitative Sozialforschung/Forum: Qualitative Social Research,* 12(3), Art. 2, http://nbn-resolving.de/urn:nbn:de:0114-fqs110327 [accessed 5 June 2015].

Valles Martínez, Miguel S., Corti, Louise, Tamboukou, Maria and Baer, Alejandro. 2011. Qualitative archives and biographical research methods. *Forum Qualitative*

Sozialforschung/Forum: Qualitative Social Research, 12(3), Art. 8, http://nbn-resolving.de/urn:nbn:de:0114-fqs110381 [accessed 5 June 2015].

Verran, Helen. 1998. Re-imagining land ownership in Australia. *Postcolonial Studies*, 1(2), 237–54.

White, Hayden. 1987. *The Content of the Form: Narrative Discourse and Historical Representation*. New York: Columbia University Press.

Whitehead, Alfred, North. 1985 [1929]. *Process and Reality* [corrected edition]. New York: The Free Press.

Whites Writing Whiteness. www.whiteswritingwhiteness.ed.ac.uk [accessed 15 June 2015].

Willcock, H.D. 1943. Mass-Observation. *American Journal of Sociology*, 48, 445–56.

Wisser, Katherine. 2011. Archival cataloguing and the archival sensibility. *RMB: Rare Books, Manuscripts and Cultural Heritage*, 12, 34–40.

Yeo, Geoffrey. 2008. Concepts of record (2): prototypes and boundary objects. *American Archivist*, 71(1), 118–43.

———— 2010. Representing the act: records and speech act theory. *Journal of the Society of Archivists*, 31(2), 95–117.

Index

Printed in the USA
CPSIA information can be obtained
at www.ICGtesting.com
LVHW051038310724
786981LV00025B/189

9 780367 596224